PHOTOGRAPHIS 79

The International Annual of Advertising and
Editorial Photography

Das internationale Jahrbuch der Werbephotographie
und der redaktionellen Photographie

Le répertoire international de la photographie
publicitaire et rédactionnelle

Edited by: / Herausgegeben von: / Réalisé par:

Walter Herdeg

Walter Herdeg, The Graphis Press, Zurich (Switzerland)

GRAPHIS PUBLICATIONS

GRAPHIS, International bi-monthly journal of graphic art and applied art
GRAPHIS ANNUAL, The international annual of advertising and editorial graphics
GRAPHIS POSTERS, The international annual of poster art
ANNUAL REPORTS, Conception and design of annual reports
GRAPHIS PACKAGING volume 2/volume 3, An international survey of package design
THE ARTIST IN THE SERVICE OF SCIENCE, Scientific and semi-scientific art
CHILDREN'S BOOK ILLUSTRATION, An international survey of children's book illustration
RECORD COVERS, The evolution of graphics reflected in record packaging
DIAGRAMS, The graphic visualization of abstract data
FILM + TV GRAPHICS 2, An international survey of the art of film animation
ARCHIGRAPHIA, Architectural and environmental graphics

GRAPHIS-PUBLIKATIONEN

GRAPHIS, Die internationale Zweimonatsschrift für Graphik und angewandte Kunst
GRAPHIS ANNUAL, Das internationale Jahrbuch der Werbegraphik und der redaktionellen Graphik
GRAPHIS POSTERS, Das internationale Jahrbuch der Plakatkunst
ANNUAL REPORTS, Konzeption und Gestaltung von Jahresberichten
GRAPHIS PACKUNGEN Band 2/Band 3, Internationales Handbuch der Packungsgestaltung
DER KÜNSTLER IM DIENST DER WISSENSCHAFT, Wissenschaftliche und populärwissenschaftliche Kunst
KINDERBUCH-ILLUSTRATION, Eine internationale Übersicht über die Kinderbuch-Illustration
PLATTENHÜLLEN, Die Schallplattenhülle als Spiegel der graphischen Entwicklung
DIAGRAMS, Die graphische Visualisierung abstrakter Gegebenheiten
FILM + TV GRAPHICS 2, Ein internationaler Überblick über die Kunst des Animationsfilms
ARCHIGRAPHIA, Architektur- und Umweltgraphik

PUBLICATIONS GRAPHIS

GRAPHIS, La revue bimestrielle internationale d'arts graphiques et d'arts appliqués
GRAPHIS ANNUAL, Le répertoire international de l'art publicitaire et l'art illustratif
GRAPHIS POSTERS, Le répertoire international de l'art de l'affiche
ANNUAL REPORTS, Conception et design de rapports annuels
GRAPHIS EMBALLAGES volume 2/volume 3, Répertoire international des formes de l'emballage
L'ARTISTE AU SERVICE DE LA SCIENCE, L'illustration scientifique et scientifique vulgarisée
ILLUSTRATIONS DE LIVRES D'ENFANTS, Un aperçu international des illustrations de livres d'enfants
CHEMISES DE DISQUES, Les pochettes de disques comme miroir du développement graphique
DIAGRAMS, La visualisation graphique de données abstraites
FILM + TV GRAPHICS 2, Un panorama international de l'art du film d'animation
ARCHIGRAPHIA, La création graphique appliquée à l'architecture et à l'environnement

Distributors / Auslieferung / Distribution:

USA: HASTINGS HOUSE, PUBLISHERS INC., 10 East 40th Street, New York, N.Y. 10016, tel (212) 689-5400
CANADA: HURTIG PUBLISHERS, 10560-105 Street, Edmonton, Alberta, T5H 2W7, tel. (403) 426-2469
FRANCE: GRAPHIS DISTRIBUTION, Milon-la-Chapelle, F - 78470 St-Rémy-lès-Chevreuse, tél. 052-13-26
ITALIA: INTER-ORBIS, Via Lorenteggio, 31/1, I - 20146 Milano, tel. 422 57 46
SPAIN: COMERCIAL ATHENEUM, S.A. Consejo de Ciento, 130-136, Barcelona 15, tel. 223 1451-3
AMERICA LATINA, AUSTRALIA, JAPAN AND OTHER ASIAN COUNTRIES, AFRICA:
FLEETBOOKS S.A., c/o Feffer & Simons, Inc., 100 Park Avenue, New York, N.Y. 10017, tel. (212) 686-0888

All other countries / Alle andern Länder / Tout autres pays:

WALTER HERDEG, THE GRAPHIS PRESS, 107, Dufourstrasse, CH - 8034 Zurich (Switzerland)

PUBLICATION No. 155 (ISBN 3-85709-279-3)

Contents　　　Inhalt　　　Sommaire

Abbreviations   Abkürzungen   Abréviations

Australia	AUS	Australien	AUS	Afrique du Sud	SAF
Austria	AUT	Belgien	BEL	Allemagne (RFA)	GER
Belgium	BEL	Brasilien	BRA	Australie	AUS
Brazil	BRA	Dänemark	DEN	Autriche	AUT
Canada	CAN	Deutschland (BRD)	GER	Belgique	BEL
Cuba	CUB	Finnland	FIN	Brésil	BRA
Czechoslovakia	CSR	Frankreich	FRA	Canada	CAN
Denmark	DEN	Griechenland	GRE	Cuba	CUB
Finland	FIN	Grossbritannien	GBR	Danemark	DEN
France	FRA	Hongkong	HGK	Espagne	SPA
Germany (West)	GER	Indien	IND	Etats-Unis	USA
Great Britain	GBR	Italien	ITA	Finlande	FIN
Greece	GRE	Japan	JPN	France	FRA
Hong Kong	HGK	Jugoslawien	YUG	Grande-Bretagne	GBR
India	IND	Kanada	CAN	Grèce	GRE
Italy	ITA	Kuba	CUB	Hongkong	HGK
Japan	JPN	Mexico	MEX	Inde	IND
Mexico	MEX	Niederlande	NLD	Italie	ITA
Netherlands	NLD	Norwegen	NOR	Japon	JPN
Norway	NOR	Österreich	AUT	Mexique	MEX
South Africa	SAF	Schweden	SWE	Norvège	NOR
Spain	SPA	Schweiz	SWI	Pays-Bas	NLD
Sweden	SWE	Spanien	SPA	Suède	SWE
Switzerland	SWI	Süd-Africa	SAF	Suisse	SWI
USA	USA	Tschechoslowakei	CSR	Tchécoslavaquie	CSR
Yugoslavia	YUG	USA	USA	Yougoslavie	YUG

While universal languages proper are making slow progress, photography can justly claim to have become a kind of universal pictorial language. Caught up in the onrush of modern communications, it is also evolving faster than ever before, and this evolution is bringing changes in the photographer's profession—a subject which is broached in the introduction to this volume. In spite of all the demands made on their time, however, many photographers continue to send us their best work, thus helping us to help them with a representative survey of what world photography has achieved in the past year. These lines convey a hearty "Thank you" to all our faithful contributors.

Während auf dem Gebiet einer Weltsprache nur wenig Fortschritte erzielt werden, kann man die Photographie mit Recht eine Welt-Bildersprache nennen. Von dem Ansturm moderner Kommunikationsmittel mitgerissen, entwickelt sich die Photographie schneller als je zuvor, und diese Entwicklung ändert auch das Berufsbild des Photographen – ein Thema, das in der Einführung zu diesem Buch aufgegriffen wird. Trotz der wachsenden Ansprüche an ihre Zeit, schicken uns sehr viele Photographen nach wie vor eine Auswahl ihrer besten Arbeiten. Sie helfen uns damit, unseren Lesern einen repräsentativen Überblick über das Geschehen in der Welt der Photographie im letzten Jahr zu vermitteln. Mit diesen Zeilen richten wir ein herzliches «Dankeschön» an alle unsere treuen Einsender.

Alors que les langues universelles proprement dites ne connaissent plus guère de perfectionnements, la photographie peut à juste titre prétendre au rang d'une langue imagière universelle. Embarquée dans le train des communications modernes, elle connaît une évolution accélérée, qui modifie entre autres la profession du photographe – sujet qui est abordé dans l'Introduction du présent volume. Malgré le peu de temps dont disposent les vedettes de la photo, de très nombreux photographes nous font parvenir régulièrement leurs meilleurs travaux, ce qui nous permet de constituer un panorama vraiment représentatif des performances de la photographie mondiale au cours de l'année écoulée. Que ces valeureux et fidèles collaborateurs trouvent ici l'expression de nos remerciements les plus chaleureux.

HUMBERT + VOGT, Studios for visual and verbal communication of Riehen, Basle, envisioned this year's dust jacket. They have been active in the photographic field for the past ten years. They also occupy themselves with design, with slide and multimedia shows and with animated films for clients inside and outside Switzerland.

HUMBERT + VOGT swb/asg/dad, Studios für visuelle und verbale Kommunikation, Riehen/Basel, sind die Gestalter unseres Schutzumschlags. Seit 10 Jahren arbeiten sie auf allen Gebieten der Photographie. Sie befassen sich ebenfalls mit Design und Gestaltungsprogrammen, mit Dia- und Multimedia-Shows sowie mit Trickfilmen für einen internationalen Kundenkreis.

HUMBERT + VOGT swb/asg/dad, Studios de communication visuelle et verbale à Riehen/Bâle, sont les auteurs de notre jaquette. Depuis 10 ans, ils œuvrent dans tous les domaines de la photographie et réalisent aussi des travaux de design, des programmes conceptuels, des expositions dias ou multimédias et des dessins animés pour une clientèle internationale.

Horst W. Staubach

Photo-Designer, a New Name
for a Growing Profession

Instead of offering a general review of the photographic scene, this introduction takes a closer look at recent developments in the photographer's profession. Since these differ to some extent from country to country, we have asked HORST W. STAUBACH to outline the present situation in West Germany. Our author discovered his love of both photography and writing during the Second World War. After demobilization, he began to write for numerous photographic magazines in Germany and elsewhere. As a photographic journalist he was specially interested in the innumerable applications of photography and film in science, industry and engineering. A mark of recognition for his work in this field came when he was called to a post in the Deutsche Gesellschaft für Photographie (German Photography Society) in 1965. In 1966 the Central Association of German Photographers awarded him their Siver Pin of Honour and the Association of Free Photo-Designers made him their correspondent and consultant.

We live in a society that depends on efficiently functioning systems of communication. In the last twenty-five years the branch today known as visual communications has gained enormously in importance; and this has led to a considerable expansion of the design professions. This is reflected in a "Report on Artists" commissioned by the West German government. "While the group of the classic fine artists, viz. painters, sculptors and object makers, has stagnated at 8000 or 10000 in the last twenty-five years, the number of professional designers in the areas of advertising, communication, product and environmental design has risen between the 1950 and the 1970 censuses by something over 50 per cent to a figure in excess of 16000."

This development—as one might expect—has included many professional photographers. They are the people who have met the rising demand for photographs in advertising, industry and fashion as well as in teaching and in the technical and scientific fields. They have been integrated ever more completely in a process involving the translation of the relevant information into visual form. Their job has thus been to turn verbal information into pictures, and to do this in a way that attracts the attention of the viewer and is qualified to stick in his memory. Now according to the existing German regulations, based on old conventions and evaluation standards, the taking of pictures by a professional photographer is a form of handicraft. The new activities just described, however, are obviously not a mere handicraft. In other words, the existing rulings fail to take account of the fact that in much photographic work the manual and technical aspects are today of minor importance and a creative mental effort is one of the first prerequisites of a successful photograph.

In the course of the last quarter of a century it has therefore become increasingly clear that the functions of many photographers working in the visual communication field have very little to do with the "official" classification of their work by society and by the law. This naturally annoyed many photographers. They were also annoyed because they had often lost their direct contacts with clients or at least with the clients' advertising agencies, since graphic designers had come along to insert themselves between the two. This led to a situation which one photographer summed up ironically by saying: "Art directors think of us as layouters' assistants." This may have been an exaggeration, but the situation was in any case unacceptable to the creative photographer.

In these circumstances it was understandable that many photographers welcomed the founding, in 1969, of the BFF = Bund Freischaffender Foto-Designer (Association of Freelance Photo-Designers). Its primary objective was the "unification of all freelance photo-designers in a professional group which is recognized as a profession". The chosen designation of this profession—"Foto-Designer", a term not in general use in other languages—was meant to specify the functions of this limited circle of photographers. The term "photo-design" is defined in *Dumont's Lexikon der Fotographie* as follows: "Photo-design is a term applied to the preparation of information by photographic means for the purposes of observation, learning and communication. The work of the photo-designer is necessarily and essentially determined, quite apart from his manual and technical skills, by his mental and creative abilities in the conception, planning and shaping of the photographic picture." This definition is based on the profession of the photo-designer as conceived by the BFF in order to ensure adequate differentiation from the idea of a merely manual and technical activity. This differentiation also has a sociological aspect, since it forces society and legislators to change their standards of evaluation for this profession. The directives of the BFF, published in 1969, make the situation clear in stipulating an equal standing for the photo-designer and the graphic designer.

In the meantime the membership of the BFF—which celebrated its tenth anniversary at the beginning of 1979—has risen to 300. Each member has had to submit his work to a committee of experts who pass judgement on his qualifications (only one applicant in three is accepted). The severe requirements of membership underline the high standards of the BFF and the prestige it offers its members.

"The profession of the photo-designer, which is an offshoot of that of the photographer, but hardly any closer to it than the electronics engineer is to the electrician, is in the budding rather than in the flowering stage (and certainly far from full maturity)," wrote Prof. Kurt Weidemann in the foreword to the list of BFF members for 1979. Just where the future of the photo-designer's profession lies is at present a matter of conjecture. Very probably the spheres of activity of photo-designers and graphic designers will tend to draw closer together. Several facts show that this is more than mere speculation. Firstly, design is studied in West Germany, as it is in the USA, in high schools and universities. Courses for "photo-design specialists" or "photo/film design" include instruction, with varying emphasis, in general and specific graphic design disciplines. The young generation of photo-designers (the first wave is just out of school) will thus be able to rely on a wider spectrum of knowledge than students of photography pure and simple and will consequently be more competent collaborators for art directors or creative directors. Secondly, there is a tendency today for graphic designers to take any photographs they happen to need them-selves, which was much less common between the thirties and the fifties. An inquiry carried out by the Bund Deutscher Grafik-Designer (Association of German Graphic Designers) showed that 65 per cent of graphic designers now make use of photography as part of their job. In these circumstances it even seems quite possible that at some time in the future there will no longer be two professional groups but only one—that of the photo-graphic designers.

Horst W. Staubach

Photo-Designer — das neue Selbstverständnis eines Berufs

Statt einen allgemeinen Überblick über die photographische Szene zu geben, beschäftigt sich diese Einführung mit der neueren Entwicklung im Berufsbild des Photographen. Da es hier von Land zu Land Unterschiede gibt, haben wir HORST W. STAUBACH gebeten, die gegenwärtige Situation in der Bundesrepublik Deutschland zu beschreiben. Der Autor entdeckte seine Liebe zur Photographie und zum Schreiben während des 2. Weltkrieges, und nach dessen Beendigung begann er für zahlreiche Photozeitschriften im In- und Ausland zu schreiben. Als Photofachschriftsteller interessierte er sich besonders für die zahllosen Anwendungsmöglichkeiten von Photographie und Film in Wissenschaft, Industrie und Technik. In Anerkennung seiner publizistischen Verdienste auf diesem Gebiet wurde er 1965 in die Deutsche Gesellschaft für Photographie (DGPh) berufen. 1966 verlieh ihm der Centralverband Deutscher Photographen die Silberne Ehrennadel, und der Bund Freischaffender Foto-Designer berief ihn zum Korrespondierenden Berater.

Wir leben in einer Gesellschaft, die auf gut funktionierende Kommunikationssysteme angewiesen ist und ohne sie gar nicht existenzfähig wäre. Auf einen kurzen Nenner gebracht, bedeutet Kommunikation die Weiter- oder Wiedergabe von Informationen an Einzelpersonen oder bestimmte Zielgruppen. Als Transportmittel für Informationen hat die visuelle Kommunikation in den zurückliegenden 25 Jahren eine ungeahnte Bedeutung gewonnen. Das wiederum führte zu einer beträchtlichen Expansion der Designerberufe. Eine Tatsache, die durch Zahlen aus dem im Auftrag der Deutschen Bundesregierung erarbeiteten «Künstler-Report» eindrucksvoll belegt wird: «Während die Gruppe der klassischen bildenden Künstler, also Maler, Bildhauer und Objektemacher, in den letzten 25 Jahren bei etwa 8000 bis 10000 stagnierte, wuchs die Zahl der hauptberuflichen Designer in den Bereichen Werbung, Kommunikation, Produkt- und Umweltgestaltung zwischen den Volkszählungen 1950 und 1970 um wahrscheinlich über 50 Prozent auf mehr als 16000 an» (Dr. Karla Fohrbeck, *Die Künstler-Enquète und ihre Folgen für Foto-Designer*).

Einbezogen in diesen Entwicklungsprozess waren — wie hätte es auch anders sein können? — viele professionelle Photographen. Sie waren es, die den zunehmenden Bedarf an photographischen Aufnahmen für Werbung, Industrie und Mode, aber auch für die Verwendung im pädagogischen, technischen und wissenschaftlichen Bereich deckten. Mehr und mehr wurden sie integriert in einen Prozess, in dem ihnen die Aufgabe zufiel, Informationen aus den genannten Bereichen zu visualisieren. Ihre Aufgabe war es dabei, verbal formulierte Konzeptionen in die Bildersprache zu transponieren, sie in eine Bildkonzeption umzusetzen und so zu realisieren, dass die Aufmerksamkeit des Betrachters geweckt und ein hoher Gedächtnis-Haftwert erzielt wird. Eine Tätigkeit mit diesen Merkmalen entspricht aber keineswegs mehr einer handwerklichen Arbeit, obwohl sie nach überkommenen Kriterien so eingestuft werden müsste. Denn nach der deutschen Handwerksordnung — auf jahrzehntealten Konventionen und Bewertungsmassstäben fussend — ist nämlich jede von einem Berufsphotographen hergestellte Aufnahme das Ergebnis einer handwerklichen Arbeit und nichts anderes. Dass aber in vielen Fällen die handwerkliche Seite eine völlig untergeordnete Rolle spielte und dass erst durch eine geistig-kreative Leistung die Realisation einer Photographie überhaupt möglich wurde, bleibt dabei völlig unberücksichtigt.

Im Laufe der Entwicklung des letzten Vierteljahrhunderts wurde immer deutlicher, dass das an den neuen Tätigkeitsmerkmalen orientierte Selbstverständnis vieler im Bereich der visuellen Kommunikation tätigen Photographen nicht mehr in Einklang zu bringen war mit der «offiziellen» Einschätzung der berufsphotographischen Tätigkeit durch Gesellschaft und Gesetzgeber. Verständlicherweise war das für viele Photographen ein Ärgernis. Ein weiteres Ärgernis war aber auch, dass die direkten Kontakte mit den Auftraggebern oder den sie vertretenden Werbeagenturen verloren gingen. Zwischen sie und die Photographen schob sich nämlich die Gruppe der Graphik-Designer. Das führte zu einem Zustand, der von einem Photographen — mit einem unüberhörbar bitter-ironischen Unterton — so gekennzeichnet wurde: «Art-Directoren halten uns doch nur für eine Art Ausführungsgehilfen des Layouters.» Wenn hier auch bewusst übertrieben wurde, so wäre auch eine näherungsweise ähnliche Situation für den kreativen Photographen unerträglich.

So war es verständlich, dass von vielen Photographen die 1969 bekanntgegebene Gründung des «Bundes Freischaffender Foto-Designer» (BFF) lebhaft begrüsst wurde. Primäres Ziel des BFF war die «Zusammenführung aller freischaffenden Photo-Designer zu einer Berufsgruppe, die als Freier Beruf anerkannt ist». Die mit Bedacht gewählte Berufsbezeichnung «Foto-Designer» signalisiert das neue Selbstverständnis einer nach Art ihrer Tätigkeit begrenzten Gruppe von Photographen. Der Begriff Photo-Design wird in

«DuMont's Lexikon der Fotografie» so definiert: «Als Foto-Design bezeichnet man die Aufbereitung von Informationen mit fotografischen Mitteln für Zwecke der Beobachtung, des Lernens und der Verständigung. Die Arbeit des Photo-Designers ist, neben seinen handwerklich-technischen Leistungen, notwendig und wesentlich bestimmt durch dessen geistig-schöpferische Fähigkeiten bei Konzeption, Entwurf und Gestaltung des fotografischen Bildes.» Diese Definition stützt sich auf das Berufsbild für Photo-Designer, das vom BFF mit dem Ziel einer Abgrenzung gegenüber einer rein handwerklichen Tätigkeit von Berufsphotographen erarbeitet wurde. Diese Abgrenzung hat insofern auch einen soziologischen Aspekt, als sie Gesellschaft und Gesetzgeber eine Neuorientierung hinsichtlich des Stellenwerts dieses Berufs abnötigt. In den 1969 veröffentlichten Grundsätzen des BFF heisst es daher auch unmissverständlich: «Gleichstellung mit den Gebrauchsgrafikern» (der Begriff Graphik-Designer wurde erst später eingeführt).

Inzwischen hat der BFF – er konnte Anfang 1979 auf zehn Jahre seines Bestehens zurückblicken – rund 300 Mitglieder. Jedes einzelne Mitglied musste sich mit seinen Arbeiten einem Gutachter-Ausschuss stellen, der über die Qualifikation des Bewerbers zu befinden hatte (im Durchschnitt werden von 30 Bewerbern nur zehn zugelassen). Die strenge Auswahl der Mitglieder unterstreicht den elitären Anspruch und den prestige-orientierten Charakter des BFF.

«Der Berufszweig der Foto-Designer, aus dem Berufsstand der Photographen hervorgegangen – und diesem kaum noch näher verbunden als der Elektroniker dem Elektriker – steht eher im Alter der Knospung als der Blüte (oder gar der Reife).» Das schreibt Prof. Kurt Weidemann im Vorwort des BFF-Mitgliederverzeichnisses 1979. Wohin die weitere Entwicklung des Photo-Designer-Berufes gehen wird, darüber kann man nur Vermutungen anstellen. Mit grosser Wahrscheinlichkeit zu erwarten ist eine zunehmende Annäherung der Tätigkeitsmerkmale von Photo-Designer und Graphik-Designer. Dass dies keine reine Spekulation ist, mögen folgende zwei Fakten belegen: 1. Ähnlich wie in den USA ist das Design-Studium in der BRD in den Hochschulen angesiedelt. Studiengänge wie «Photo-Design-Spezialist» oder «Photo-/Film-Design» berücksichtigen mit unterschiedlicher Gewichtung allgemeine und spezifisch graphische Grundlagen des Designs im Lehrangebot. Die junge Generation der Photo-Designer (die ersten Absolventen haben gerade die Hochschule verlassen) wird sich also auf eine breitere Kenntnisbasis stützen können als der rein photographisch ausgebildete Student und daher ein kompetenterer Gesprächspartner für den Art-Director bzw. den Creative-Director sein können.
2. Gehörte es in den dreissiger bis fünfziger Jahren noch zur Ausnahme, so kann man heute bei Graphik-Designern schon von dem Trend sprechen, etwa benötigte photographische Aufnahmen selbst herzustellen. Eine Umfrage des Bundes Deutscher Grafik-Designer ergab, dass 65 Prozent der Graphik-Designer das Medium Photographie in ihrer Tätigkeit einsetzen. So scheint die Vermutung nicht von der Hand zu weisen zu sein, dass es in absehbarer Zukunft keine Unterscheidung mehr zwischen Graphik-Designer und Photo-Designer geben wird. Vielmehr ist die Integration dieser beiden Berufsgruppen zum Photo-Graphik-Designer sehr wahrscheinlich.

Horst W. Staubach

Le designer photographe — redéfinition d'une profession

Au lieu de passer en revue l'ensemble de la scène photographique, l'introduction que l'on va lire traite de l'évolution récente de la profession de photographe. Le tableau se présente différemment de pays en pays. Aussi avons-nous demandé à HORST W. STAUBACH de nous décrire la situation qui prévaut actuellement en République fédérale d'Allemagne. C'est de la Seconde Guerre mondiale que date l'engouement de l'auteur pour la photo et le journalisme. Au lendemain de la guerre, il s'est mis à écrire pour de nombreux magazines photo allemands et étrangers. Publiciste spécialisé dans le domaine de la photographie, il s'est intéressé en particulier aux nombreuses applications scientifiques, industrielles et techniques de la photographie et du cinéma. Ses travaux d'écrivain lui ont valu sa nomination au sein de la Deutsche Gesellschaft für Photographie DGPh (Société allemande de photographie) en 1965. En 1966, le Centralverband Deutscher Photographen (Fédération centrale des photographes allemands) lui conférait son Insigne d'honneur en argent et le Bund Freischaffender Foto-Designer (Fédération allemande des designers photographes indépendants) le nommait conseiller correspondant.

Nous vivons dans une société qui dépend du bon fonctionnement des réseaux de communication sans lesquels elle ne serait pas viable. En bref, communication veut dire ici la transmission ou reproduction d'informations destinées à des individus ou à des segments déterminés de la population. En tant que moyen de transport d'informations, la communication visuelle a pris une importance extrême au cours du quart de siècle écoulé. Il en est résulté une expansion considérable des professions du design, comme le montrent de façon impressionnante les chiffres compilés dans le «Künstler-Report» (Rapport sur l'état de l'art) pour le gouvernement de l'Allemagne fédérale: «Alors que le groupe des artistes plastiques au sens classique du terme – peintres, sculpteurs, créateurs d'objets – s'est stabilisé autour des 8 à 10 000 ces 25 dernières années, les designers à temps complet engagés dans la publicité, la communication, l'esthétique industrielle et l'aménagement de l'environnement ont vu probablement plus que doubler leur nombre entre les recensements de 1950 et 1970 et sont aujourd'hui plus de 16 000» (Dr Karla Fohrbeck, *Die Künstler-Enquete und ihre Folgen für Foto-Designer,* L'Enquête relative à l'état de l'art et ses conséquences pour la profession des designers photographes).

Il va sans dire que nombre de photographes professionnels ont participé à cette évolution. Il leur appartenait en effet de satisfaire à la boulimie photographique grandissante de la publicité, de l'industrie et de la mode, mais aussi de l'enseignement, de la technologie et des sciences. Ils ont ainsi été progressivement intégrés dans un processus où ils étaient chargés de visualiser l'information émanant de ces différents secteurs. Leur tâche consistait à transposer dans le langage des images des concepts verbalisés, d'en faire des concepts visuels et de mettre ces messages en œuvre de manière à accrocher l'attention et à déclencher une réaction mnémonique durable. Une activité répondant à ces critères n'a toutefois plus rien à faire avec les principes artisanaux qui guident traditionnellement le métier de photographe. Le règlement qui régit l'artisanat en Allemagne et qui est basé sur des conventions et principes d'évaluation vieux de plusieurs décennies veut que toute photo réalisée par un photographe professionnel soit le résultat d'un travail artisanal, sans plus. C'est ne pas tenir compte du fait que l'aspect artisanal de nombre de réalisations ne joue plus qu'un rôle infinitésimal et que l'intelligence créatrice est de loin ce qui s'affirme dans une photographie bien venue au plan du design.

Au cours de l'évolution intervenue ces 25 dernières années, il est apparu de plus en plus clairement que la conception nouvelle que se faisaient de leur métier un grand nombre de photographes engagés dans des réalisations de communication visuelle en fonction des critères d'appréciation nouveaux de leur activité ne cadrait plus du tout avec l'idée «officielle» que s'en faisaient la société et le législateur rivés à la notion de l'artisan photographe professionnel. Si cet état de choses était déjà de nature à irriter de nombreux professionnels, un nouveau sujet d'irritation naissait du fait que le contact direct avec les clients ou les agences de publicité représentant les clients était rompu par l'intercalage des designers graphiques. Les photographes avaient finalement l'impression d'être ravalés aux yeux des directeurs artistiques au rang de simples auxiliaires de l'exécution d'un lay-out. Ce constat mi-ironique, mi-amer comportait certes quelque exagération. Et pourtant, semblable situation ou toute situation pouvant s'en rapprocher ne pouvait être tolérée par les photographes créatifs.

C'est ainsi que la fondation, en 1969, du «Bund Freischaffender Foto-Designer» BFF (Fédération allemande des designers photographes indépendants) fut accueillie avec joie et soulagement par nombre de photographes. Cette organisation s'est tracée pour but de «regrouper tous les designers photographes indépendants en un groupement professionnel à qui puisse être reconnue la qualité de profession libérale». L'appellation «designer photographe» est choisie de manière à refléter la conception nouvelle que se fait de son métier un groupe de photographes limité par la nature même de ses fonctions. Le «Lexikon der Fotografie» (Encyclopédie de la photo) de DuMont donne la définition suivante: «Par design photographique, on entend le traitement de l'information par des moyens photographiques aux fins d'observation, d'apprentissage et de communication. Le travail du designer photographe, outre ses prestations artisanales et techniques, est nécessairement et essentiellement axé sur des compétences intellectuelles créatrices lors de la conception du projet et de la réalisation de l'image photographique.» Cette définition s'appuie sur le profil professionnel élaboré par la BFF pour le designer photographe en vue de délimiter son activité par rapport aux tâches purement artisanales du photographe professionnel. Cette délimitation a aussi valeur sociologique en obligeant la société et le législateur à redéfinir l'importance de cette profession. Les principes de la BFF publiés en 1969 sont sans équivoque à cet égard: «Assimilation des professions de designer photographique et d'artiste publicitaire» (par la suite rebaptisé en designer graphique).

Début 1979, la BFF avait 10 années d'existence et comptait près de 300 membres. Chaque candidat doit présenter ses travaux à un comité d'experts qui statue sur son admission et refuse en moyenne 20 candidats sur 30. Cette sélection rigoureuse souligne le caractère élitiste de la Fédération et l'auréole de prestige dont elle se pare.

«La profession de designer photographe, qui s'est séparée du tronc commun des photographes professionnels et n'a avec ce dernier plus que les vagues relations qui unissent par exemple l'électronicien et l'électricien n'en est encore qu'à sa phase de bourgeonnement avant de passer à celle de la floraison et de la maturation.» Voici ce qu'on pouvait lire sous la plume du Pr Kurt Weidemann dans l'avant-propos de la liste des membres BFF de 1979. On ne peut que conjecturer l'évolution future de la profession de designer photographe. Ce qui semble fort probable, c'est que les activités du designer photographe et celle du designer graphique vont s'aligner toujours davantage l'une sur l'autre. Ce n'est pas pure spéculation, comme tendent à le montrer les deux facteurs suivants: 1. L'étude du design est en Allemagne fédérale, comme aux Etats-Unis, affaire des universités. Il existe désormais des curriculums de «spécialiste en design photographique» ou «design photo/cinéma» qui tiennent compte de cette spécialisation au sein du design. La toute jeune génération de designers photographes (qui compte les premiers diplômés de ces branches frais émoulus de l'université) bénéficie d'une formation de base plus large et plus complète que celle qui n'a étudié que la photo, et pourra donc s'affirmer comme interlocuteur plus compétent face aux directeurs artistiques et aux directeurs créatifs. 2. Ce qui, durant les années 30, 40 et 50, était encore l'exception se généralise de plus en plus chez les graphistes, à savoir la production personnelle des photos nécessaires à leur travail. Un sondage de la Fédération allemande des designers graphiques (Bund Deutscher Grafik-Designer) révèle que 65% de ses membres font appel à la photographie dans leur activité professionnelle. Il semble donc difficile d'écarter à la légère l'hypothèse selon laquelle, dans un avenir proche, la distinction entre designer photographe et designer graphique sera entièrement abolie. Il paraît au contraire tout à fait probable que ces deux groupes professionnels fusionneront un jour pour donner naissance au designer photo/graphique.

Index to Photographers
Verzeichnis der Photographen
Index des photographes

Index to Designers
Verzeichnis der Gestalter
Index des maquettistes

Index to Art Directors
Verzeichnis der künstlerischen Leiter
Index des directeurs artistiques

Index to Agencies and Studios
Verzeichnis der Agenturen und Studios
Index des agences et studios

Index to Publishers
Verzeichnis der Verleger
Index des éditeurs

Index to Advertisers
Verzeichnis der Auftraggeber
Index des clients

■ Entry instructions may be requested by anyone interested in submitting samples of exceptional photography or graphics for possible inclusion in our annuals. No fees involved. Closing dates for entries:
PHOTOGRAPHIS (advertising and editorial photography): 30 June
GRAPHIS ANNUAL (advertising and editorial art and design): 31 January
GRAPHIS POSTERS (an annual of poster art): 30 June
Write to: The Graphis Press, Dufourstrasse 107, 8034 Zurich, Switzerland

■ Einsendebedingungen können von jedermann angefordert werden, der uns Beispiele hervorragender Photographie oder Graphik zur Auswahl für unsere Jahrbücher unterbreiten möchte. Es werden keine Gebühren erhoben. Einsendetermine:
PHOTOGRAPHIS (Werbe- und redaktionelle Photographie): 30. Juni
GRAPHIS ANNUAL (Werbe- und redaktionelle Graphik): 31. Januar
GRAPHIS POSTERS (ein Jahrbuch der Plakatkunst): 30. Juni
Adresse: Graphis Verlag, Dufourstrasse 107, 8034 Zürich, Schweiz

■ Tout intéressé à la soumission de travaux photographiques et graphiques recevra les informations nécessaires sur demande. Sans charge de participation. Dates limites:
PHOTOGRAPHIS (photographie publicitaire et rédactionnelle): 30 juin
GRAPHIS ANNUAL (art graphique publicitaire et rédactionnel): 31 janvier
GRAPHIS POSTERS (annuaire sur l'art de l'affiche): 30 juin
S'adresser à: Editions Graphis, Dufourstrasse 107, 8034 Zurich, Suisse

Editor and Art Director: Walter Herdeg
Assistant Editors: Stanley Mason
Project Manager: Heinke Jenssen
Designers: Ulrich Kemmner, Klaus Schröder
Art Assistants: Martin Byland, Willy Müller, Peter R. Wittwer

1

Magazine Advertisements

Newspaper Advertisements

Zeitschriften-Inserate

Zeitungs-Inserate

Annonces de revues

Annonces de presse

1 Magazine advertisement for *Kraft* mayonnaise, which is made with eggs. Full page, full colour. (USA)
2, 3 Trade magazine advertisements from a series about the services offered by *Durkee* to bakers. (USA)
4, 5, 9 Complete double-spread magazine advertisements and photograph used for one of them, from a campaign of the *Migros* grocery stores, here for fresh vegetables and fruit. (SWI)
6, 7 Two editorial-type magazine advertisements from a campaign for *Iglo* deep-frozen foods. Colour illustrations. (GER)
8 Double-spread colour magazine advertisement for *Energen* low-calorie jams and marmalades. (GBR)

1 Zeitschrifteninserat für *Kraft*-Mayonnaise, die mit Eiern hergestellt wird. Ganze Seite, in Farbe. (USA)
2, 3 Aus einer Reihe von Fachzeitschriften-Inseraten für *Durkee*-Bäckereiprodukte. (USA)
4, 5, 9 Komplette, doppelseitige Zeitschrifteninserate und eine Aufnahme daraus, aus einer Kampagne des schweizerischen Einzelhandelsgiganten *Migros*, unter dem Motto «frisch von der *Migros*»; hier für Gemüse und Obst. (SWI)
6, 7 Farbinserate aus einer Magazin-Kampagne für *Iglo*-Tiefkühlkost, mit Kochrezepten im redaktionellen Stil. (GER)
8 Doppelseitiges Zeitschriften-Inserat in Farbe für kalorienarme *Energen*-Konfiture. (GBR)

DESIGNER / GESTALTER / MAQUETTISTE:

1 John Koelle
2 Bob Rath
3 Frank Bartucci
4, 5, 9 Max Rindlisbacher
6, 7 Wolfgang Schönholz
8 Ian Whapshott

ART DIRECTOR / DIRECTEUR ARTISTIQUE:

1 John Koelle
2 Bob Rath
3 Ray Galigardi
4, 5, 9 Max Rindlisbacher
6, 7 Wolfram Dörr/Klaus-Jürgen Hergert
8 Ian Whapshott

AGENCY / AGENTUR / AGENCE – STUDIO:

1 J. Walter Thompson
2, 3 Meldrum and Fewsmith, Inc.
4, 5, 9 Gisler & Gisler
6, 7 Heumann, Ogilvy & Mather
8 FGA/Kenyon & Eckhardt Ltd.

Frisch von der Migros-woher denn sonst.

MIGROSfrisch

5

You've got to break some eggs to make real mayonnaise. At Kraft we do.

1

Presenting Beta Plus with SSL.
An easier way to put your bread together.

Durkee
We stay one step ahead of tomorrow.

2

Any way you slice it, new B-40 can cut your costs.

Durkee
We stay one step ahead of tomorrow.

3

1 «On ne fait pas de mayonnaise sans casser des œufs – chez *Kraft* du moins.» Annonce de magazine polychrome. (USA)
2, 3 Annonces figurant dans une série pour un service *Durkee* offert aux boulangers. (USA)
4, 5, 9 Annonces de magazine double page et photographie utilisée pour l'une d'elles. Elles figurent dans une campagne en faveur de la chaîne des magasins *Migros*. Ici on présente des fruits et des légumes «toujours frais de chez *Migros*». (SWI)
6, 7 «Il n'y a pratiquement rien qu'on ne puisse faire avec des Steaklets.» – «La pâte feuilletée surgelée incitera même les gens les plus honnêtes à tricher.» Pour produits surgelés. (GER)
8 Pour une confiture basse en calories. Polychromie. (GBR)

PHOTOGRAPHER / PHOTOGRAPH / PHOTOGRAPHE:

1 Clay Taylor
2 Phil Marco
3 Shigeta-Wright
4, 5, 9 Marcel Hayoz
6, 7 Richard Stradtmann
8 Martin McGlone

Es gibt fast nichts, was Sie mit Steaklets nicht machen können.

Iglo
Du weißt man, daß es schmeckt.

6

Blätterteig aus der Tiefkühltruhe verleitet die ehrlichsten Leute zum Schwindeln.

Iglo
Du weißt man, daß es schmeckt.

7

Advertisements / Inserate / Annonces

4

Energen have always held the belief that slimmers have taste buds, just like everyone else.

So when they brought out their new range of low calorie jams and marmalades they made absolutely certain that first and foremost, they tasted nice.

You might even find that you prefer Energen jams and marmalades to the ordinary ones.

Some people think that taking out some of the sugar makes them taste more fruity.

There are three fruit-filled Energen jams, strawberry, raspberry and blackcurrant. And two marmalades, orange jelly and thick cut.

And they have only half the calories of ordinary jams and marmalades.

That means from now on you can have your diet — with jam on it.

Energen low calorie jams and marmalades.

It isn't jam packed with calories.

8

Frisch von der Migros-woher denn sonst.

Ideales Klima, beste Anbaugebiete, ständig kontrolliertes Wachsen und Gedeihen, sehr sorgfältiges Pflücken und ein ausgeklügeltes Kühlschnelltransport-System, das sind die guten Gründe für unsere fruchtig frischen Früchte.

Nicht nur eine Augenweide, auch eine herzhafte, vitaminreiche Abwechslung für den Gaumen.

Das erwartet Sie jetzt täglich in Hülle und Fülle in Ihrer Migros – immer Migrosfrisch und immer zum Migros-Preis.

MIGROSfrisch
weil alles frisch weggeht

9

10

11

12

14

PHOTOGRAPHER / PHOTOGRAPH / PHOTOGRAPHE:

10, 11 Julian Cottrell
12 Jim Brady
13 Larry Sillen
14 Paul Bussell
15, 16 John Paul Endress

DESIGNER / GESTALTER / MAQUETTISTE:

12 Jean Claude Goldberg
13 Jim Scalfone
14 Allen Lofts

10, 11 Two advertisements from a magazine campaign for *Majala* cream desserts. (GER)
12 Full-page colour magazine advertisement for *Marlboro* cigarettes. No copy. (FRA)
13 Full-page magazine advertisement for *Chivas Regal* whisky. Full colour, from a campaign. (USA)
14 Advertisement for *Chivers* thick-cut marmalade. (GBR)
15, 16 Detail of the photography and complete double-spread trade magazine ad for packages made by The Continental Group, serving for instance to protect tomatoes. (USA)

10, 11 Zwei Anzeigen aus einer Werbekampagne für *Majala*-Cremedessert, das ohne Kochen zubereitet wird. (GER)
12 Ganzseitiges farbiges Zeitschrifteninserat für *Marlboro*-Zigaretten, ohne Worte. (FRA)
13 Ganzseitiges Inserat, farbig, aus einer Zeitschriftenkampagne für *Chivas-Regal*-Whisky. (USA)
14 Inserat für Orangen-Konfiture von *Chivers,* nach altem englischem Rezept hergestellt. (GBR)
15, 16 Detail der Photographie und Doppelseite eines Inserats für Verpackungen der *Continental Group.* Hier wird am Beispiel der Tomaten erklärt, auf welche Weise ihre natürliche Haltbarkeit verlängert werden kann. (USA)

10, 11 Deux annonces d'une campagne publicitaire en faveur des desserts *Majala.* (GER)
12 Annonce de magazine pleine page (en couleurs) pour les cigarettes *Marlboro.* Il n'y a aucun texte. (FRA)
13 Annonce de magazine pour une marque de whisky. Pleine page en couleurs figurant dans une campagne. (USA)
14 Annonce pour une confiture à l'orange, faite d'après une vieille recette anglaise. (GBR)
15, 16 Détail de la photo et page double complète d'un magazine professionnel pour une marque d'emballages. Ici on explique comment les tomates peuvent être conservées en les emballant comme il faut. (USA)

ART DIRECTOR / DIRECTEUR ARTISTIQUE:

10, 11 Uwe Duvendack
12 Jean Claude Goldberg
13 Jim Scalfone
14 Allen Lofts
15, 16 Arvale Rogers

AGENCY / AGENTUR / AGENCE — STUDIO:

10, 11 TBWA
12 Leo Burnett
13 Doyle Dane Bernbach, Inc.
14 Ted Bates
15, 16 Young & Rubicam

If you think people buy Chivas Regal just for the bottle,
try selling this one.

13

16

15

17

20

17, 20 Detail of the colour shot and complete double-spread trade magazine advertisement for a new range of *Hartley's* sauces marketed for convenience in portion packs. (GBR)
18 Full-page magazine advertisement in full colour for a brand of English *State Express* cigarettes. Gold pack. (USA)
19 "My Parisienne." Full-page colour magazine advertisement for *Parisienne* cigarettes. (SWI)
21, 22 Two double-spread magazine advertisements in full colour from a series about the "impeccable pedigree" of *Hennessy* cognac. This pedigree was obviously best embodied in St. Bernards as legendary carriers of cognac to travellers in distress. (GBR)

17, 20 «Bekommen Ihre Kunden zuviel von einer guten Sache?» Detail und Doppelseite einer Fachzeitschriftenanzeige für *Hartley's*-Saucen, abgefüllt in praktischen Portionspackungen. (GBR)
18 Ganzseitiges Zeitschrifteninserat in Farbe für *555-International*-Zigaretten mit Anspielung auf «die feine englische Art». Angabe des Teer- und Nikotingehalts einer Zigarre. (USA)
19 Ganzseitiges farbiges Inserat für *Parisienne*-Zigaretten aus einer Kampagne unter dem Slogan «meine Parisienne», zu der auch Plakate gehören. (SWI)
21, 22 Zwei doppelseitige, farbige Zeitschrifteninserate aus einer Serie über den «tadellosen Stammbaum» des *Hennessy*-Cognacs. (GBR)

17, 20 «Vos clients, ont-ils trop de quelque chose de bon?» Détail et page double d'un magazine professionnel pour les sauces *Hartley's*, qui sont vendues par portions. (GBR)
18 Annonce de magazine pleine page (en couleurs) pour une marque de cigarettes avec une allusion aux «bonnes manières anglaises». Indications de la teneur en nicotine. (USA)
19 Annonce pleine page pour les cigarettes *Parisienne*, figurant dans un campagne lancée avec le slogan «ma parisienne». En polychromie. (SWI)
21, 22 Deux annonces de magazine double page, en polychromie, tirées d'une série consacrée au «pedigree impeccable» du cognac *Hennessy*. (GBR)

Advertisements / Inserate / Annonces

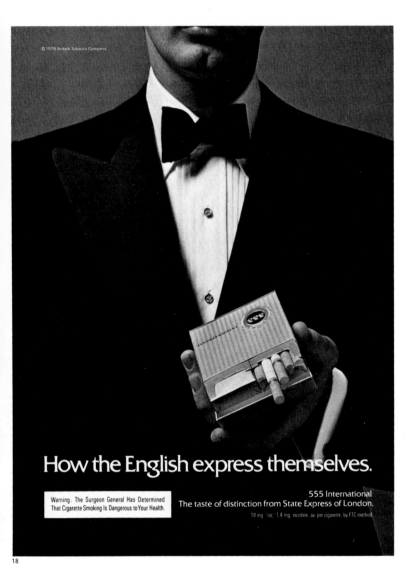

18

19

21

22

23 Full-page magazine advertisement against a sailing background for *Booth's* gin. Full colour. (USA)
24 "Sometimes it's quite easy to be faithful." Magazine advertisement for *Cinzano* white vermouth. Full-colour illustration. (ITA)
25 A humorous who-dun-it magazine advertisement for a *Seagram* whisky. Dark blue ground, gold embroidery. (USA)
26, 27 "Green *Tuborg* makes life a bit greener." Two full-colour advertisements from a campaign for *Tuborg* beer. (DEN)
28 "*Harveys Bristol Cream* costs only 10 Kr. more than a good bottle of sherry." Colour magazine advertisement for *Harveys* sherry. (DEN)
29, 30 Complete magazine advertisement and detail of the shot of an old glass for *Herrenhäuser* beer. Title: "Drinking culture." (GER)

23 Ganzseitiges, farbiges Zeitschrifteninserat für *Booth/s*-Gin. (Martini ist in den USA ein Aperitif, der mit Gin gemixt wird.) (USA)
24 Ganzseitige Zeitschriftenanzeige in Farbe für *Cinzano Bianco*. (ITA)
25 «Der Butler war es.» Ganzseitiges, farbiges Zeitschrifteninserat für *Seagram's* kanadischen Whisky *Crown Royal*. (USA)
26, 27 Zwei ganzseitige, farbige Zeitschrifteninserate aus einer Kampagne für *Tuborg*-Bier, mit dem Slogan «das grüne *Tuborg* macht das Leben ein bisschen grüner». (DEN)
28 «*Harveys Bristol Cream* kostet nur 10 Kronen mehr als eine gute Flasche Sherry.» Ganzseitiges Zeitschrifteninserat für spanischen Sherry. (DEN)
29, 30 Ganzseitige Zeitschriftenanzeige und Detail der Aufnahme für *Herrenhäuser Pilsner*, hier in einem kostbaren alten Glas. (GER)

PHOTOGRAPHER / PHOTOGRAPH:
23 Klaus Lucka
24 Philip Jude
25 Arthur Beck
26–28 Finn Rosted
29, 30 K. Ohlenforst

DESIGNER / GESTALTER:
23 Eric Overkamp
29, 30 W. Würdinger

ART DIRECTOR:
23 Eric Overkamp
24 Renato Deandrea
25 Jerry Prestomburgo
26, 27 Peter Wibroe
28 Gorm Larsen
29, 30 W. Würdinger

AGENCY / AGENTUR:
23 J. Walter Thompson
24 Young & Rubicam
25 Arthur Beck
26, 27 Partners
28 Gorm Larsen & Partners I/S
29, 30 Gottschling & Würdinger

Advertisements
Inserate
Annonces

23 Annonce de magazine pleine page, en couleurs, pour le gin *Booth's*. (Aux Etats-Unis le «martini» est un apéritif contenant du gin.) (USA)
24 «Des fois il est facile d'être fidèle.» Annonce de magazine pour *Cinzano Bianco*. Illustration en polychromie. (ITA)
25 «C'était le butler.» Annonce de magazine pour une marque de whisky. Broderie dorée sur fond bleu foncé. (USA)
26, 27 «La *Tuborg* verte rend la vie un peu plus verte.» Annonces figurant dans une campagne en faveur de la bière *Tuborg*. En polychromie. (DEN)
28 «*Harveys Bristol Cream* ne coûte que 10 couronnes de plus qu'une bonne bouteille de sherry.» Annonce en couleurs pour un sherry. (DEN)
29, 30 Annonce de magazine et détail de la photo présentant un ancien verre pour la bière *Herrenhäuser*. Slogan: «Culture du boisson.» (GER)

30

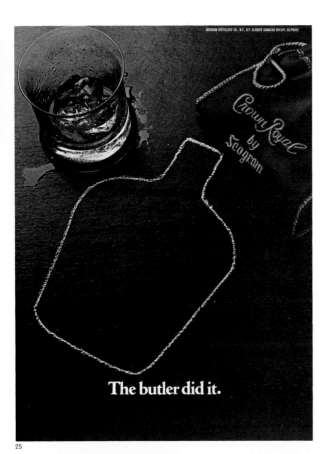

25

28

29

31

34

32

Born in Israel
The essence of the Jaffa orange with just a hint of fine chocolate.
Sabra Liqueur

33

31, 32 Photographs for advertisements and posters forming part of a campaign for *Benson & Hedges* cigarettes. (GBR)
33 Colour magazine advertisement for the orange liqueur *Sabra* made in Israel. (USA)
34, 35 Magazine advertisements with colour illustrations from a series that uses big names to popularize *Puerto Rican* rums for mixed drinks—here white rum and tonic and white rum and soda. (USA)

31, 32 Aufnahmen, beide farbig, aus einer Werbekampagne in Form von Zeitschrifteninseraten und Plakaten, für *Benson-&-Hedges*-Zigaretten. (GBR)
33 Farbiges Inserat für den israelischen *Sabra*-Likör, «hergestellt aus Jaffa-Orangen und einer Spur feiner Schokolade». (USA)
34, 35 Zwei farbige Beispiele aus einer Inseratenkampagne für weissen Rum aus Puerto Rico, beide mit einer Rahmengeschichte zu der entsprechenden Titelzeile. (USA)

31, 32 Photographies utilisées pour des annonces et affiches qui faisaient partie d'une campagne publicitaire lancée en faveur des cigarettes *Benson & Hedges*. (GBR)
33 «Née en Israël.» Annonce de magazine (en polychromie) pour une liqueur à l'orange provenant de l'Israël. (USA)
34, 35 Annonces figurant dans une campagne publicitaire en faveur d'un rhum blanc du Puerto Rico. Chacune présente une petite historie portant sur le rhum. (USA)

PHOTOGRAPHER / PHOTOGRAPH / PHOTOGRAPHE:
31, 32 Adrian Flowers
34, 35 Alen MacWeeney

DESIGNER / GESTALTER / MAQUETTISTE:
31, 32 Graham Watson/John O'Donnell
34, 35 Carol Nelson

ART DIRECTOR / DIRECTEUR ARTISTIQUE:
31, 32 Graham Watson
34, 35 Carol Nelson

AGENCY / AGENTUR / AGENCE – STUDIO:
31, 32 Collett Dickenson Pearce & Partners Ltd.
34, 35 Kenyon & Eckhardt, Inc.

"Ilie Nastase introduced us to white rum and tonic."

"One day when I was photographing a match for a tennis magazine, Ilie Nastase came over to say hello. He displayed his usual charm—and then proceeded to tell me how much he hated one of my pictures of him in a recent issue.

That night, in a spirit of atonement, Ilie took Bob and me out to a Japanese restaurant. Before dinner, he ordered Puerto Rican white rum and tonic, a drink we had never tried before. We were intrigued, so we ordered the same.

When Ilie is right, he's right. White rum and tonic were made for each other.

A Rumanian in a Japanese restaurant introducing two Americans to Puerto Rican white rum.

That's how we got on to a good thing."

Convert yourself.
Instead of automatically ordering gin and tonic, try white rum and Canada Dry Tonic next time. Canada Dry is the classic summer tonic. And Puerto Rican Rum makes a smoother drink than gin or vodka—for a very good reason. Unlike gin or vodka, white rum from Puerto Rico is aged for at least a full year before it's bottled. And when it comes to smoothness, aging is the name of the game.

PUERTO RICAN RUMS
Aged for smoothness and taste.
For free "Light Rums of Puerto Rico" recipes, write: Puerto Rican Rums, Dept. XXX, 1290 Avenue of the Americas, N.Y., N.Y. 10019 © 1978 Commonwealth of Puerto Rico.

34

"Liza introduced us to white rum and soda at an Andy Warhol party."

We were introduced to Liza Minnelli at a party Andy Warhol gave for his magazine "Interview." What amazed us about her was that the personality she projects on stage is not an act at all. It's simply Liza. She radiates such warmth and enthusiasm that after an hour of conversation we both felt as if we'd known her all our lives.

During the evening I asked Liza if I could get her a drink and she ordered something I'd never tasted before: white rum and soda. It sounded interesting (Liza has a way of making everything sound interesting) so I tried one. Then my wife tried one. From that moment, white rum and soda has been one of our favorite drinks.

White rum also mixes marvelously with tonic.

is fantastic with orange juice and makes a better martini than gin or vodka.

A Warhol party, the start of a friendship with Liza Minnelli and an introduction to white rum. Not bad for one evening.

Convert yourself.
Instead of automatically ordering a vodka and soda, try white rum and soda next time. You'll find it makes a smoother drink than vodka for gin for a very good reason. Unlike gin and vodka, white rum is aged for at least a full year before it's bottled. And when it comes to smoothness, aging is the name of the game.

PUERTO RICAN RUMS
Aged for smoothness and taste.
For free "Light Rums of Puerto Rico" recipes, write: Puerto Rican Rums, Dept. XXX, 1290 Avenue of the Americas, N.Y., N.Y. 10019 © 1977 Commonwealth of Puerto Rico.

35

36

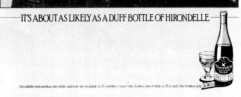

37

39

Advertisements / Inserate / Annonces

38

36, 37 From a series of black-and-white magazine advertisements presenting unlikely contingencies, for *Hirondelle* wines. (GBR)
38 "Forty-six countries have water sent from Germany." Advertisement for *Apollinaris* mineral water. (GER)
39, 40 Complete double-spread magazine advertisement and detail of the photograph in actual size, for a mineral water that was already being drunk all over the world 200 years ago. (GER)

36, 37 Aus einer Serie von Schwarzweiss-Zeitschrifteninseraten für *Hirondelle*-Weine. «Eine schlechte Flasche *Hirondelle* ist so wahrscheinlich wie das in den Aufnahmen Gezeigte.» (GBR)
38 Anzeige für *Apollinaris*-Mineralwasser, aus einer Kampagne zu der auch Plakate gehören. (GER)
39, 40 Doppelseitiges Zeitschrifteninserat für *Staatl.-Selters*-Mineralwasser und Aufnahme in Originalgrösse. (GER)

36, 37 D'une série d'annonces pour les vins *Hirondelle* dont le défaut de qualité est comparé à des événements impossibles. (GBR)
38 «46 pays se font envoyer de l'eau depuis l'Allemagne.» Annonce en faveur de l'eau minérale *Apollinaris*. (GER)
39, 40 Annonces de magazine double page et détail de la photographie (en grandeur nature) pour une eau minérale qu'on a déjà bue il y a 200 ans dans le monde entier. (GER)

41

42

Spis deg mett med god samvittighet

43

44

PHOTOGRAPHER / PHOTOGRAPH / PHOTOGRAPHE:
41, 42 Jim Marvy/Kerry Peterson
43 Jon Halvorsen
44 Perazzoli
45 Carl Fischer

DESIGNER / GESTALTER / MAQUETTISTE:
41, 42 Ken Morrison
45 George Lois

ART DIRECTOR / DIRECTEUR ARTISTIQUE:
41, 42 Ken Morrison
43 Trygve Foss
44 Aldo Lanfranco
45 George Lois

AGENCY / AGENTUR / AGENCE – STUDIO:
41, 42 Martin/Williams
43 Idé Reklame & Marketing
44 Studio Armando Testa
45 Lois Holland Callaway

41, 42 Photographic illustration in roughly actual size and complete ad for a new ADM low-calorie corn sweetener. (USA)
43 Advertisement for a fruit and vegetable information office presenting food you can eat "with a good conscience". (NOR)
44 "Try turning it over, it doesn't fall out." Advertisement for a *Liebig* "home-made" tomato sauce. Red sauce. (ITA)
45 Tennis star Ilie Nastase advertises non-stop flights of Royal Air Maroc from New York to Morocco. (USA)

41, 42 Aufnahme, ungefähr Originalgrösse, und doppelseitiges Inserat für einen neuen kalorienarmen Süssstoff aus Mais. (USA)
43 Inserat einer Informationsstelle über Früchte und Gemüse, «Speisen, die man mit gutem Gewissen essen kann». (NOR)
44 «Versuch' es umzukippen, es läuft nichts heraus». Farbige Anzeige für «hausgemachte» *Liebig*-Tomatensauce. (ITA)
45 Tennis-Star Ilie Nastase wirbt für die Non-Stop-Flüge New York–Marokko der Royal Air Maroc. (USA)

41, 42 Photo (approx. grandeur nature) et annonce double page pour un édulcorant à base de maïs, basse en calories. (USA)
43 Un bureau d'information pour fruits et légumes présente des plats qu'on peut manger «sans mauvaise conscience». (NOR)
44 «Essaie de le renverser, il n'y a rien qui coule.» Pour une sauce aux tomates «faite à la maison». Polychromie. (ITA)
45 Nastase, champion de tennis, fait de la publicité pour les vols directs de la Royal Air Maroc à destination de ce pays. (USA)

45

PHOTOGRAPHER / PHOTOGRAPH / PHOTOGRAPHE:
46 Albert Schöpflin
47–49 Jay Maisel

DESIGNER / GESTALTER / MAQUETTISTE:
46 Lombacher

ART DIRECTOR / DIRECTEUR ARTISTIQUE:
46 Manfred Schmidt
47–49 Michael Winslow

AGENCY / AGENTUR / AGENCE – STUDIO:
46 Young & Rubicam
47–49 McKinney, Rockett & Silver

46

47

North Carolina is like that. From the mountains to the fertile midlands, all the way to the sea that brought the British colonists to the New World. Because a lot of things have changed, but in some ways nothing has. And, once you've been here, you might never be quite the same yourself. **NORTH CAROLINA**

48

46 "Those who defend their land should also be able to build on it." Double-spread black-and-white magazine advertisement for a building society, drawing attention to state contributions for men in military service. (GER)
47–49 Double-spread tourist ads and detail of the photography from one of them (actual size) for North Carolina. The pictures show "the world's second oldest river" and "the great blue hills of God". (USA)

46 Doppelseitiges Zeitschrifteninserat in Schwarzweiss aus einer Anzeigenkampagne der Bausparkasse *Wüstenrot*. (GER)
47–49 Doppelseiten und eine Aufnahme davon in Originalgrösse aus einer Touristen-Werbekampagne des amerikanischen Bundesstaates North Carolina. Die Aufnahmen zeigen den «zweitältesten Fluss der Welt», der kurioserweise «New River» heisst, und die «grossen blauen Hügel Gottes» der Cherokees. (USA)

Advertisements / Inserate / Annonces

46 «Ceux qui savent défendre leur terrain devraient pouvoir y construire.» Annonce double page (noir-blanc) d'une caisse d'épargne-construction signalant que les militaires ont droit à des contributions gouvernementales. (GER)
47–49 Annonces touristiques (pages doubles) et détail de la photo (en grandeur nature) pour la Caroline du Nord. Les photos montrent «l'un des plus vieux fleuves du monde» et les «grandes collines bleues de Dieu». (USA)

EVER GET THE FEELING ALL BRANDIES ARE THE SAME?

What's more, the people who make it have been making fine brandies for years.

It's made just as expertly as the world-famous brandies.

But a bottle doesn't cost you the earth.

Grand Empereur is smooth, warming and mellow.

Slip down a glass sometime.

And, as you do so, by all means strike a posture.

Slip your right hand under your jacket, and over the left side of your chest.

Let your heart beat proudly.

You may have noticed a tendency among brandy manufacturers to whack Napoleon on the bottle at the drop of a bicorn hat.

The trouble is, the gap between one brandy and the next, whether it's thought of as a 'Napoleon' brandy or not, can be as wide as the gap

between Moscow and Paris.

Something the great man knew all about.

You can rest assured with Grand Empereur.

It has every right to be so named.

To start with, it comes from France, where the most famous brandies originate.

Because you'll be toasting the Great Emperor in a style he would have labelled authentic.

GRAND EMPEREUR
Fine French Brandy

50

Meet Aunt Agatha

(Ronrico's Spanish Screwdriver)

Drink orange juice and vodka and you taste orange juice. But drink orange juice and Ronrico Rum and you taste Columbus discovering America, Cortez taking Mexico, and the seven most beautiful dancing girls on earth (all Spanish). In other words, Ronrico Rum transforms orange juice into a spectacular drink. Anything vodka can do, Ronrico Rum can do better. It is one of the world's great liquors, exquisitely light, clear and fragrant. (What's that, Aunt Agatha? You say you'd like another?) **RONRICO FROM PUERTO RICO**

PUERTO RICAN RUM, 80 PROOF. WHITE OR GOLD LABEL, GENERAL WINE AND SPIRITS COMPANY, NEW YORK 22

51

Ziehen Sie sich mal was Anständiges an.

Wenn Sie scharf auf ein anständiges Hemd mit bestem Schnitt, aus unverwüstlichem Denim und rostfreien Knöpfen sind, das dazu nicht anständig

teuer ist, wird Ihnen dieses Hemd passen. Denn Wrangler ist Qualität. Die echten Wrangler Jeans & Jackets & Shirts gibt es in allen möglichen Formen, Farben und Größen.

Wrangler

53

SOME PEOPLE WILL DO ANYTHING FOR A FREE BEER.

The competitors in this year's Whitbread Round The World Yacht Race will each take a free supply of Whitbread Pale Ale. They could hardly be expected to sail over 27,000 miles and remain dry.

We're not suggesting it's the *only* reason they entered. But, we can't think of a better travelling companion.

WHITBREAD

54

PHOTOGRAPHER / PHOTOGRAPH / PHOTOGRAPHE:

50 Alan Brooking/Jeremy Parkin
51 Carl Fischer
52 Bill Stettner
53 Sylvain Corrodi
54 Jonathan Eastland
55, 56 Peter Lindbergh

DESIGNER / GESTALTER / MAQUETTISTE:

51 George Lois
52 Michael Tesch
54 Edward Floyd

ART DIRECTOR / DIRECTEUR ARTISTIQUE:

50 Tony Muranka
51 George Lois
52 Michael Tesch
53 Stefan Hagemeister
54 Edward Floyd
55, 56 Bernd Kreutz

50 J. Walter Thompson Co. Ltd.
51 Papert, Koenig, Lois Inc.
52 Ally & Gargano
53 Doyle Dane Bernbach GmbH
54 Collett Dickenson Pearce & Partners Ltd.
55, 56 GGK

According to the Farmers' Almanac, you'll be able to take full advantage of Burberry and Aquascutum 74 times this year.

Not to mention Gleneagles, London Fog, Harbor Master, Christian Dior, Giorgio Armani, Nino Cerutti. Also not to mention the 291 sunny days when the fashions in Barney's Rainmaker Room also shine.

Barney's Rainmaker Room

7th Avenue and 17th Street. Open 9 AM to 9:30 PM. Free parking. We honor the American Express Card, Master Charge, BankAmericard/Visa. And, of course, your Barney's Card.

52

50 Colour magazine advertisement for *Grand Empereur* French brandy. (GBR)
51 Colour magazine advertisement for *Ronrico* rum. It stirred up comment because it showed a lady about to indulge in liquor. (USA)
52 Full-page magazine advertisement for men's fashions in rainwear from *Barney's*. (USA)
53 "Put on something decent for once." Magazine advertisement for *Wrangler* shirts. (GER)
54 Double-spread colour magazine advertisement for *Whitbread* beers, referring to the round-the-world yacht race organized by this brewing company. (GBR)
55, 56 From a series of black-and-white magazine advertisements with anecdotal copy for *Louis London* fashions. (GER)

50 Farbiges Zeitschrifteninserat für den französischen Cognac *Grand Empereur*. (GBR)
51 Farbiges Zeitschrifteninserat für *Ronrico*-Rum. Wegen der in Verbindung mit Alkoholkonsum gezeigten Dame (Tante Agatha) wurde Anstoss an dieser Werbung genommen. (USA)
52 Ganzseitiges Zeitschrifteninserat für Herren-Regenmode von *Barney's*, mit einer Aufstellung der nach dem hundertjährigen Kalender zu erwartenden Regentage im Jahr. (USA)
53 Zeitschrifteninserat aus einer Kampagne für *Wrangler*-Jeanskleidung. (GER)
54 Doppelseitiges Zeitschrifteninserat für *Whitbread*-Biere, farbig. (GBR)
55, 56 Aus einer Serie von Schwarzweiss-Zeitschrifteninseraten für Kleidung von *Louis London*, «eine Mode voller Leben». (GER)

50 Annonce de magazine en couleurs pour le cognac français *Grand Empereur*. (GBR)
51 Annonce de magazine polychrome pour le rhum *Ronrico*. Elle a fait sensation en montrant une femme prenant vraiment plaisir à boire. (USA)
52 «D'après l'almanach, vous porterez votre imper *Barney's* 74 fois cette année.» (USA)
53 «Pour une fois, mettez quelque chose de décent.» Pour les chemises *Wrangler*. (GER)
54 Annonce de magazine double page, en couleurs, pour les bières *Whitbread*, évoquant la course de voiliers autour du monde organisée par ce brasseur. (GBR)
55, 56 Exemples d'une série d'annonces de magazine en noir et blanc en faveur des modes *Louis London*, «la mode pleine de vie». (GER)

Samstag. Es gibt doch *liebe* **Polizisten.** Heute Mittag hat mir einer *mein* **Protokoll** so nett erklärt, daß ich ihm *beinahe* noch eins **abgekauft** hätte. **Louis London®**
Eine Mode voller Leben.

Freitag. Läuft mir doch meine alte **Schulfreundin** Elke über den Weg. **Meine Güte,** bist Du reif geworden«, *flötet sie.* Flöte ich: »*Vielleicht hol'ich Dich eines Tages* sogar ein.« **Louis London®**
Eine Mode voller Leben.

57

58

60

61

Advertisements / Inserate / Annonces

57–62 Full-page and double-spread advertisements from a campaign for *Wrangler* jeans. The copy, in some cases on the suggestive side, refers to the hard-wearing qualities of the jeans and zip fasteners. (GER)
63, 64 From a series of magazine advertisements for *Gant*, shirtmakers, here for shirts and sweaters (Fig. 63) and for rugger shirts (Fig. 64). (USA)
65 Colour advertisement in a trade magazine for *Scherle* knitted goods. (GER)

57–62 Ganzseitige und doppelseitige Inserate aus einer Werbekampagne für *Wrangler*-Jeans. Die Texte, mit teilweise leicht anzüglichem Charakter, beziehen sich auf die Dauerhaftigkeit der Jeans und Reissverschlüsse. (GER)
63, 64 Aus einer Serie von Zeitschrifteninseraten für *Gant*-Textilien. Hier geht es um Hemden und Pullover (Abb. 63) und Trainingshemden (Abb. 64). (USA)
65 Farbiges Fachzeitschrifteninserat für *Scherle*-Tricots. (GER)

57–62 Annonces pleine page et double page pour une campagne des jeans *Wrangler*. Les textes, parfois très suggestifs, se rapportent aux qualités de ces jeans et de leurs fermetures éclair jugés inusables. Cette campagne a fait passer la marque de la seconde à la première place du marché allemand. (GER)
63, 64 D'une série d'annonces de magazine pour les chemises *Gant*, ici pour les chemises et pullovers (fig. 63) et des chemises de sport (fig. 64). (USA)
65 Annonce parue dans la presse professionnelle en faveur des articles en tricot de *Scherle*. (GER)

63

44

59

62

PHOTOGRAPHER / PHOTOGRAPH / PHOTOGRAPHE:
57–62 Roberto Petrin
63, 64 Gary Bernstein
65 H. P. Mühlemann

DESIGNER / GESTALTER / MAQUETTISTE:
63, 64 Howard Title
65 Kreativ-Team Ulrich & Fehlmann

ART DIRECTOR / DIRECTEUR ARTISTIQUE:
57–62 Stefan Hagemeister
63, 64 Howard Title

AGENCY / AGENTUR / AGENCE – STUDIO:
57–62 Doyle Dane Bernbach GmbH
63, 64 Waring & LaRosa, Inc.
65 Kreativ-Team Ulrich & Fehlmann

THE GANT ATTITUDE

64

65

66 Magazine advertisement in full colour (red tube) for a *Hayfield* blend of wool and acrylic that claims to be "sexier" than plain wool. (GBR)
67 Magazine advertisement in grey tones for *Cacharel* fashions sold in a special room by *Dayton's* stores, Minneapolis. (USA)
68, 69 "... One thing is certain—it's platinum..." Double-spread black-and-white advertisements from a series for platinum jewellery. (GER)
70, 71 Detail of the photography in actual size and complete magazine advertisement for fashionable spectacle frames from *Rodenstock.* (FRA)

66 Annonce de magazine (tube rouge) pour un mélange *Hayfield* de laine et de fibres acryliques réputé plus sexy que la laine ordinaire. (GBR)
67 Annonce de magazine en tons gris pour les articles de mode *Cacharel* que le grand magasin *Dayton's* vend dans un rayon spécial. (USA)
68, 69 «Ce qui est sûr... c'est qu'il est de platine.» Annonces de magazine double page (en noir et blanc) figurant dans une campagne en faveur de bijoux en platine. (GER)
70, 71 Détail de la photo (en grandeur nature) et annonce de magazine complète pour une marque de montures à la mode. (FRA)

66 Farbiges Zeitschrifteninserat (roter Schlauch) für *Hayfield Superblend,* ein Mischgarn aus Wolle und Acryl, das für Grossvaters Weste als ungeeignet angesehen wird. (GBR)
67 Zeitschrifteninserat in Grautönen für *Cacharel*-Mode, die im Kaufhaus *Dayton's,* Minneapolis, in einem speziellen Raum angeboten wird. (USA)
68, 69 Doppelseitige Zeitschrifteninserate, schwarzweiss, aus einer Werbekampagne der *Platin Gilde* unter dem Slogan «... Eines ist Gewissheit – es ist Platin...». (GER)
70, 71 Detail der Aufnahme in Originalgrösse und komplettes Zeitschrifteninserat für modische Brillengestelle von *Rodenstock.* (FRA)

66

67

68

69

PHOTOGRAPHER / PHOTOGRAPH:

66 John Thornton
67 Kyle Ericksen
68, 69 Jerry Plucer-Sarna
70, 71 Christian v. Alvensleben

DESIGNER / GESTALTER:

66 Alan Midgley
67 Karen Brown
70, 71 Vis-Studio/Werbeabteilung Rodenstock

ART DIRECTOR:

66 Alan Midgley
67 Karen Brown
68, 69 Harald Winter
70, 71 P. Kinzer

AGENCY / AGENTUR / AGENCE:

66 Saatchi & Saatchi
   Garland-Compton Ltd.
67 Dayton's Adv.
68, 69 J. Walter Thompson
70, 71 Vis-Studio

70

Advertisements
Inserate
Annonces

71

72

PHOTOGRAPHER / PHOTOGRAPH / PHOTOGRAPHE:

72, 73 Chris von Wangenheim
74, 76 Robert Huber
75 Steve Campbell

DESIGNER / GESTALTER / MAQUETTISTE:

72, 73 Gene Federico
75 Frank Sully

ART DIRECTOR / DIRECTEUR ARTISTIQUE:

72, 73 Gene Federico
74, 76 Jean Pierre Rocher
75 Frank Sully

AGENCY / AGENTUR / AGENCE – STUDIO:

72, 73 Lord, Geller, Federico, Einstein, Inc.
74, 76 Service Publicité Bally France
75 Landsdowne Marketing

73

74

Goggles is a beautiful new range of sunglasses – stylish, comfortable and of high quality.

Every model has been specially selected by Oliver Goldsmith, the internationally renowned designer of fashion frames and leading authority on the sunglasses market.

Goggles are the greatest thing to happen to eyes – and their combination of excellent lenses and superb frames makes them outstanding value.

Goggles is a highly individual and memorable brand name – supremely important in a vast market with great potential: £46 million retail and trading up!

Three out of every four existing owners buy new sunglasses each year; and next year a lot of them will be choosing Goggles!

GOGGLES: BIGGEST-EVER ADVERTISING BUDGET. Nothing but the best promotional support would be good enough for sunglasses like ours – so we're spending a total of one million pounds on consumer advertising alone!

This colossal campaign will include 130 spots on television, 200 radio spots and no fewer than 50 full-colour pages in the top-circulation magazines.

GOGGLES: MASSIVE MERCHANDISING SUPPORT. Throughout the season there will be eye-catching point-of-sale material with stunning display stands which show Goggles off to perfection.

These stands, which make maximum use of minimum space, feature full-face mirrors, leaflet dispensers and a distinctive headboard.

Every pair of Goggles is colour-coded to indicate the lens type, and comes in a free Goggles-branded carrying case.

Every model also carries a replacement guarantee service.

GOGGLES: LENSES AND FRAMES. There are 102 models in the Goggles range: with five lens types, 53 frame styles (excluding 12 clip-on versions) and in seven price categories.

Goggles: fashion, quality, style – right on the nose! goggles

75

72, 73 From a series of advertisements applying changing adjectives to *Dior* fashions—here for a scarf collection. Photographic illustration in actual size and complete page. (USA)
74, 76 Complete magazine advertisement for a *Bally* shoe model and detail of the photographic illustration in actual size. (FRA)
75 Double-spread trade magazine advertisement in colour for *Goggles* sunglasses. (GBR)

72, 73 Aus einer Serie von Inseraten mit verschiedenen Attributen für *Dior*-Mode, hier für eine Schalkollektion. Aufnahme in Originalgrösse und komplette Seite. (USA)
74, 76 Komplettes, ganzseitiges Zeitschrifteninserat für Schuhkreationen von *Bally* und Aufnahme in Originalgrösse. (FRA)
75 Doppelseitiges Fachzeitschrifteninserat in Farbe für *Goggles*-Sonnenbrillen. (GBR)

72, 73 D'une série d'annonces présentant les modes *Dior* avec des attributs divers – ici une collection de foulards. Illustration en grandeur nature et annonce complète. (USA)
74, 76 Annonce de magazine complète et détail de la photographie (en grandeur originale) pour un nouveau modèle de chaussures *Bally*. (FRA)
75 Annonce de revue professionnelle pour les lunettes *Goggles*. Double page en couleurs. (GBR)

Advertisements / Inserate / Annonces

76

77

78

PHOTOGRAPHER / PHOTOGRAPH / PHOTOGRAPHE:

77, 78 Rosemary Howard
79, 81, 82 Guy Bourdin
80 Jerry Abramowitz

DESIGNER / GESTALTER / MAQUETTISTE:

80 Ron Becker

ART DIRECTOR / DIRECTEUR ARTISTIQUE:

79, 81, 82 Freimut Steiger
80 Ron Becker

AGENCY / AGENTUR / AGENCE – STUDIO:

77, 78 William Seltzer Advertising
80 DKG Advertising

79

"THE DIRECTOR HAD ME DO 28 STUNTS TODAY. MY ZIPPER DIDN'T FALL ONCE."

"Whenever the director says, 'Action!' he means *action*.

And that's where I fall in. Through windows. Over walls. From fast cars. Anything.

Of course, everyone thinks I'm crazy, but I love being a stuntman. And while the work is easy for me, it's tough on my pants. Especially on my zipper.

That's why I always make sure my pants have a Talon Channel-Zip® nylon zipper. It was designed to take this kind of punishment.

For instance, last week I was in a scene where I had to jump from a speeding train. I did six takes, and my zipper never even left the track. Now that's what I call a terrific performance.

The point is, I can always depend on my Talon® zipper.

Look for me the next time you see an "action" film. Whether I'm playing a good guy or a bad guy, I always have to be a tough guy.

With an even tougher zipper."

The Talon Channel-Zip zipper says a lot about the pants it's in.

80

77, 78 Complete double-spread magazine advertisement and detail of the photography from a campaign for men's clothing with a European look by *Adolfo.* Full colour. (USA)
79 Colour spread from *Vogue* advertising *Charles Jourdan* shoes. (FRA)
80 Double-spread magazine advertisement from a campaign for *Talon* zip fasteners, here with reference to the strenuous day of a stuntman. (USA)
81, 82 Two full-colour double spreads from *Vogue* for *Charles Jourdan* shoe fashions. See also Fig. 79. (FRA)

77, 78 Komplettes, doppelseitiges Inserat und Detail der Aufnahme aus einer Kampagne für Herrenkleidung im europäischen Stil von *Adolfo.* Farbig. (USA)
79 Doppelseitiges Inserat aus *Vogue* für Schuhe von *Charles Jourdan.* (FRA)
80 Doppelseitiges Zeitschrifteninserat aus einer Kampagne für *Talon*-Reissverschlüsse; hier wird die aufreibende Arbeit eines Doubles bei Filmaufnahmen gezeigt. (USA)
81, 82 Zwei weitere farbige Doppelseiten aus *Vogue* für Schuhe von *Charles Jourdan.* Siehe auch Abb. 79. (FRA)

77, 78 Annonce double page complète et détail de la photo: campagne pour la confection messieurs d'*Adolfo,* de style européen. En polychromie. (USA)
79 Page double en couleurs servant à la promotion des chaussures *Charles Jourdan.* (FRA)
80 Annonce double page figurant dans une campagne publicitaire pour l'indestructible fermeture éclair *Talon*; ici on fait allusion au travail dur d'un cascadeur. (USA)
81, 82 Deux autres annonces double page publiées dans le magazine *Vogue* en faveur des chaussures de *Charles Jourdan.* Voir aussi fig. 79. (FRA)

81

82

83 Double-spread advertisement for *Adidas* track shoes. It refers to the Cross du Figaro race in Paris and wishes participants a happy New Year. (FRA)
84 Advertisement for *Cacharel* fashions for men. (FRA)
85 Full-colour ad for clothing from *Levi's*. (USA)
86 Black-and-white ad for Italian Western-style fashions sold by a San Francisco store. (USA)
87, 88 Double-spread black-and-white ad, with photograph, for boots from the *Stéfano* store in Chicago. (USA)
89, 90 Complete advertisement and photograph in roughly actual size, announcing the winter collection of *Eli Colaj* to be presented in Milan and Florence. (ITA)

83 Doppelseitiges Inserat für *Adidas*-Sportschuhe, mit Anspielung auf den Cross-du-Figaro-Lauf in Paris, dessen Teilnehmern ein glückliches Jahr gewünscht wird. (FRA)
84 Anzeige für *Cacharel*-Herrenmode. (FRA)
85 Farbiges Inserat für *Levi's*-Kleidung. (USA)
86 Schwarzweiss-Inserat für italienische Mode im Western-stil, von einem Geschäft in San Francisco. (USA)
87, 88 Doppelseitiges Schwarzweiss-Inserat und Aufnahme für Stiefel des Geschäftes *Stéfano*, Chicago. (USA)
89, 90 Komplettes Inserat und Aufnahme, ungefähr Originalgrösse, für die Herbst/Winter-Kollektion von *Eli Colaj*, die in Mailand und Florenz gezeigt wird. (ITA)

ART DIRECTOR / DIRECTEUR ARTISTIQUE:

83 M. Delacroix/Ph. Martignoni
84 Robert Delpire
85 Connie Yuvan
86 Walter Sparks
87, 88 Jim Cox

AGENCY / AGENTUR / AGENCE – STUDIO:

83 Mandarine
84 Ideodis
85 Foote, Cone, Belding
86 Gauger Sparks Silva
87, 88 Jim Cox Associates

87

83

Bonne année, bonne santé.

adidas
La marque aux 3 bandes

84

83 Annonce double page pour les chaussures de sport *Adidas*. Elle se réfère au grand footing Cross du Figaro et souhaite aux participants une bonne année. (FRA)
84 Annonce pour les modes masculines *Cacharel*. (FRA)
85 Annonce couleurs pour les vêtements *Levi's*. (USA)
86 Annonce noir-blanc pour les modes italiennes style Western, vendues par un magasin de San Francisco. (USA)
87, 88 Annonce double page (noir-blanc) et photo pour les bottes vendues par *Stéfano* à Chicago. (USA)
89, 90 Annonce complète et photo (approx. grandeur nature) annonçant une présentation de la collection d'hiver de *Eli Colaj* à Milan et Florence. (ITA)

PHOTOGRAPHER / PHOTOGRAPH / PHOTOGRAPHE:

83 Daniel Hamot (Hauptmann Groupe)
84 Art Kane
85 Robert Blakeman
86 Peter Olgivie
87, 88 François Robert
89, 90 Alberta Tiburzi

DESIGNER / GESTALTER / MAQUETTISTE:

86 Walter Sparks
87, 88 Jim Cox

LET YOURSELF LEVI'S!

85

Wilkes Bashford
La moda italiana riflette il West ... San Francisco (415) 986-4380

86

89

Advertisements / Inserate / Annonces

88

90

53

91

Cadillac £16·99, Chevrolet £17·99, Camaro £17·99.
Low running costs, leather upholstery, two-tone finish optional.

Polyveldt Cruisers by *Clarks*

93

PHOTOGRAPHER / PHOTOGRAPH / PHOTOGRAPHE:

91, 92 Kou Chifusa
93 Tony May
94, 95 Iver Hansen

DESIGNER / GESTALTER / MAQUETTISTE:

91, 92 Tsuyoshi Morita
93 Nigel Rose

ART DIRECTOR / DIRECTEUR ARTISTIQUE:

91, 92 Tsuyoshi Fukuda
93 Nigel Rose
94, 95 Erwin Schmidt

AGENCY / AGENTUR / AGENCE – STUDIO:

91, 92 Chameleon
93 Collett Dickenson Pearce & Partners Ltd.
94, 95 Doyle Dane Bernbach GmbH

Advertisements / Inserate / Annonces

92

Christian Dior

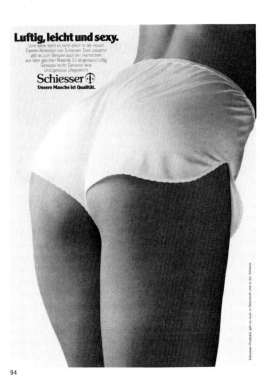

Luftig, leicht und sexy.
Und dabei steht es nicht allein in der neuen Damen-Kollektion von Schiesser. Dazu passend gibt es zum Beispiel auch ein Hemdchen aus dem gleichen Material. Es ist genauso luftig. Genauso leicht. Genauso sexy. Und genauso pflegeleicht.

Schiesser ⊕
Unsere Masche ist Qualität.

Sind sie nicht süß, unsere Zitronen?
Und damit Sie nicht sauer werden, haben wir sie aus dem gleichen Material gemacht wie das ganze Hemd: Aus bester Baumwolle. Aber damit nicht genug: Wir haben sie bestens verarbeitet. So daß Sie wie auf den Gedanken kommen, wir würden mit Zitronen handeln.

Schiesser ⊕
Unsere Masche ist Qualität.

94

95

55

96

97

PHOTOGRAPHER / PHOTOGRAPH:

96, 97 Cosimo
98 Michel Tcherevkoff
99 David Bailey
100, 101 François Lamy

AGENCY / AGENTUR / AGENCE—STUDIO:

96, 97 Harvard Peskin & Edrick, Inc.
99 Young & Rubicam
100, 101 Mafia

DESIGNER / GESTALTER / MAQUETTISTE:

96, 97 Aric Frons
98 Bob Anastasio

ART DIRECTOR / DIRECTEUR ARTISTIQUE:

96, 97 Aric Frons
98 Bob Anastasio
99 René Turini
100, 101 Alexandre Wolkoff

98

Desideri di donna
faber

99

96, 97 Illustration in actual size and complete magazine advertisement for "electrifying" jewellery made by *Jose Hess*. (USA)
98 Magazine advertisement in blue-grey and grey-green shades for jewellery from Les Bernard, Inc., here presenting a necklace in Honan jade. (USA)
99 Double-spread black-and-white magazine advertisement for *Faber* lingerie. (ITA)
100, 101 Full-page colour illustration and complete double-spread advertisement for children's clothing from *Absorba*, "the first years of life". (FRA)

96, 97 Aufnahme und komplettes Fachzeitschrifteninserat für «spannungsgeladenen» Schmuck von dem Designer *Jose Hess*. (USA)
98 Ganzseitiges Zeitschrifteninserat in Farbe für Schmuck aus «Honan-Jade», einem blassgrünem Halbedelstein, der aus der chinesischen Provinz Honan importiert wird. Hier wird als Beispiel eine Halskette mit kleinen handgeformten Fischen gezeigt. (USA)
99 Doppelseitiges Schwarzweiss-Inserat für Damenwäsche von *Faber*. (ITA)
100, 101 Ganzseitige Aufnahme in Farbe und komplettes, doppelseitiges Zeitschrifteninserat für *Absorba*-Kinderkleidung. «Die ersten Jahre des Lebens.» (FRA)

96, 97 Illustration en grandeur nature et annonce de magazine complète pour des bijoux «électrisants» créés par *Jose Hess*. (USA)
98 Annonce de magazine pleine page pour un joaillier, présentant ici un collier en jade de Ho-nan. Prédominance de tons bleu gris et gris vert. (USA)
99 Annonce page double (en noir et blanc) pour la lingerie *Faber*. (ITA)
100, 101 Illustration pleine page (en couleurs) et annonce de magazine complète pour les vêtements *Absorba*, «dans lesquels les enfants se sentent bien». (FRA)

absorba
Absorba habille les enfants. Tout simplement.

100

Absorba, les premières années de la vie.

absorba

101

102

103

102 Colour magazine advertisement for matching shoes and handbag by *Etienne Aigner*. (FRA)
103 Colour magazine advertisement for rare jewels from Harry Winston Inc. It shows the Washington Diamond of 89.23 carats. (USA)
104–108 Complete magazine advertisement in full colour and the shots used in four ads from the same series for *Christian Dior*. They advertise sun glasses (Fig. 105), bathing suits (Fig. 106), lingerie (Fig. 107) and handbags (Fig. 108). (FRA)

102 Farbige Magazinanzeige für Schuhe und passendes Zubehör von *Etienne Aigner*. (FRA)
103 Farbiges Zeitschrifteninserat für seltene Juwelen von Harry Winston Inc. Es zeigt den Washington-Diamanten mit 89,23 Karat. (USA)
104–108 Komplettes Inserat in Farbe und Aufnahmen aus vier Anzeigen der gleichen Serie für *Christian Dior*. Es geht um Sonnenbrillen (Abb. 105), Bademode (Abb. 106), Wäsche (Abb. 107) und Handtaschen (Abb. 108). (FRA)

102 Annonce couleur pour les chaussures et sacs à main assortis d'*Etienne Aigner*. (FRA)
103 Annonce de magazine en couleurs en faveur de rares pierres précieuses de la Harry Winston Inc. On y présente le diamant Washington de 89.23 carats. (USA)
104–108 Annonce de magazine (en polychromie) et photos utilisées pour quatre annonces figurant dans la même série de *Christian Dior*. Elles servent à la publicité pour les lunettes de soleil (fig. 105), les bikinis (fig. 106), la lingerie (fig. 107) et les sacs à main (fig. 108). (FRA)

PHOTOGRAPHER / PHOTOGRAPH / PHOTOGRAPHE:

102 E.T. Werlen
103 Onofrio Paccione
104–108 Hans Feurer

DESIGNER / GESTALTER / MAQUETTISTE:

102 Manfred Gerden
103 Ronald Winston
104–108 Studio graphique Christian Dior

ART DIRECTOR / DIRECTEUR ARTISTIQUE:

102 Manfred Gerden
103 Ronald Winston

AGENCY / AGENTUR / AGENCE – STUDIO:

102 Fashion Promotion STAAB GmbH
103 Stan Merritt
104–108 Studio graphique Christian Dior

104

Advertisements / Inserate / Annonces

105

106

107

108

109

110

111

112

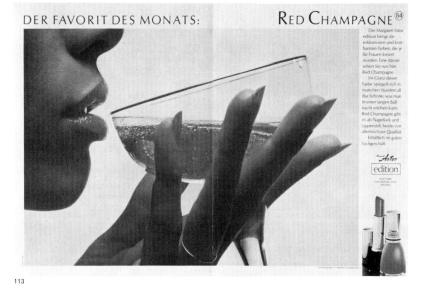

113

114

Advertisements
Inserate
Annonces

109, 111 Two double-spread magazine advertisements for *Shiseido* cosmetics. Full colour. (JPN)
110 Double-spread magazine advertisement for *Coty* skin care products with portraits of an actress at a sixteen-year interval. Full colour. (GBR)
112 "When leather is haute couture." Double spread in grey-brown shades for *Sicons* leather clothing. (ITA)
113 "Favourite of the month: Red Champagne." Double-spread magazine advertisement in full colour for *Margaret Astor* lipstick and nail varnish. (GER)
114 Magazine advertisement with colour illustration for *Babe* lipsticks made by *Fabergé*. (USA)
115 Magazine advertisement for *Aimée* toilet water. (SWI)
116 Magazine advertisement for the *Yves Saint Laurent* range of cosmetics. Red lips on black. (FRA)

109, 111 Zwei doppelseitige Zeitschrifteninserate in Farbe für *Shiseido*-Kosmetik. (JPN)
110 Doppelseitiges Zeitschrifteninserat in Farbe für *Coty*-Kosmetik. Gezeigt werden zwei Aufnahmen der Schauspielerin Jean Shrimpton, zwischen denen 16 Jahre liegen. (GBR)
112 «Wenn Leder Haute Couture ist.» Doppelseitiges Inserat in Grau-Braun-Tönen für *Sicons*-Lederkleidung. (ITA)
113 Doppelseitiges Zeitschrifteninserat in Farbe für Lippenstifte und Nagellack von *Margaret Astor*. Hier für den Farbton «Roter Champagner». (GER)
114 Ganzseitiges Zeitschrifteninserat in Farbe für *Babe*-Lippenstifte von *Fabergé*. (USA)
115 Zeitschrifteninserat für *Aimée*, Eau de Parfum. (SWI)
116 Zeitschrifteninserat für die Kosmetikreihe von *Yves Saint Laurent*. Roter Mund auf schwarzem Hintergrund. (FRA)

109, 111 Annonces de magazine double page d'une série pour les produits cosmétiques *Shiseido*. En polychromie. (JPN)
110 Annonce de magazine double page pour les produits *Coty* pour les soins de la peau, montrant le visage d'une actrice sans grande modification à 16 ans d'intervalle. (GBR)
112 «Quand le cuire est haute couture.» Annonce double page en tons brun gris pour les vêtements en cuire de *Sicon*. (ITA)
113 «Le favorit du mois: le Champagne rouge.» Annonce de magazine double page pour les rouges à lèvres et vernis à ongle de *Margaret Astor*. (GER)
114 Annonce de magazine avec illustration en couleurs pour les rouges à lèvres *Babe* de *Fabergé*. (USA)
115 Annonce de magazine pour une eau de toilette. (SWI)
116 Annonce de magazine pour une gamme de produits cosmétiques de *Yves Saint Laurent*. Lèvres rouges sur noir. (FRA)

115

116

PHOTOGRAPHER / PHOTOGRAPH / PHOTOGRAPHE:

109, 111 Bishin Jumonji
110 David Bailey
112 Photostudio Giob
113 Jean Loup Sieff
114 Richard Avedon
115 Jost Wildbolz
116 Jean-Luc Buyo

DESIGNER / GESTALTER / MAQUETTISTE:

110 John Foster
112 Rinaldo Del Sordo/Giuseppe Berlinghieri
113 Ernst Meier/Lürzer & Conrad
114 Irwin Goldberg
115 Domenig K. Geissbühler

ART DIRECTOR / DIRECTEUR ARTISTIQUE:

109 Takashi Mizuno/Kazuhiko Ohta
110 John Foster
111 Tatsuhiro Inuyama/Kunio Hachimura
112 Rinaldo Del Sordo/Giuseppe Berlinghieri
113 Ernst Meier
114 Irwin Goldberg
115 Domenig K. Geissbühler
116 Philippe Sauter

AGENCY / AGENTUR / AGENCE–STUDIO:

110 Collett Dickenson Pearce & Partners Ltd.
112 Studio Giob
113 Lürzer, Conrad
114 Nadler & Larimer, Inc.
115 Domenig K. Geissbühler
116 Mafia

PHOTOGRAPHER / PHOTOGRAPH:

117, 118 Sarah Moon/Alain Mery
119 J. Frederick Smith
121 David Hamilton
122 Alberto Rizzo

DESIGNER / GESTALTER / MAQUETTISTE:

117, 118 Serge Mansau
122 Martin Stevens

ART DIRECTOR / DIRECTEUR ARTISTIQUE:

117, 118 Serge Mansau
119 Nel Rustom
122 Martin Stevens

AGENCY / AGENTUR / AGENCE – STUDIO:

119 Norman Craig & Kummel
121 Edifrance
122 50th Floor Workshop

119

117

118

120

I f you're going to do something about beauty care,
do it very, very well. Princess Marcella Borghese

Special beauty treatment and uncommon color. Available internationally.

122

121

117, 118 Complete double-spread magazine advertisement and detail of the photography. For the *Revillon* perfume *Detchema*, "surprising and mysterious as the goddess whose name it bears". (FRA)
119 Full-colour magazine advertisement for an *Old Spice* after-shave lotion. (USA)
120 Magazine advertisement for *Chanel No. 5* perfume. Full colour. (USA)
121 Magazine advertisement in pale flesh and green shades with a "canvas" effect for the *Nina Ricci* perfume *Farouche*. (FRA)
122 Institutional magazine advertisement with colour illustration for the beauty treatments of Princess Marcella Borghese Inc. (USA)

117, 118 Komplettes, doppelseitiges Zeitschrifteninserat und Detail der Aufnahme für das Parfum *Detchema* von *Revillon*. «Überraschend und geheimnisvoll wie die Göttin, deren Namen es trägt.» (FRA)
119 «Sehr überzeugend.» Farbiges Zeitschrifteninserat für die After-Shave-Lotion *Old Spice Musk*. (USA)
120 Zeitschrifteninserat für das Parfum *Chanel No. 5*. In Farbe. (USA)
121 Zeitschrifteninserat in blassen Haut- und Grüntönen mit «Leinwand»-Effekt für das Parfum *Farouche* von *Nina Ricci*. (FRA)
122 Image-Werbung mit farbiger Aufnahme für pflegende und dekorative Kosmetik von Princess Marcella Borghese Inc. (USA)

117, 118 Annonce de magazine double page complète et détail de la photographie pour le parfum *Detchema* de *Revillon*. (FRA)
119 Annonce de magazine en couleurs pour une lotion après-rasage. (USA)
120 Annonce de magazine en faveur du parfum *Chanel No. 5*. En polychromie. (USA)
121 Annonce de magazine pour le parfum *Farouche* de *Nina Ricci*. Tons rose pâle et verts avec effet de toile. (FRA)
122 Annonce de prestige avec photo couleur en faveur des produits de beauté de la Princess Marcella Borghese Inc. (USA)

Are you wild enough to wear it?

The top, a brilliant lamé butterfly by Julio.
The ornaments, golden hoops and
spears by Ted Muehling.
The fragrance, Tigress by Fabergé.
Provoking. Compelling.
The scent you dare to wear.

Tigress

Put a little wild in your life.

123

PHOTOGRAPHER / PHOTOGRAPH / PHOTOGRAPHE:

123, 125 Neal Barr
126 Giorgio & Valerio Lari
127 Pete Turner/Cailor/Resnick
128 Yosh Inouye

DESIGNER / GESTALTER / MAQUETTISTE:

123, 125 Gary Shapiro
126 Rinaldo Del Sordo/Giuseppe Berlinghieri
128 Raymond Lee

ART DIRECTOR / DIRECTEUR ARTISTIQUE:

123, 125 Gary Shapiro
126 Rinaldo Del Sordo/Giuseppe Berlinghieri
127 Bob Phillips
128 Raymond Lee

AGENCY / AGENTUR / AGENCE – STUDIO:

123, 125 Nadler & Larimer
126 Studio Giob
127 Levine, Huntley, Schmidt, Plapler & Beaver
128 Raymond Lee & Associates Ltd.

pour chaque courbe, chaque creux, chaque   douceur de votre corps...   un parfum fou de vous.

VU
PAR
TED LAPIDUS

124

Advertisements / Inserate / Annonces

123 Double-spread magazine advertisement (dress in gold lamé) for the *Fabergé* perfume *Tigress*. (USA)
124 "For each curve, each hollow, each softness of your body..." Double-spread colour magazine advertisement for the perfume *Vu* by *Ted Lapidus*. (FRA)
125 Advertisement from the same campaign as Fig. 123 for *Tigress* perfume. White crêpe jumpsuit. (USA)
126 Colour magazine advertisement for beachwear from a campaign for *Ermenegildo Zegna*. (ITA)
127 Double-spread magazine advertisement in full colour for an eau-de-cologne spray called *Embracing*. (USA)
128 Magazine ad for *McGregor's* deodorant socks. (USA)

123, 125 «Sind Sie mutig genug, es zu tragen?» Zwei doppel-seitige Zeitschrifteninserate in Farbe für das Parfum *Tigress* (Tigerin) von *Fabergé*. (USA)
124 «Für jede Rundung, jede Vertiefung, jede Weichheit Ihres Körpers...» Doppelseitiges Farbinserat für das Parfum *Vu* von *Ted Lapidus*. (FRA)
126 Farbiges Zeitschrifteninserat aus einer Kampagne für Strandmode von *Ermenegildo Zegna*. (ITA)
127 Doppelseitiges Zeitschrifteninserat in Farbe für das Eau-de-Cologne «Embracing» (umarmend). (USA)
128 «Socken für Nasen». Zeitschrifteninserat für *McGregor*-Socken mit desodorierender Ausrüstung. (USA)

123 Annonce de magazine double page (robe en lamé doré) pour le parfum *Tigress* de *Fabergé*. (USA)
124 Annonce de magazine double page (en polychromie) pour le parfum *Vu* de *Ted Lapidus*. (FRA)
125 Annonce figurant dans la même campagne que fig. 123. Costume en crêpe blanc. (USA)
126 Annonce en couleurs tirée d'une campagne publicitaire en faveur des modes de plage d'*Ermenegildo Zegna*. (ITA)
127 Annonce de magazine double page (en polychromie) pour un vaporisateur d'eau de Cologne *Embracing*. (USA)
128 «Les chaussettes pour le nez.» Annonce de magazine pour les chaussettes désodorisantes de *McGregor*. (USA)

125

126

127

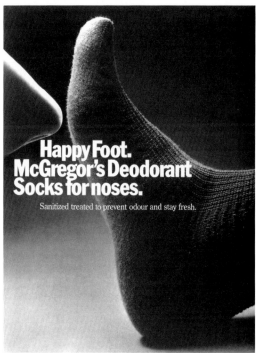

128

65

129

130

131

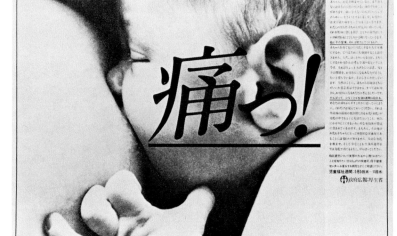

132

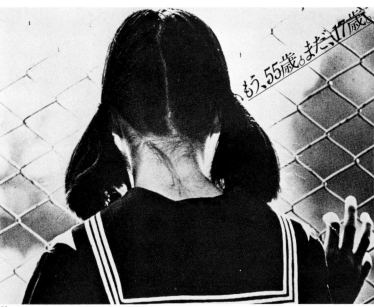

133

129, 130 Two double-spread trade magazine advertisements with colour illustrations for *Chilton* publications, which are backed by a marketing assistance programme. Fig. 129 refers particularly to the tourist magazine *Going Places* published by this company. (USA)
131 Newspaper advertisement for the governmental National Land and Fire Protection Agencies. Black and white. (JPN)
132 Newspaper advertisement for the Ministry of Health and Welfare. (JPN)
133 Newspaper advertisement for the Ministry of Labour. (JPN)
134 "*Ritmo*. Evolution of the species." Black-and-white newspaper advertisement for a new *Fiat* model. The name *Ritmo* means "rhythm". (ITA)
135 Black-and-white newspaper advertisement for *Real Estate 10*, who offer to prevent the selling of a house from becoming a nightmare. (USA)
136 "That's how beautiful the winter's going to be." Newspaper ad for *Modissa* fashions. (SWI)

129, 130 Doppelseitige, farbige Zeitschrifteninserate des Verlagshauses *Chilton*. Abb. 129 informiert über *Chiltons* Reisejournal «Going Places», Abb. 130 über das «Marketing Assistance Program», das Fachpublikationen, Marktforschungsinstrumente, Datenbanken etc. umfasst. (USA)
131–133 Von Mitgliedern des Nippon Design Center gestaltete Zeitungsinserate. Abb. 131 wirbt für die Ämter für Landschaftsschutz und Brandverhütung, Abb. 132 für das Gesundheits- und Sozialamt, Abb. 133 für das Arbeitsamt. (JPN)
134 Doppelseite in Schwarzweiss für das neue Modell *Ritmo* (Rhythmus) des Automobilherstellers *Fiat*, mit detaillierten Angaben über die Eigenschaften des Fahrzeugs. (ITA)
135 «Ihr Haus zu verkaufen muss kein Alptraum sein». Mit diesem Schwarzweiss-Inserat bietet eine Maklerfirma ihre Dienste an. (USA)
136 Ganzseitiges Zeitungsinserat in Braunweiss. Das Zürcher Modehaus *Modissa* wirbt mit einem italienischen Mantelmodell für die neue Winterkollektion. (SWI)

129, 130 Annonces de magazine pour les publications *Chilton*. Fig. 129 donne des informations sur le magazine touristique *Going Places*, fig. 130 se réfère au «Marketing Assistance Program», comprenant des publications professionnelles, instruments de prospection, etc. (USA)
131 Annonce de journal publiée par les offices nationaux de l'environnement et de la lutte anti-sinistres. (JPN)
132 Annonce de journal pour le Ministère de la Santé et de la Sécurité Sociale. (JPN)
133 Annonce de journal pour le Ministère du Travail. (JPN)
134 «*Ritmo*. L'évolution d'une espèce.» Annonce de journal en noir et blanc pour un nouveau modèle de *Fiat*. Le nom *Ritmo* signifie «rythme». (ITA)
135 «La vente d'une maison ne devrait être un cauchemare.» Annonce de journal par laquelle un agent immobilier offre ses services. (USA)
136 Annonce de journal pour la nouvelle collection d'hiver de la maison *Modissa* à Zurich. (SWI)

Advertisements / Inserate / Annonces

PHOTOGRAPHER / PHOTOGRAPH:

129 Larry Kanefsky
130 Joe Baker
131 Koji Suzuki
132 Kenneth Heyman
133 Mamoru Sugiyama
134 M. Zappala
135 Kent Severson
136 Ernst Wirz

DESIGNER / GESTALTER / MAQUETTISTE:

129, 130 Jack Taylor
131, 133 Hideyo Matsuda/Yutaka Sasaki
132 Hideyo Matsuda
135 Sue Crolick
136 Jacques Lehnen

ART DIRECTOR / DIRECTEUR ARTISTIQUE:

129, 130 Jack Taylor
131–133 Hideyo Matsuda
134 M. Göttsche
135 Sue Crolick
136 Erich Hartmann

134

135

136

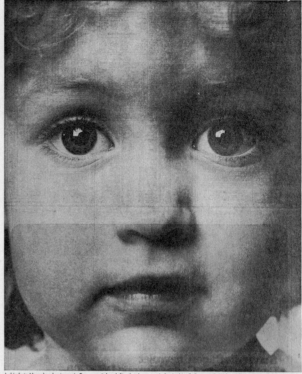

In den neuen Telefon-Nahbereichen können viele Groß-eltern mit ihren Enkeln 30 kostenlose 8-Minuten-Ge-spräche führen. Ab 1. Januar 1980 führt die Post nach und nach die neuen Telefon-Nahbereiche und den Zeittakt von 8 Minuten ein. Ein Telefon-Nahbereich ist etwa 20mal größer als ein Ortsnetz heute. In den neuen Telefon-Nahbereichen gibt es keine Ferngespräche mehr, sondern nur noch Nahgespräche. Ein 8-Minuten-Gespräch, das heute noch 3,68 DM kostet, weil es ein Ferngespräch ist, kostet dann nur noch 23 Pfennig, weil es ein Nahgespräch ist. Der Zeittakt gilt dann auch in den heutigen Ortsnetzen. Alle Gespräche in den heutigen Orts-netzen, die nicht länger als 8 Minuten sind, kosten dann so viel wie ein Ortsgespräch heute, nämlich 23 Pfennig. Nach 8 Minuten kosten sie dann allerdings 23 Pfennig mehr, nach weiteren 8 Minuten wieder 23 Pfennig mehr usw. Da man bei Gesprächen in den neuen Telefon-Nahbereichen viel mehr spart, als man bei sehr langen Gesprächen im heutigen Ortsnetz zuzahlt, wird Telefonieren billiger. Die Telefon-kunden werden insgesamt jedes Jahr rund 1 Milliarde DM an Ge-bühren sparen. Nun hat die Post aber festgestellt, daß viele alte und behinderte Menschen heute wenig Ferngespräche, dafür aber lange Ortsgespräche führen. Sie hätten also kaum Vorteile von der Verbilli-gung der Gespräche in den neuen Telefon-Nahbereichen. Deshalb bekommen sie von der Post jeden Monat eine Gutschrift von 30 Ge-bühreneinheiten. Das sind monatlich 30 kostenlose 8-Minuten-Ge-spräche im Ortsnetz oder Telefon-Nahbereich. Hier haben wir Ihnen einmal ganz genau aufgeschrieben, wer die Gutschrift von 30 Ge-bühreneinheiten im Monat bekommt. Das sind erst einmal alle Telefon-kunden, die einen Sozialanschluß haben und alleine wohnen. Das sind weiterhin alle Rentner, die Wohngeld beziehen und alleine wohnen. Dazu kommen alle Empfänger von Witwen- oder Witwerrente, die das 60. Lebensjahr vollendet haben, Wohngeld beziehen und alleine wohnen. Alle Personen, die wenigstens 80 Prozent in ihrer Erwerbstätig-keit gemindert und durch ihr Leiden ständig an ihre Wohnung gebunden sind, erhalten ebenfalls die Gutschrift von 30 Gebühreneinheiten im Monat. Dabei spielt es keine Rolle, ob sie alleine wohnen oder nicht. Viele alte Menschen können sich ab 1. Januar 1980 also ruhig ein bißchen länger mit ihren Enkeln am Telefon unterhalten. **Ihre Post.**

137

139

PHOTOGRAPHER:

137 Ben Oyne
138 Tony Mandarino
139, 140 Ken Griffiths
141 David Hamilton

DESIGNER:

138 Tony Mandarino
139, 140 TBWA

ART DIRECTOR:

137 Helmut Rottke
138 Tony Mandarino
139, 140 Charlotte
    Sherwood

AGENCY / AGENTUR:

137 GGK
138 Frankfurt
    Communications
139, 140 TBWA
141 Walther
    & Leuenberger AG

140

137 Double-spread newspaper advertisement in which the German Post Office announces 30 free local telephone conversations monthly for old people and invalids. Black and white. (GER)
138 Newspaper advertisement for the magazine *Parade*, with a story of an oil sultan's shopping expedition in the West. Black and white. (USA)
139, 140 Complete full-page newspaper advertisement and detail of the photograph for the services of *Singapore Airlines* from Europe to the Middle and Far East. Black and white. (SWI)
141 Black-and-white newspaper advertisement for a new perfume by *Nina Ricci*. (SWI)

137 Doppelseitiges Zeitungsinserat aus einer Werbekampagne der Deutschen Bundespost, mit welcher über Vergünstigungen im Fernmeldebereich, u. a. für ältere und behinderte Personen, informiert wird. (GER)
138 Ganzseitiges Inserat der Zeitschrift *Parade*. Der Text bezieht sich auf einen Bericht über die Einkäufe eines Sultans. (USA)
139, 140 Komplettes, ganzseitiges Zeitungsinserat und Detail der Aufnahme für *Singapore Airlines*. Angepriesen wird unter anderem der Bordservice, «von dem andere Fluggesellschaften nur reden». (SWI)
141 Schwarzweisses Zeitungsinserat für *farouche*, ein neues Parfum von *Nina Ricci*. (SWI)

137 Annonce de journal double page des P & T allemandes annonçant que 30 conversations téléphoniques locales par mois sont gratuites pour les vieux gens et les invalides. En noir et blanc. (GER)
138 Annonce de journal pour le magazine *Parade* qui publie l'histoire d'un magnat de l'industrie pétrolière qui a fait ses emplettes dans les pays occidentaux. En noir et blanc. (USA)
139, 140 Annonce de presse pleine page et détail de la photographie en faveur des services offerts par *Singapore Airlines* durant les vols à destination du Moyen et de l'Extrême Orient. (SWI)
141 Annonce de journal en noir et blanc pour un nouveau parfum de *Nina Ricci*. (SWI)

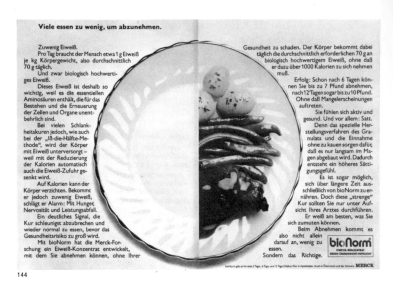

144

142

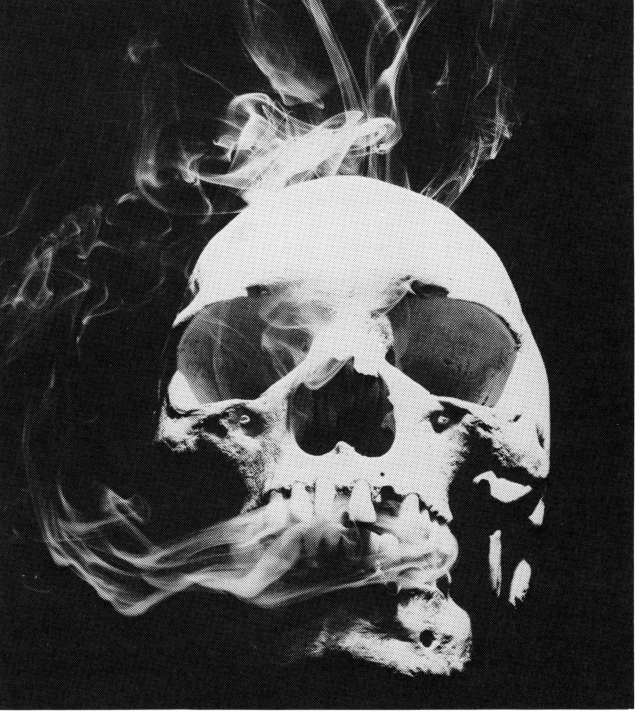

143

Seja discreta.   o.b.

145

o.b. A grande vedete das últimas Olimpíadas.   o.b.

146

"Group Therapy"

Aristocort
Triamcinolone Acetonide
Topicals

a form and strength for every pediatric patient...every type of steroid-responsive dermatosis

Available in low potency 0.025% Cream-effective for many common pediatric dermatoses.

Also available in regular and high potency Creams and Ointments for conditions requiring higher strength treatment...and as ARISTOGEL® Triamcinolone Acetonide Gel 0.1%.

The first triamcinolone preparation to remove common sensitizers—contains no parabens, phenol preservatives, lanolin...in bases that are "kind" to tender young skin.

One of the most economical topical steroids available.

147

PHOTOGRAPHER / PHOTOGRAPH / PHOTOGRAPHE:

142, 143 Pierre Hinch
144 Hans Hansen
145, 146 Moacir Lugato
147 Harold Krieger
148 Reid Miles

DESIGNER / GESTALTER / MAQUETTISTE:

142, 143 Derek Spaull
145, 146 José Zaragoza
147 Eric Rathje
148 Karen Crowley

ART DIRECTOR / DIRECTEUR ARTISTIQUE:

142, 143 Derek Spaull
144 Thomas Rempen
145, 146 José Zaragoza
147 Eric Rathje
148 Peter Belliveau

AGENCY / AGENTUR / AGENCE – STUDIO:

142, 143 Derek Spaull Graphics
144 Hildmann, Simon, Rempen & Schmitz
145, 146 Duailibi, Petit, Zaragoza Propaganda S.A.
147 Dugan/Farley Communications
148 William Douglas McAdams

In harmony with his antihypertensive life-style

Apresoline®
(hydralazine)

Avoids many troublesome side effects that limit daily activities

Added to your usual diuretic, Apresoline helps lower blood pressure without many of the problems associated with adrenergic inhibitors or beta blockers: sexual dysfunction, drowsiness, lethargy, and sedation are unlikely to occur. Postural hypotension is rare.

Acts on main hemodynamic abnormality

Through direct attention to arteriolar smooth muscle, Apresoline works by lowering excessive peripheral resistance—the main hemodynamic disturbance in most hypertension.

Compatible with a diuretic and virtually all antihypertensive regimens

Differing in action from most other oral antihypertensives, Apresoline often enhances and complements their effectiveness—thus permitting lower individual drug dosages.

Accompanying a fall in blood pressure from Apresoline is an increase in cardiac rate and output. As with any antihypertensive agent, use with caution in patients with advanced renal damage. Contraindicated in coronary artery disease.

CIBA

148

142, 143 Complete black-and-white newspaper advertisement for *Lobidan,* a cure for smoking, and detail of the shot. (SAF)
144 Double-spread magazine advertisement with colour illustration for a *Merck* albumin concentrate as a slimming aid. (GER)
145, 146 "Be discreet."—"The great star of the last Olympics." Magazine advertisements for *o.b.* sanitary tampons. Colour illustrations. (BRA)
147 Double-spread colour advertisement in the medical press for *Lederle* creams and ointments against dermatoses. (USA)
148 Double-spread advertisement in the medical press for a CIBA antihypertensive. Man and dog in colour. (USA)

142, 143 Komplettes Schwarzweiss-Inserat und Detail der Aufnahme für ein Medikament gegen Nikotinsucht. (SAF)
144 Doppelseitiges Inserat in Farbe für *bionorm*-Eiweisskonzentrat von *Merck,* empfohlen für Abmagerungskuren. (GER)
145, 146 Aus einer Serie von farbigen Zeitschrifteninseraten für *o.b.*-Tampons. Die Aufnahmen sollen die Unsichtbarkeit und Sicherheit der Tampons demonstrieren. (BRA)
147 Doppelseitiges Fachzeitschrifteninserat in Farbe für *Aristocort*-Salbe gegen Hautkrankheiten bei Kindern. (USA)
148 Farbige Doppelseite aus einer Fachzeitschrift für das Antistress-Mittel *Apresoline* von CIBA. (USA)

142, 143 Annonce de journal noir-blanc et détail de la photo pour un médicament anti-tabac. (SAF)
144 Annonce de magazine double page (illustration couleur) pour une préparation de protides pour amaigrir. (GER)
145, 146 D'une série d'annonces de magazine (en couleurs) pour les tampons *o.b.* (BRA)
147 Annonce de magazine professionnel pour un onguent contre la dermatose. Page double en couleurs. (USA)
148 Annonce double page publiée dans la presse médicale en faveur d'un produit de CIBA contre l'hypertension. (USA)

149

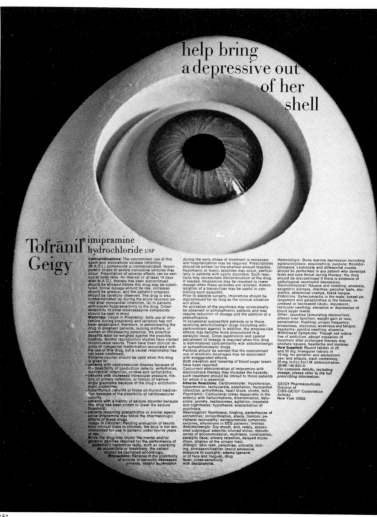

151

152

Advertisements
Inserate
Annonces

150

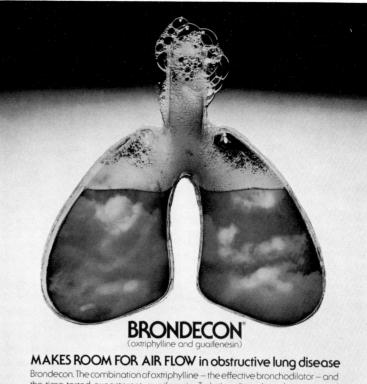

153

CROTALE
Système de défense
anti-aérienne
basse altitude tous temps.
Terre et mer.

THOMSON-CSF
DIVISION SYSTÈMES ÉLECTRONIQUES
1, RUE DES MATHURINS / B.P. 10 / 92222 BAGNEUX / FRANCE
TÉL. (1) 657.10.60

154

BRAUN

155

149, 152 Colour illustration and complete double-spread advertisement in medical magazines for a *Pfizer* drug against psychotic symptoms in the elderly. (USA)
150 Illustration of an institutional magazine advertisement for Kawakichi Wallpaper Co. (JPN)
151 Full-page magazine advertisement for a *Geigy* antidepressant. Green eye, blue ground. (USA)
153 Magazine ad for a *Warner-Chilcott* drug to relieve lung complaints. Blue lungs. (USA)
154 Magazine advertisement for an electronic anti-aircraft defence system. Yellow sky. (FRA)
155 Black-and-white shot for a newspaper campaign for *Braun* electric shavers. (SWI)
156 Double-spread trade press advertisement for *AlphaComp* typesetting machines, which even a girl typist can use after a little instruction. (USA)

149, 152 Farbaufnahme und Doppelseite eines Fachzeitschrifteninserats für das Medikament *Navane* gegen psychische Störungen, wie Verwirrung, Depressionen etc., im Alter. (USA)
150 Photographische Illustration zur Image-Werbung eines Tapetenherstellers. (JPN)
151 Ganzseitiges Inserat für das Antidepressivum *Tofranil*. Grünes Auge, blauer Grund. (USA)
153 Farbiges Fachzeitschrifteninserat für ein Medikament gegen Atembeschwerden. (USA)
154 Ganzseitiges Fachzeitschrifteninserat für ein elektronisches Abwehrsystem. (FRA)
155 Schwarzweiss-Aufnahme aus einer Zeitungskampagne für *Braun*-Rasierapparate. (SWI)
156 Doppelseitiges Fachzeitschrifteninserat für die *AlphaComp*-Setzmaschine («Der richtige Setzer möge aufstehen!»): Nach kurzer Einarbeitung kann eine Schreibkraft sie bedienen. (USA)

149, 152 Illustration en couleurs et annonce double page publiée dans la presse médicale pour un produit pharmaceutique contre les troubles psychotiques des gens âgés. (USA)
150 Illustration d'une annonce de prestige pour un fabricant de papiers peints. (JPN)
151 Annonce de magazine pleine page pour un antidépresseur. Œil vert, fond bleu. (USA)
153 Annonce de magazine pour un produit pharmaceutique contre les troubles respiratoires. (USA)
154 Annonce de magazine pour un système de défense anti-aérienne de *Thomson-CSF*. (FRA)
155 Photo en noir et blanc figurant dans une campagne de presse pour les rasoirs *Braun*. (SWI)
156 Annonce professionnelle double page pour les composeuses *AlphaComp*: «Le vrai typo est prié de se lever» – c'est une dactylo rapidement mise au courant de la frappe très facile. (USA)

PHOTOGRAPHER / PHOTOGRAPH / PHOTOGRAPHE:

149, 152 Peter Simon
150 Koji Suzuki
151 Joachim Laube
153 John Olivio
154 J. P. Ragot
155 Jost Wildbolz
156 Carl Fischer

DESIGNER / GESTALTER / MAQUETTISTE:

149, 152 Mike Lyons
150 Akido Terada
153 Dick Russinko
154 G. Briot
155 Domenig K. Geissbühler
156 Herb Lubalin

ART DIRECTOR / DIRECTEUR ARTISTIQUE:

149, 152 Mike Lyons
150 Norimitsu Mamada
151 Jackie Rose
153 Dick Russinko
155 Domenig K. Geissbühler
156 Herb Lubalin

AGENCY / AGENTUR / AGENCE – STUDIO:

149, 152, 153 Sudler & Hennessey, Inc.
150 Nippon Design Center
151 Geigy Pharmaceuticals
154 Bazaine
155 F. Huhle
156 LSC&P Design Group

Will the real typesetter please stand up!

Alpha Comp

156

157

158

Advertisements
Inserate
Annonces

157, 158 Complete full-page trade magazine advertisement and detail of the photography for an antiflatulent made by Stuart Pharmaceuticals. (USA)
159 Double-spread black-and-white magazine advertisement placed in the medical press for a CIBA antihypertensive drug. (USA)
160 Double-spread trade magazine advertisement in full colour for a *Geigy* pharmaceutical for the treatment of depression. (USA)
161 "A dog is a man's best friend. But it isn't a human being." Double-spread magazine advertisement for a *Pierrel* range of products for dogs. (ITA)
162, 163 Detail of the colour shot and complete double-spread trade magazine advertisement for a *Geigy* drug for the treatment of arthritis. (USA)

157, 158 Ganzseitiges Fachzeitschrifteninserat und photographische Illustration für *Mylicon,* ein Medikament gegen Blähungen. (USA)
159 «Auch Mammas erster Schritt ist wichtig.» Gemeint ist der Beginn einer Antistress-Therapie mit dem Medikament *Esidrix* von CIBA. Doppelseitiges Fachzeitschrifteninserat. (USA)
160 Farbige Doppelseite eines Zeitschrifteninserats für *Tofranil-PM,* ein Medikament von *Geigy* gegen Symptome der Depression. Auf einer weiteren Seite Angaben über das Medikament. (USA)
161 «Der Hund ist der beste Freund des Menschen, aber er ist kein Mensch.» Doppelseitiges Zeitschrifteninserat für eine Ernährungs- und Pflegeproduktreihe für den Hund. (ITA)
162, 163 «Äpfel und Orangen lassen sich ebensowenig vergleichen wie *Butazolidin alka (Geigy)* mit neueren Antiarthritis-Medikamenten.» Inserat und Detail der Aufnahme. (USA)

159

160

162

163

157, 158 Annonce professionnelle pleine page et détail de la photographie pour un produit pharmaceutique contre la flatulence. (USA)
159 Annonce double page en noir et blanc publiée dans la presse médicale en faveur d'un produit pharmaceutique contre l'hypertension. (USA)
160 Annonce publiée dans la presse médicale pour un antidepresseur de *Geigy*. Page double en polychromie. (USA)
161 «Le chien est le meilleur ami de l'homme. Mais il n'est pas un être humain.» Annonce de magazine double page pour une gamme de produits *Pierrel* pour chiens. (ITA)
162, 163 «La différence entre les pommes et les oranges est aussi grande qu'entre *Butazolidin alka* (*Geigy*) et les autres produits contre l'arthrite.» Annonce et détail de la photo. (USA)

161

PHOTOGRAPHER / PHOTOGRAPH:

157, 158 Ryszard Horowitz
159 Reid Miles
160 Whitney Lane
161 B Communications
162, 163 Ed Gallucci

DESIGNER / GESTALTER / MAQUETTISTE:

157, 158 Marc Rubin
159 Peter Belliveau
160, 162, 163 Ron Vareltzis
161 B Communications

ART DIRECTOR / DIRECTEUR ARTISTIQUE:

157, 158 Marc Rubin
159 Peter Belliveau
160, 162, 163 Ron Vareltzis
161 B Communications

AGENCY / AGENTUR / AGENCE – STUDIO:

157, 158 Sudler & Hennessey, Inc.
159 William Douglas McAdams
160, 162, 163 Ciba-Geigy Design
161 B Communications

164

Advertisements / Inserate / Annonces

PHOTOGRAPHER / PHOTOGRAPH:

164–166 Marvin Koner
168, 169 Jake Wallis
170, 171 James Joern

IN SOME WAYS IT'S A PITY MOTORISTS CAN'T FALL OFF THEIR CARS.

IT DOESN'T TAKE MUCH TO BLOT OUT A MOTORCYCLIST.

We spread the risk   because you can't.

MGIC

170

168   169

DESIGNER / GESTALTER / MAQUETTISTE:

164–166 Mario Giuriceo
170, 171 Howland Blackiston

ART DIRECTOR / DIRECTEUR ARTISTIQUE:

164–166 Mario Giuriceo
168, 169 Clinton Firth
170, 171 Howland Blackiston

AGENCY / AGENTUR / AGENCE – STUDIO:

164–166 Edwin Bird Wilson
167 Présence
168 TBWA Ltd.
170, 171 Ries Cappiello Colwell

The Naturists...

...Pollution control systems provided by our equipment financing/leasing subsidiary, one of the largest in the U.S. gives industry the means to protect the environment for future generations. Consider the source.

MANUFACTURERS HANOVER
The financial source.Worldwide.

165

The Futurists...

...Our innovative lending techniques enable industry to channel more funds into research and development—with breakthroughs that mean more jobs and better ways to do business around the world. Consider the source.

MANUFACTURERS HANOVER
The financial source.Worldwide.

166

Erich Landert Styliste 5445680

167

164–166 Photograph and two complete double-spread advertisements for the financial services of Manufacturers Hanover, here for pollution control systems and technical research. (USA)
167 Self-promotion for a designer: double-spread black-and-white magazine advertisement. (FRA)
168, 169 Full-page newspaper advertisements from a series in which the Institute of Motorcycling gives safety tips and warnings to motorcyclists. (GBR)
170, 171 Complete double-spread magazine advertisement and photograph. The basket represents the USA, over which the Mortgage Guaranty Insurance Corporation spreads the risk. (USA)

164–166 Aufnahme von Abb. 165 und komplette doppelseitige Anzeigen der Finanzierungsgesellschaft Manufacturers Hanover, hier für Umweltschutz und technische Forschung. (USA)
167 Doppelseitiges Zeitschrifteninserat in Schwarzweiss. Eigenwerbung eines Designers. (FRA)
168, 169 Ganzseitige Inserate aus einer Schwarzweiss-Serie, womit das Institut für Motorradsport den Motorradfahrern Ratschläge gibt und auf Gefahren aufmerksam macht. (GBR)
170, 171 Komplettes Inserat und farbige Aufnahme für eine Hypothekarversicherungsgesellschaft. Der Korb in Form der USA soll die breite geographische Basis der Firma deutlich machen. (USA)

164–166 Photographie et deux annonces double page pour la «source financière mondiale» de Manufacturers Hanover, ici se référant au contrôle de la pollution et à la recherche technique. (USA)
167 Annonce autopromotionnelle d'un designer. Double page en noir et blanc. (FRA)
168, 169 Annonces pleine page en noir et blanc figurant dans une série de l'Institut de Motocyclisme qui avertit les motocyclistes des dangers et de la prévention d'accidents. (GBR)
170, 171 Annonce de magazine complète et détail de la photo couleur pour une compagnie d'assurance foncière. La corbeille représentant les Etats-Unis devrait symboliser le rayon d'action de cette entreprise. (USA)

171

176

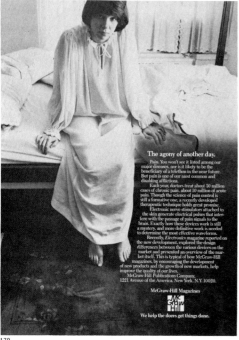

172

173

178

174

175

180

All the body money can buy.

"The Men Who Spend Your Money to Keep You Healthy," by Donald Robinson
September 11, 1977 issue

Money may not buy happiness, but the men and women who serve us in Washington are out to see if it won't buy health.

That's your health, of course. And it's your money. In 1976 $2.4 billion. This year $2.7 billion. For medical research alone.

Oddly enough, the decision as to how this money should be spent is up to 12 men — six Senators, five Representatives, and one Cabinet member — a sort of jury of your peers, who may not always agree.

Parade's article on the subject underlines the sincerity of the effort by these men to preserve the body politic — and suggests that many of them find their motivation in tragedy in their own lives. They may argue over pet projects, but they agree on basic purpose.

What happens to health is a primary concern of Parade's 41,000,000 readers. So Parade takes what time and space is needed to elaborate on the subject. But wastes no words that might

be better spent bringing other news items to their attention.

Our editors cover the world — its health, its happiness, and its many horizons — in as few words as possible. Our readers like it that way. After all, they're in a Sunday mood — not just to read, but to go out and buy, and time is of the essence.

Take a position in Parade with your advertising message some Sunday soon. And look toward healthy sales. Call (212) 953-7650.

parade
It wouldn't be Sunday without a Parade

177

The $600,000 man.

'Intelligence Report'
November 28, 1976 issue

There's nothing heroic about him. He's an average European male. He works, his wife does n't. He has two children. And, according to the Rotterdam Savings Bank and its computer, he will have spent $640,000 in his lifetime, if he dies at the age of 69.

The figure includes the cost of his funeral and a modest $4,000 estate for his heirs.

To no one's surprise — certainly not

that of Parade's 40 million readers — the largest item of expense in his lifetime is taxes $108,000, followed closely by the cost of his house ($96,000), food ($88,000), car ($48,000), coffee, tea, booze, and sweets ($24,000) and $10,000 for postage and phone service.

For Parade's readers, Europe's $600,000 man has one big advantage over America's seven-figure television

character. He is real. His problems are real. And Parade readers are nothing if not realists. They identify.

Parade's editors serve up brief, brightly-edited bits of reality Sunday after Sunday. The subject matter is broad and varied. The editorial treatment is deft and crisp. Readers respond to it in 114 Sunday newspapers. So do advertisers. Call (212) 953-7650 for details.

parade
It wouldn't be Sunday without a Parade

179

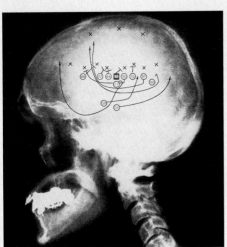

Michigan's winningest game plan.

'A Pep Talk from Coach Bo Schembechler,' by Joe Falls
October 31, 1976, issue

It did not figure in the Wolverines' recent Rose Bowl appearance.

This particular game plan is one Coach Bo Schembechler 'X-ed' and 'O-ed' for himself to see him through open-heart surgery.

Parade detailed the Coach's game plan which, among other things, found

him going over his own X-rays, as though they were last week's films showing him what he had to beat. Once he saw what needed doing, he ordered it done.

The Coach, notoriously secretive about most game plans, shares this one happily with all who are interested.

Parade's 40 million readers are among the first, because Parade is usually around where the meaningful, interesting things happen. And Parade reports them promptly, and with feeling.

For a piece of the action, call (212) 953-7650. Parade. It isn't very heavy but it carries a lot of weight.

parade
It wouldn't be Sunday without a Parade

181

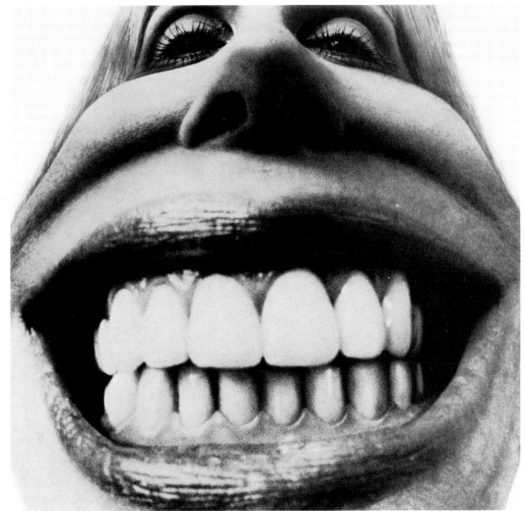

182

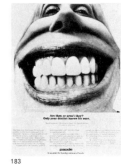

183

Advertisements / Inserate / Annonces

"Dear American Tourister: I went east, you went west."

"Dear American Tourister: I fell flat on my attache."

"Dear American Tourister: My life was resting on your suitcase."

Your antifreeze will freeze before our oil will.

Mobil 1 The oil that saves you gas.

"No gossip."

ANDY WARHOL, ARTIST. A READER SINCE 1968.

U.S.News & WORLD REPORT We spare our readers unimportant news. We spare our advertisers unimportant readers.

"No recipes."

CRAIG CLAIBORNE, FOOD CRITIC. A READER SINCE 1972.

U.S.News & WORLD REPORT We spare our readers unimportant news. We spare our advertisers unimportant readers.

184–186 Magazine ads from a long and continuing campaign stressing the toughness of *American Tourister* suitcases. (USA)
187 Magazine ad for a *Mobil* oil that doesn't freeze even at very low temperatures. (USA)
188, 189 Black-and-white ads from a campaign for *U.S. News and World Report*, here showing Andy Warhol and the food critic Craig Claiborne. (USA)
190 Double-spread magazine ad in full colour on the subject of trust, for Employers Reinsurance Corporation. (USA)
191 Advertisement from a campaign for Portfolio Management Inc. Black and white. (USA)
192, 193 Complete self-promotion advertisement for the design studio Frank Delano & Associates, Inc., with black-and-white photograph in roughly actual size. (USA)

184–186 Ganzseitige, farbige Zeitschrifteninserate für strapazierfähige *American-Tourister*-Koffer. (USA)
187 Zeitschrifteninserat für *Mobil*-Motorenöl, das auch bei strengstem Frost zuverlässig sein soll. (USA)
188, 189 Schwarzweiss-Inserate aus einer Kampagne für die Zeitschrift *U.S. News and World Report*. Hier Andy Warhol unter dem Titel «kein Klatsch», unter «keine Rezepte» Craig Claiborne, ein Gastronom. (USA)
190 Doppelseitiges Zeitschrifteninserat in Farbe für eine Rückversicherungsgesellschaft. Das Thema: «Vertrauen». (USA)
191 «Zu gut um anzudauern» steht über der Aufnahme zu einem Schwarzweiss-Inserat der Portfolio Management, Inc. (USA)
192, 193 Schwarzweiss-Inserat einer Werbeagentur, mit eingestreuten Attributen, die sie auszeichnen sollen. (USA)

184–186 Annonces de magazine figurant dans une longue série pour les valises *American Tourister* super-robustes. (USA)
187 Annonce de magazine en faveur d'une huile *Mobil* qui ne se congèle pas même par forte gelée. (USA)
188, 189 Annonce noir-blanc en faveur du *U.S. News and World Report* où il n'y a «pas de bavardage» (Andy Warhol) et «pas de recettes» (Craig Claiborne). (USA)
190 Annonce de magazine double page (en couleurs) pour une compagnie de réassurance. Sujet: «confiance». (USA)
191 Annonce tirée d'une campagne noir-blanc en faveur de la Portfolio Management, Inc. (USA)
192, 193 Annonce autopromotionnelle publiée par un studio de design américain et détail de la photographie en noir et blanc (approx. grandeur nature). (USA)

PHOTOGRAPHER / PHOTOGRAPH / PHOTOGRAPHE:
184–186 Cosimo
187 Henry Sandbank
188, 189 Mick Pateman
190 Jay Maisel
191 L. Payne/J. Baraban/C. McGrath/J. Brooks
192, 193 Jamie Odgers

DESIGNER / GESTALTER / MAQUETTISTE:
192, 193 Frank Delano/April Greiman

192

190

191

ART DIRECTOR / DIRECTEUR ARTISTIQUE:

184–186 Jack Maricucci/Roy Grace
187 Ron Arnold
188, 189 J. Ryder
190 Tim Hamill
191 Jack Amuny/Dean Narahara
192, 193 Frank Delano

AGENCY / AGENTUR / AGENCE – STUDIO:

184–187 Doyle Dand Bernbach
188, 189 Ted Chin & Company
190 Brewer Advertising
191 Art City
192, 193 Frank Delano & Associates Inc.

193

YOU'RE ALL WET.

Take a Boeing Holiday.

Almost every minute of every day there's a Boeing jetliner going somewhere. To sunshine. Good food. Good friends. And good times. Call your travel agent or your airline and say "I've had it. I'm going where the sun is shining." **BOEING**
Put me on a Boeing. *Getting people together*

194

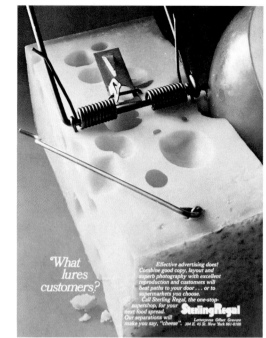

'What lures customers?'

Effective advertising does! Combine good copy, layout and superb photography with excellent reproduction and customers will beat paths to your door . . . or to supermarkets you choose. *Call Sterling Regal, the one-stop-supershop, for your next food spread. Our separations will make you say, "cheese".*

Sterling Regal
Letterpress Offset Gravure
104 E. 45 St. New York 661-0100

196

what price design?

If you believe the best must cost you more, then the Sadler Suite will surprise you.
Take a look. Clean, simple lines. No sharp corners. Beautifully finished. You'll notice we've hidden all the fixing screws – a feature of the Sadler Suite range.
And that really is the point. Hiding the screws has improved the style. Yet all our fittings are as easy to fit as more conventional styles. And painting is made a lot easier.
So what price design? You pay no more for Sadler Suite fittings than you would for many more ordinary designs. Which means you can count the eye-pleasing style and functional good sense of Sadler Suite design as a very welcome bonus – that costs you nothing!
Look into the Sadler Suite range. We believe you'll find it worthwhile. Send for our full and comprehensive catalogue. R. Lilly & Sons Limited, Baltimore Road, Birmingham 22b. Telephone: 021-357 1761.

The Sadler Suite by **LILLY**

200

Advertisements

WHITE.
Purest expression of a Sherle Wagner classic.

FORM, SO SURE OF ITSELF, IT SPURNS DECORATION. A TRIUMPH OVER THE OBVIOUS. TODAY A BEAUTIFUL ARTIFACT, TOMORROW THE PRIDE OF COLLECTORS. 60 EAST 57 ST. NEW YORK, **SHERLE WAGNER** N.Y. 10022 PLAZA 8-3300

195

197   198   199

201   202   203

204

205

206

207

204 Full-colour magazine advertisement, without copy, for *Pentax* cameras. (USA)
205 Magazine advertisement in full colour for an "invisible" *Laverne* chair. The diffraction effect in the copy underlines the chair's transparency. (USA)
206, 207 From a series of double-spread black-and-white advertisements for *Colt* heating and ventilating systems, here with reference to the dulling effect of heat in summer and to the nuisance of draughts in winter. (GER)
208, 209 Detail of the photography and complete double-spread magazine advertisement ("Colours show life") for *Gebr. Schmidt* printing inks. (GER)

204 Annonce de magazine en couleurs, sans texte, pour les caméras *Pentax*. (USA)
205 Annonce de magazine en polychromie pour une chaise *Laverne* «invisible», jouant sur l'effet de diffraction entre la chaise et le texte. (USA)
206, 207 Annonces double page en noir et blanc figurant dans une série pour les systèmes de ventilation et de chauffage *Colt*, avec référence à l'effet endormant de la chaleur estivale et aux courants d'air embêtants de l'hiver. (GER)
208, 209 Détail de la photo et annonce de magazine double page d'un fabricant d'encres d'imprimerie qui «reproduisent la vie». (GER)

204 Ganzseitiges Fachzeitschrifteninserat in Farbe für *Pentax*-Kameras, ohne Worte. (USA)
205 Farbiges Zeitschrifteninserat für einen Sessel von *Laverne*, «durch den man hindurchsehen kann..., der scheinbar keinen Platz wegnimmt». (USA)
206, 207 Doppelseitige Schwarzweiss-Inserate für *Colt International*, Hersteller von Lüftungssystemen, die im Sommer wie im Winter für das richtige «Arbeitsklima» sorgen sollen. Abb. 206 bezieht sich auf die «Urlaubsreife» im Sommer, Abb. 207 auf Durchzug im Winter. (GER)
208, 209 Detail der Aufnahme und komplettes doppelseitiges Zeitschrifteninserat für Druckfarben der Gebr. Schmidt GmbH: «Diese Farben machen wir». (GER)

Advertisements / Inserate / Annonces

PHOTOGRAPHER / PHOTOGRAPH:

205 Carl Fischer
206, 207 Franz-Erwin Wagner
208, 209 Klaus M. Lang

DESIGNER / GESTALTER / MAQUETTISTE:

205 George Lois
206, 207 Walter Hugelshofer
208, 209 Olaf Leu/Fritz Hofrichter

ART DIRECTOR / DIRECTEUR ARTISTIQUE:

205 George Lois
206, 207 Walter Hugelshofer

AGENCY / AGENTUR / AGENCE – STUDIO:

205 Papert, Koenig, Lois Inc.
206, 207 Doyle Dane Bernbach GmbH
208, 209 Olaf Leu Design

209

208

212

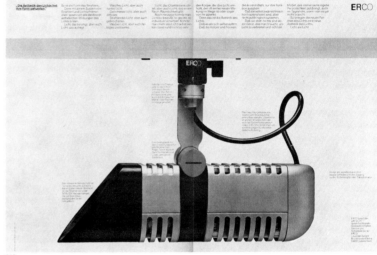

213

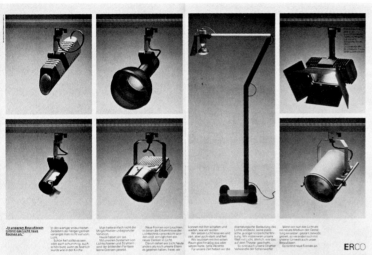

214

215

211

ERCO

216

210, 211 Photographic illustration in actual size and complete double-spread magazine advertisement for a *Westvaco* art paper. (USA)
212, 213 Double-spread magazine ads from campaigns for BMW cars in which their speed and sporting qualitites are underlined. (USA)
214—216 "Light takes on new forms in our consciousness."—"The aesthetics of light have found their form."—"Exemplary design is also exhibited in the Museum of Modern Art." Double-spread magazine advertisements from a full-colour campaign for *Erco* lamps, which are also represented in the Museum of Modern Art. (GER)

210, 211 Aufnahme und komplettes, doppelseitiges Zeitschrifteninserat für ein *Westvaco*-Papier. Es wird die gute Qualität der Wiedergabe auf diesem Papier hervorgehoben. (USA)
212, 213 Doppelseitige Zeitschrifteninserate aus Kampagnen für BMW-Automodelle, die sich auch auf dem Nürburgring sehen lassen könnten. (GER)
214—216 Drei doppelseitige Zeitschrifteninserate in Farbe aus einer Werbekampagne für *Erco*-Leuchten, die helfen sollen, Licht bewusst, gezielt und individuell einzusetzen. Einige der Leuchten werden als beispielhaftes Design im Museum of Modern Art, New York, gezeigt. (GER)

210, 211 Illustration en grandeur nature et annonce de magazine double page soulignant la qualité des papiers *Westvaco*. (USA)
212, 213 Annonces double page tirées de campagnes BMW où l'on met l'accent sur le côté sportif de ces voitures qui ne dépareraient pas un circuit automobile. (USA)
214—216 Annonces de magazine double page figurant dans une campagne lancée en faveur des lampes *Erco* pour l'usage individuel. Quelques-unes des lampes *Erco* sont exposées au Museum of Modern Art, New York. (GER)

Advertisements

PHOTOGRAPHER / PHOTOGRAPH / PHOTOGRAPHE:

210, 211 Phil Marco
212, 213 Dick James/David Thorpe
214—216 Hans Hansen

DESIGNER / GESTALTER / MAQUETTISTE:

210, 211 Ted McNeil

ART DIRECTOR / DIRECTEUR ARTISTIQUE:

210, 211 Ted McNeil
212, 213 Clem McCarthy
214—216 Thomas Rempen

AGENCY / AGENTUR / AGENCE – STUDIO:

210, 211 McCaffrey & McCall
212, 213 Ammirati Puris Avrutick
214—216 Hildmann, Simon, Rempen & Schmitz

The phones that serve your office.

Mountain Bell's new communications system for local governments.

217

DESIGNER / GESTALTER / MAQUETTISTE:

218 Zezito Marques da Costa
221 Sam Scali/Peter Kingman
222 Carlos Zintra Mauro
223 Charles Davidson

ART DIRECTOR / DIRECTEUR ARTISTIQUE:

217 Jerry Murff
218 Carlos Cintra Mauro
219 Anne Shaver
220 Helmut Krone
221 Sam Scali/Peter Kingman
222 Zezito Marques da Costa
223 Charles Davidson

AGENCY / AGENTUR / AGENCE – STUDIO:

217 Tracy-Locke, Inc.
218, 222 Marques da Costa Propaganda
219 Cargil Wilson & Acree, Inc.
220 Doyle Dane Bernbach
221 Scali, McCabe, Sloves
223 Harry Viola Advertising

HOW AMARLITE ANACONDA CAN INSULATE YOUR CLIENTS AGAINST HIGH ENERGY COSTS.

In today's energy-conscious economy, a building has to work as good as it looks.

And that's why Amarlite Anaconda offers a broad line of thermally-improved architectural aluminum. Five curtain wall systems and six low-rise framing systems. Each designed to keep nature outside and energy inside with specially constructed thermal barriers between indoors and outdoors.

In the final analysis, it's the lifecycle costs that concern a building owner. So our thermally-improved products are designed to minimize long-term energy expenses. And to keep a building operating at a constant and economical temperature.

But even with such a broad line, we never stop improving our thermally-improved products.

Amarlite Anaconda is constantly innovating. Refining our refinements. Our challenge is to stay ahead of the challenges facing you.

Which is part of the reason our architectural aluminum also comes with a design assistance team. To help you adapt Amarlite's special products to your project's special needs.

So specify Amarlite thermally-improved products for your next project.

Your building design will look better with each passing year.

Whether you're involved with one story, or thirty stories, you'll want to hear our story. Send for our catalogs, "Thermally-Improved Curtain Walls" and "Entrances and Storefront Systems." Write to Amarlite Anaconda, P.O. Box 1719, Atlanta, Ga. 30301. Or read about us in "Sweets 8.11/AN and 8.14/AN." Or you can call our home office at (404) 691-5750.

AMARLITE
ANACONDA ▲ Aluminum Division

219

218

Advertisements / Inserate / Annonces

220

221

222

223

224

225

226

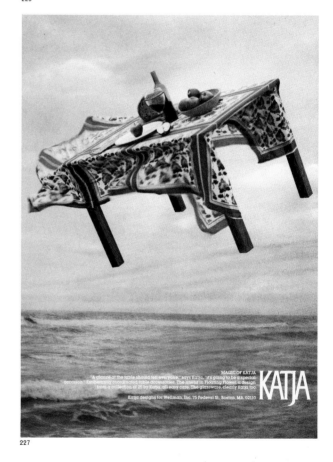

227

224 Colour ad for French china, glass and silver from *Baccarat*. (USA)
225 Colour magazine ad for a *Pentax* camera as a "third eye". (NOR)
226 Black-and-white advertisement for *Taylor's* discount stores, Elsternwick, where bargaining is encouraged. (AUS)
227 Magazine ad for *Katja* table accessories. Mainly blue shades. (USA)
228 Double-spread magazine ad for *Pyral* musical instruments. (FRA)
229, 230 Photographic illustration of an advertisement for a store selling wicker goods and other gift articles. (GER)

224 Pour une marque de procelaine, de cristal et de services en argent. (USA)
225 «*Asahi Pentax*, le troisième œil.» Annonce de magazine (NOR)
226 Annonce de magazine en noir et blanc en faveur d'une chaîne de magasins discount où l'on est encouragé à marchander. (AUS)
227 Annonce pour les accessoires de table *Katja*. Tons bleus. (USA)
228 Annonce double page (en couleurs) pour les instruments *Pyral*. (FRA)
229, 230 Annonce complète et détail de la photo publiée par un magasin qui vend des cadeaux. (GER)

224 Inserat für französisches Kristall, Porzellan und Tafelsilber. (USA)
225 «*Asahi Pentax*, das dritte Auge.» Farbiges Magazininserat. (NOR)
226 Schwarzweiss-Inserat für ein australisches Discountwarenhaus. (AUS)
227 Farbiges Inserat für Geschirr und Tischdecken von *Katja*. (USA)
228 Doppelseitiges Farbinserat für *Pyral*-Musikinstrumente. (FRA)
229, 230 Komplettes Inserat und Detail der Aufnahme für ein Geschenkartikelgeschäft, mit Hinweis auf die Frankfurter Messe. (GER)

PYRAL

228

229

230

ipoteruso

design
Achille Castiglioni

231

SCHÖN WÄR'S:
Bestimmtes aussagen.
Ins Konzept passen.
Ausgesprochenes tun.
Genau machen.
So lassen.
Mit KS geht's.

KALKSANDSTEINE

232

PHOTOGRAPHER / PHOTOGRAPH / PHOTOGRAPHE:

231 Jurgen Beker
232 Klaus Kinold
236 Paul Kluber
237 Dennis Eilers
238 Frank Lafitte

DESIGNER / GESTALTER / MAQUETTISTE:

232 Klaus Kinold
233–235 David Kennedy
236 Paul Kluber
238 Myron Polenberg

ART DIRECTOR / DIRECTEUR ARTISTIQUE:

231 P. Tavoglia
232 Klaus Kinold
233–235 David Kennedy
237 Barbara Hood
238 Myron Polenberg

AGENCY / AGENTUR / AGENCE – STUDIO:

231 P. Tavoglia
232 Atelier Kinold
233–235 Art Kane
236 Brooke Lemburg Photography
237 D'Arcy MacManus & Masius
238 CBS Records

233

THE POWER TO MOVE YOU, EVEN WHEN IT'S STANDING STILL.

The 1978 Harley-Davidson Sportster.

This is the motorcycle whose owners are frequently described as a "cult."

The one machine every red-blooded American sooner or later dreams of owning.

Fast, maneuverable, powerful. The kind of machine that turns heads even when it's standing still.

Low, lean, sleek.

Powered by a classic V-Twin... in our opinion, still the best engine configuration for a heavyweight motorcycle.

The Sportster looks like a motorcycle should look. Sounds like a motorcycle should sound. Performs in a way that turns converts into fanatics.

Incredible low-end torque. Quick, responsive handling. Solid, stable ride.

For 1978 we've mounted dual front disc brakes onto a laced wheel that's tastily pinstriped, added a solid state voltage regulator, and popped on a 3-D nameplate for no other reason than it looks good.

The Harley-Davidson Sportster is an American classic. Someday you'll see it in the art museums.

Right now, no museum can hold it.

Harley-Davidson

UNTIL YOU'VE BEEN ON A HARLEY-DAVIDSON, YOU HAVEN'T BEEN ON A MOTORCYCLE.

We believe in safety first. Always ride with lights and helmet. Help keep insurance costs down, lock your bike. Follow owner's manual for maintenance. Specifications subject to change without notice. For nearest dealer call 800-221-3333 toll free. In New York State call 212-775-1395 collect.

231 Double-spread magazine advertisement for *Flos* lamps. (ITA)
232 Advertisement for hewn stone placed in architectural magazines. Olive-brown foreground, white stone, blue sky. (GER)
233–235 Double-spread magazine ads from a campaign for *Harley-Davidson* motorcycles. (USA)
236 Self-promotional shot for Brooke Lemburg Photography. Glasses chiefly in shades of blue and red, green and red background. (USA)
237 Institutional advertisement for Whirlpool Corporation referring to the white-headed (American) eagle, now threatened by extinction. Double spread, black and white. (USA)
238 Ad for *Epic Records*, to promote four successful recordings by the Boston group. (USA)

231 Doppelseitiges Inserat für Lampen von *Flos*, Design A. Costiglioni. (ITA)
232 Ganzseitiges Zeitschrifteninserat in Farbe für *Kalksandstein-Information*. (GER)
233–235 «Solange man nicht auf einer *Harley-Davidson* gesessen hat, ist man nicht motorradgefahren.» Drei Beispiele aus einer Werbekampagne für *Harley-Davidson*-Motorräder. (USA)
236 Farbiges Eigenwerbungs-Inserat eines Photostudios. Die photographische Illustration soll die Möglichkeiten des Studios demonstrieren. (USA)
237 «Lektion einer aussterbenden Spezies.» Der Adler steht als Symbol für Eigenschaften, die in Vergessenheit zu geraten drohen: Stolz, Würde, Aufrichtigkeit, Eigenschaften, welche die Whirlpool Corporation, Hersteller von elektrischen Apparaten, nicht vergessen will. (USA)
238 Inserat für Erfolgsaufnahmen der Gruppe Boston auf *Epic*-Schallplatten und -Bändern. (USA)

231 Annonce de magazine double page en faveur des lampes *Flos*. (ITA)
232 Annonce publiée dans les magazines d'architecture en faveur des pierres taillées. Fond olive brun, pierre blanche, ciel bleu. (GER)
233–235 D'une campagne d'annonces double page pour une marque de motocyclettes. (USA)
236 Photo d'une annonce autopromotionnelle d'un studio de photographie. Verres en tons bleus et rouges prédominant, fond vert et rouge. (USA)
237 Annonce de prestige avec référence à l'aigle qui symbolise des caractéristiques (fierté, dignité sincérité) en voie d'être oubliées, caractéristiques que cette firme cultive. (USA)
238 Annonce pour la promotion d'un enregistrement du groupe Boston. (USA)

Advertisements / Inserate / Annonces

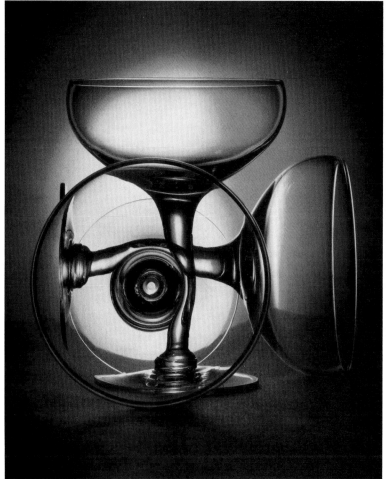

236

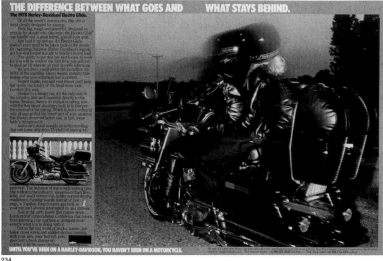

234

237

235

238

2

Booklets

Folders

Catalogues

Invitations

Programmes

Broschüren

Faltprospekte

Kataloge

Einladungen

Programme

Brochures

Dépliants

Catalogues

Invitations

Programmes

239

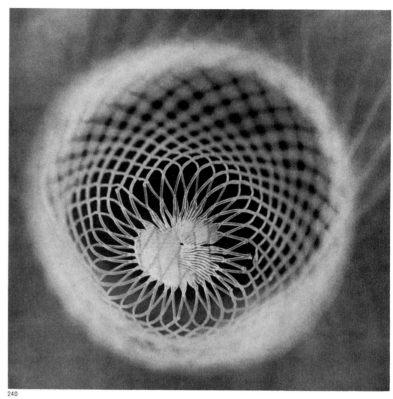

240

optimum packaging

242

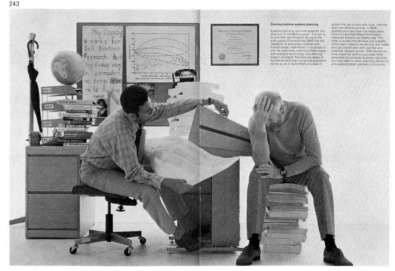

243

Pemco Tests & Controls

Frit is made in continuous smelters. To maintain quality standards Pemco takes a representative sample for every lot of frit produced. The sample is put through a battery of tests in our Quality Control Laboratory to be sure that it is suitable for its generally accepted use.

Certain control tests are basic but none the less important. For example, test plates are made on every run of porcelain enamel frit. These plates will be examined for consistency of color, quality of finish, strength of adherence, reflectance, cleanability, acid-resistance, alkali-resistance and many other properties.

Control Equipment

Custom test equipment is frequently designed and made by personnel in the Pemco Research & Development Laboratories. Special customer requirements, unique specifications, unusual situations tax the ingenuity of Pemco scientists.

Development work

In addition to meeting the current and changing needs of frit customers, Pemco's ceramic engineers are constantly exploring techniques and formulations that may improve performance.

Since the earliest years, the Pemco Research & Development Laboratories have served as a training ground for people in the ceramic industry.

Technical manuals on ceramic coating technology are written by Pemco personnel and supplied to university ceramic engineering departments as well as to industrial management.

FRIT by Pemco

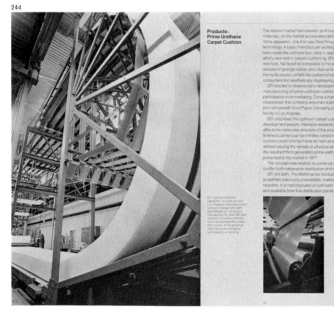

244

Products: Prime Urethane Carpet Cushion

The rebond market had opened up through the availability of scrap materials. As the market accelerated and the price rose, a new market niche appeared, one that was filled through the emergence of new technology. A basic manufacturer working with prime chemicals could now create the urethane bun, slice it, apply a backing, and offer it as a wholly new look in carpet cushioning. (Prime urethane had literally a new look, flat-faced as compared to the air-trapping bubbles and textures of sponge rubber, and clean and single-toned as compared to the multicolored confetti-like pattern of rebond, which some consumers find aesthetically displeasing.)

GFI elected to observe early developments and failures in the manufacturing of prime urethane cushion, and to undertake limited participation in its marketing. Once a marketing opportunity had been established, the company assumed a position of strength through a joint venture with Scott Paper Company, plus GFI's own prime urethane facility in Los Angeles.

GFI described the optimum carpet cushion to Scott's research and development people. Intensive research provided a technique that affects the molecular structure of the processed chemicals so the finished cushion can be infinitely varied in resistance. Simply stated, cushion could now be made as hard as a rock or as soft as a feather without varying the density or physical profile of the product. Matrix, the resultant third-generation prime urethane carpet cushion, was promoted to the market in 1977.

The concept was twofold: to come out with a superior product, and to offer both nationwide distribution and multiple f.o.b. points.

GFI did both. The Matrix series revolutionized the market with properties previously unavailable, making other urethane products obsolete. It is manufactured at both east coast and west coast plants, and available from five distribution points.

245

Products: Synthetic Grass

GFI is the world's largest producer of quality synthetic grass, having assumed the lead less than two years after entering the market. Discerning a niche in the synthetic turf market, the company's management was able to progress quickly through its engineering capability and strong, flexible distribution mechanism.

Synthetic grass was introduced as a nylon product for professional athletic field use. The wide publicity resulting from that application evoked a consumer demand, for which the nylon product was unsuitable. GFI designed an alternative product for the consumer market, replacing nylon with ribbons of solution-dyed olefin yarn, which simulates grass effectively.

GFI pioneered the use of synthetic grass for playgrounds, swimming pool areas and patios. But the company did not permit the product to reach a plateau at those applications. Newer applications include bleachers, indoor floorcoverings, and ski lodge walls, for which synthetic grass is a sturdy protective cover, with zero absorbency. Because of the indoor uses, product sales in the north are not far behind those in the sun belt.

239, 240 Cover (blue shades) and black-and-white page of a packaging booklet for Sarabhai Research Centre, Bombay. (IND)
241 Two panels of a folder in which Dresser Industries thank the American petroleum industry. Full colour. (USA)
242 Double spread from a booklet about a special *Pemco* glass, here referring to testing. Full-colour illustrations. (USA)
243 From a capabilities brochure for Bell-Northern Research. (CAN)
244, 245 Double spreads with colour illustrations from a large booklet introducing General Felt Industries. (USA)
246 Complete cover of a booklet about the David J. Joseph Company, dealers in scrap iron and steel. Grey and yellow shades. (USA)

239, 240 Umschlag in Blautönen und Schwarzweiss-Seite aus einer Broschüre über Verpackungsentwicklung. (IND)
241 Aus einem Faltprospekt der Dresser Industries, die sich bei der amerikanischen Petroleum-Industrie bedanken. Farbig. (USA)
242 Doppelseite aus einer Broschüre für Spezialglas der SMC Corporation, hier über Testmethoden. In Farbe. (USA)
243 Farbige Doppelseite aus einer Broschüre der Telephongesellschaft Bell Northern Research, hier über Planung. (CAN)
244, 245 Farbige Doppelseiten aus einer Broschüre, mit der ein Hersteller von Teppichprodukten vorgestellt wird. (USA)
246 Umschlag eines Prospektes der Altmetallhändler David J. Joseph Company. In Grau- und Gelbtönen. (USA)

239, 240 Couverture (tons bleus) et page noir-blanc d'une brochure consacrée au développement des emballages. (IND)
241 Deux panneaux d'un dépliant par laquelle Dresser Industries remercient l'industrie pétrolière américaine. En polychromie. (USA)
242 Page double d'une brochure sur un verre spéciale, avec référence aux méthodes des tests. En polychromie. (USA)
243 Page double (en couleurs) de la brochure d'une société de télécommunications, ici se référant au planning. (CAN)
244, 245 Pages doubles avec illustrations en couleurs tirées d'une brochure d'un fabricant de tapis. (USA)
246 Couverture d'un prospectus publié par un marchant de ferraille. Prédominance de tons jaunes et gris. (USA)

241

246

PHOTOGRAPHER / PHOTOGRAPH / PHOTOGRAPHE:

241 Henry Wolf
242 James Lightner
243 Richard Crump
244, 245 Hank Gans/C. E. Furones
246 Roy Stevens

DESIGNER / GESTALTER / MAQUETTISTE:

239, 240 V. V. Dukle
241 Charles Hivley
242 Thomas Zgorski
243 Frank Haveman
244, 245 Philip Gips
246 George Tscherny

ART DIRECTOR / DIRECTEUR ARTISTIQUE:

239, 240 Sunil Sen
241 Charles Hivley
242 William Schneider
243 Richard Crump
244, 245 Philip Gips
246 George Tscherny

AGENCY / AGENTUR / AGENCE – STUDIO:

239, 240 Shilpi Adv. Ltd.
241 Metzdorf Advertising
242 Schneider Design Associates, Inc.
243 Design Interpretive
244, 245 Gips & Balkind, Inc.
246 Rubenstein, Wolfson & Co., Inc.

Booklets
Prospekte
Brochures

247, 248 Cover of a booklet about Gulf Oil Chemicals Company, showing a plant in Texas, and inside double spread (yellow sky). (USA)
249, 250 Cover and opening spread, both in full colour, of a brochure about computerized animation as offered by Cinetron Computer Systems, Inc. (USA)
251, 252 Double spread with narrow interleaved pages and full-page illustration in actual size from a booklet about the American Forest Products Corporation. The booklet is printed on heavy stock with all illustrations in full colour. (USA)

PHOTOGRAPHER / PHOTOGRAPH / PHOTOGRAPHE:

247, 248 Jay Maisel
249, 250 Arington Hendley
251, 252 Nick Pavloff/Ted Kurihara/Thom LaPerle

247, 248 Umschlag einer Broschüre über die Gulf Oil Chemicals Company, mit Aufnahme der Werkanlagen in Texas, und Doppelseite daraus (gelber Himmel). (USA)
249, 250 Umschlagseite und einleitende Doppelseite, beide farbig, aus einer Broschüre über computergesteuerte Bewegungsabläufe beim Film, von einem Computer-Hersteller. (USA)
251, 252 Doppelseite mit schmaleren Zwischenseiten und ganzseitige photographische Illustration in Originalgrösse aus einer Broschüre der American Forest Products Corporation. Alle Abbildungen sind farbig, auf festem Papier gedruckt. (USA)

247, 248 Couverture d'une brochure de la Gulf Oil Chemicals Company présentant une usine au Texas et page double y figurant (ciel jaune). (USA)
249, 250 Couverture et première page double (les deux en couleurs) tirées d'une brochure sur les systèmes électroniques pour la production de films d'animation. (USA)
251, 252 Page double avec des pages intercalées et illustration pleine page (en grandeur nature) figurant dans une brochure publiée par l'American Forest Products Corporation. Toutes les illustrations sont en couleurs et imprimées sur papier fort. (USA)

Gulf Oil Chemicals Company in Profile

247

249

248

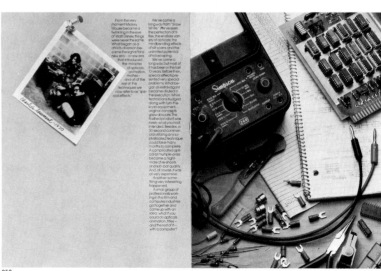

250

Booklets / Prospekte / Brochures

DESIGNER / GESTALTER / MAQUETTISTE:

249, 250 Ed Martel
251, 252 Thom LaPerle

ART DIRECTOR / DIRECTEUR ARTISTIQUE:

247, 248 Tom Jennison
249, 250 Ed Martel
251, 252 Thom LaPerle

AGENCY / AGENTUR / AGENCE – STUDIO:

247, 248 Brewer Advertising
251, 252 LaPerle/Assoc., Inc.

251

252

253

254

257

PHOTOGRAPHER / PHOTOGRAPH:

253 Dave Bartruff
254 Pierre Berdoy
255 M. Lacroix
256 Richard Schenkirz
257, 258 Tim Street-Porter
259 Rudi Schmutz
260 Andres Puech

DESIGNER / GESTALTER / MAQUETTISTE:

253 Sal Vergara
254–259 Massimo Vignelli
260 S. Puech

ART DIRECTOR / DIRECTEUR ARTISTIQUE:

253 Sal Vergara
254–259 Rudolf Beck/Wolf Kaiser
260 Andres Puech

AGENCY / AGENTUR / AGENCE – STUDIO:

253 Botsford Ketchum, Inc.
260 MP/Andres Puech

Booklets
Prospekte
Brochures

255

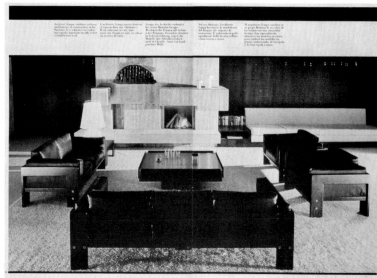

256

258

259

253 Photographic illustration from a brochure for *Japan Airlines*. (USA)
254–256 Cover and two double spreads from a booklet about furniture for the home made by Knoll International, here showing a furnished interior and the Bastiano suite designed by Scarpa. All illustrations are in full colour; the texts are in four languages so that the booklet can be used internationally. (GER)
257–259 Cover and two double spreads from a second *Knoll* booklet similar in presentation but dealing with furniture for business premises and public rooms. (GER)
260 "Where there is a lesion of the tissue, it is a matter of urgency to calm the pain." One side of a promotional card about the powerful analgesic *Vanadian*. Full colour. (SPA)

253 Photographische Illustration aus einer Broschüre für *Japan Airlines*. (USA)
254–256 Umschlag und zwei Doppelseiten aus einer Broschüre über Möbel zum Wohnen von Knoll International. Hier ein möblierter Wohnraum und die von dem Architekten Scarpa entworfene Bastiano-Gruppe. Alle Abbildungen in Farbe, die Texte in vier Sprachen. (GER)
257–259 Umschlag und zwei Doppelseiten einer weiteren Broschüre von *Knoll*, ähnlich in der Aufmachung, hier jedoch Möbeln für Büros und öffentliche Räume gewidmet. Die in Abb. 258 gezeigten Möbel wurden nach Entwürfen von Mies van der Rohe hergestellt. (GER)
260 «Bei einer Verletzung des Gewebes muss der Schmerz dringend gestillt werden.» Seite eines Promotionsblattes für das schmerzstillende Mittel *Vanadian*. (SPA)

253 Illustration tirée d'une brochure de la compagnie aérienne *Japan Airlines*. (USA)
254–256 Couverture et deux pages doubles d'une brochure consacrée aux meubles créés par Knoll International. On y présente un intérieur meublé ainsi qu'une suite Bastiano réalisée par l'architecte Scarpa. Les illustrations sont en couleurs, les textes en quatre langues. (GER)
257–259 Couverture et deux pages doubles figurant dans une autre brochure *Knoll* de conception pareille. Celle-là est consacrée aux meubles pour le bureau et pour les salles publiques. Les meubles présentés sous fig. 258 ont été créés par Mies von der Rohe. (GER)
260 «Si le tissu est lésé, la douleur doit être apaisée d'urgence.» Recto d'une carte promotionnelle pour un analgésique. En polychromie. (SPA)

260

PHOTOGRAPHER / PHOTOGRAPH / PHOTOGRAPHE:

261 Richard Crump
262–265 Foto Fiat
266 Ed Gallucci
267, 268 Karl W. Henschel/Bengt Fosshag

DESIGNER / GESTALTER / MAQUETTISTE:

261 Richard Crump
262, 263 Felix Humm
264, 265 CGSS
266 Bob Paganucci
267, 268 Studio Feuerstein

262

Ritmo: qualità della vita in auto

Dopo l'epoca in cui l'automobile era considerata oggetto di lusso e simbolo di condizione sociale, altre esigenze sono emerse. Prima fra tutte, quella di dare all'automobile le caratteristiche necessarie a farne un razionale strumento di lavoro oltre che un comodo mezzo di svago. L'intatta validità della motorizzazione privata, ha reso però necessario di rivedere il modo di usare l'automobile. Ci si è resi conto che sia per il lavoro sia nel tempo libero, si spendono molte ore della giornata in automobile. E si è arrivati alla conclusione che viaggiando in automobile è necessario disporre dello stesso livello di confort di cui si gode in casa. La qualità della vita in automobile ha dunque assunto primaria importanza, divenendo uno degli elementi di base della progettazione della Ritmo.

Si è capito che non ci si doveva più limitare alla creazione di una vettura dall'abitacolo spazioso, dotata di una meccanica solida e affidabile, di sospensioni e di un telaio la cui flessibilità fosse quella più adatta all'organismo umano e con sedili ergonomici e comandi collocati in modo razionale. Era necessario andare oltre.

Per la Ritmo sono così intervenuti esperti di altri settori, che hanno messo la loro cultura a disposizione del progettista, per rendere l'intera vettura rispondente alla primaria esigenza della qualità della vita in automobile.

Si è fatto ricorso a tecniche nuove, a indagini mai volte prima, a ricerche tese a fornire il meglio in fatto di materiali, sfruttando tutto ciò che la scienza ha saputo fornire all'industria attraverso l'esteso impiego dell'elettronica.

Così è nata la Ritmo, la prima Fiat degli anni 80.

Ritmo: affidabilità

L'affidabilità di una automobile si valuta in base alla continuità di funzionamento che essa è in grado di garantire nel tempo. È importantissimo disporre di una vettura affidabile, che non abbia ad accusare un guasto che molto raramente. Fra gli elementi-base del progetto di massima della Ritmo, fu presa in considerazione anche l'affidabilità, e doveva garantire l'utente dagli imprevisti per almeno 100.000 chilometri. Fu anche per questo motivo che si scelse come punto di partenza la meccanica della 128, ritenuta giustamente fra le più durature ed affidabili grazie ai continui interventi di affinamento che il modello subì nel corso degli anni. Naturalmente si è proceduto a ulteriori migliorie di progetto per aumentare la durata dei principali organi di usura: frizione, cambio, freni, pneumatici. Anche l'impianto elettrico ha potuto di migliorie qualitative grazie all'adesione del sistema a centralina con cavi modulari.

Per verificare che le premesse fossero poi mantenute in produzione, alcuni prototipi sono stati sottoposti ad una lunga serie di verifiche; un milione e mezzo di chilometri percorsi a bordo esperti collaudatori incaricati esclusivamente di trovare imperfezioni. Sul grande anello per l'alta velocità di Nardò e sulla pista speciale della Mandria, le Ritmo hanno girato per settimane, in una prova di affaticamento che veniva fatta proprio per verificarne l'affidabilità.

Un test realizzato in tutte le condizioni di impiego: ad alta velocità, in curva, in frenata, sui pavé, sullo sterrato, su fondi asciutti e bagnati, in guadi di acqua salata. I risultati sono stati sorprendenti. Con l'uso di tecniche e di materiali di elevata qualità (come ad esempio lo Zincrometal per combattere l'assalto della ruggine nei punti più esposti) la Ritmo, a resa dei conti, offre un elevato grado di affidabilità, che i tecnici hanno valutato in 0,5 guasti critici per 100.000 chilometri.

In questo quadro, è da sottolineare anche il passaggio della cadenza chilometrica per l'assistenza periodica da 15.000 a 20.000 chilometri. Nell'arco di vita media di una vettura, dunque, per la Ritmo sono necessari meno interventi di controllo, con una consistente riduzione delle spese di manutenzione a parità di efficienza del mezzo.

263

261

Two kinds of pneumonitis confused with asthma
By Michael H. Grieco, M.D.

Dr. Grieco is Director, R. A. Cooke Institute of Allergy, The Roosevelt Hospital, and Assistant Professor of Clinical Medicine, Columbia University College of Physicians and Surgeons, New York City.

266

Il promiscuo 238 E si presta a ogni combinazione di trasporto: da 9 persone e 4 quintali a 1 conducente e 9,6 quintali. Togliendo i sedili, si può ottenere un vano di carico di dimensione analoga a quella del furgone. L'accresciuta comodità dei sedili favorisce il confort dei passeggeri. Il promiscuo adotta, per la sicurezza, le nuove serrature tridirezionali.

238 E promiscuo: 9 persone e 4 quintali di cose

264

L'autobus 238 E serve le esigenze di trasporto di comunità, aziende, gruppi sportivi, alberghi, complessi musicali, club, eccetera. Trasporta su comode poltrone 11 persone e 140 kg nel razionale vano-bagagli, accessibile dalla porta posteriore. È adatto al trasporto-navetta come ai lunghi trasferimenti. Ottimo il confort: anche questa versione ha pavimenti rivestiti in moquette e pareti e padiglione interamente imbottiti. È dotato di serie di un efficace impianto di riscaldamento e aerazione.

238 E autobus: 11 posti in poltrona e 140 kg di bagaglio

265

261 Figure from a mural for telephone stores issued by Bell Canada. Full colour. (CAN)
262, 263 Spreads from a booklet about a new *Fiat* model, the *Ritmo*, here referring to "quality of life" and "reliability". Illustrations in full colour. (ITA)
264, 265 Double spreads from a catalogue presenting *Fiat* commercial vehicles, here a general-purpose van and a minibus. Full-colour illustrations. (ITA)
266 Spread from a booklet containing articles for physicians on the subject of asthma, issued by Geigy Pharmaceuticals. Black and white with orange band. (USA)
267, 268 Photograph (green glass) and complete cover of a folder about *Ecrylon* bullet-proof glass. (GER)

261 Aus einer Wanddekoration für Telephon-Geschäfte, herausgegeben von der *Bell*-Telephongesellschaft. (CAN)
262, 263 Doppelseiten aus einem Prospekt für das neue *Fiat*-Modell *Ritmo,* hier mit Bezug auf «Lebensqualität» und «Zuverlässigkeit». In Farbe. (ITA)
264, 265 Doppelseiten aus einem Prospekt über Nutzfahrzeuge von *Fiat,* hier ein Allzweck-Transporter und ein Mini-Bus. Abbildungen in Farbe. (ITA)
266 Doppelseite aus einer Broschüre für Ärzte mit Artikeln über das Thema Asthma, herausgegeben von Geigy Pharmaceuticals. Schwarzweiss. (USA)
267, 268 Detail der Aufnahme und komplette Umschlagseite eines Prospektes über *Ecrylon,* ein kugelsicheres Glas. Illustration in Grüntönen. (GER)

261 Figure d'une décoration murale pour les magasins d'articles de télécommunication. En polychromie. (CAN)
262, 263 D'une brochure présentant la nouvelle *Fiat Ritmo* avec référence à «la qualité de vie» et à «la fiabilité». En polychromie. (ITA)
264, 265 Pages doubles d'un prospectus consacré aux nouveaux véhicules utilitaires de *Fiat,* présentant ici une camionnette «à tout faire» et un minibus. (ITA)
266 Page double d'une brochure *Geigy* destinée au corps médical. Elle est entièrement consacrée à l'asthme. (USA)
267, 268 Détail de la photo (verre vert) et couverture complète d'un dépliant publié par un fabricant de verres antiballes. (GER)

LE VERRE ECRYLON
La protection contre les tirs et les cambriolages

268

ART DIRECTOR / DIRECTEUR ARTISTIQUE:

261 Richard Crump
262, 263 Fiat – Pubblicità e Immagine
264, 265 CGSS
266 Bob Paganucci
267, 268 Karl W. Henschel/Bengt Fosshag

AGENCY / AGENTUR / AGENCE – STUDIO:

261 Design Interpretive
262, 263 Fiat – Pubblicità e Immagine
264, 265 CGSS
266 Ciba-Geigy
267, 268 Studio Sign

267

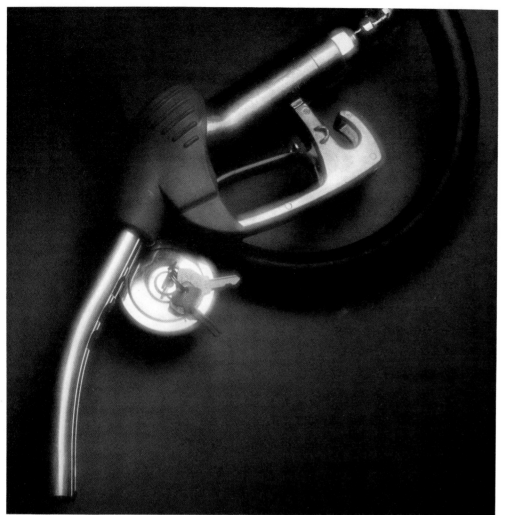

269

271

273

272

269–272 Two full-page illustrations (Fig. 269 chiefly in shades of green) and the corresponding double spreads from a booklet about *Frisol* oils. Figs. 269/270 refer to petrol stations, Figs. 271/272 to inland trade and the blending of lubricating oils. (NLD)
273, 274 Double spread and illustration in actual size from a booklet about Grow Chemical Corporation, makers of chemical coatings. Fig. 274 shows part of the Golden Gate Bridge, San Francisco on which a *Grow* product was tested. (USA)

269–272 Zwei ganzseitige Illustrationen (Abb. 269 vorwiegend in Grüntönen) und die entsprechenden Doppelseiten aus einem Katalog über *Frisol*-Öl. Abb. 269/270 beziehen sich auf Tankstellen, Abb. 271/272 auf den Binnenhandel und Schmierölmischungen. (NLD)
273, 274 Doppelseite und photographische Illustration in Originalgrösse aus einer Broschüre über Grow Chemical Corporation, Hersteller von chemischen Belägen. Abb. 274 zeigt einen Teil der Golden Gate Bridge, San Francisco, an welcher ein *Grow*-Produkt getestet wurde. (USA)

269–272 Deux illustrations pleine pages (fig. 269 en tons verts prédominant) et pages doubles correspondantes figurant dans un catalogue sur les huiles *Frisol*. Les figs. 269 et 270 se réfèrent aux postes d'essence, les figs. 271 et 272 au commerce intérieur et aux huiles de graissage. (NLD)
273, 274 Page double et illustration en grandeur nature tirées de la brochure d'un fabricant de revêtements chimiques. Fig. 274 présente une partie du Golden Gate Bridge à San Francisco où un produit *Grow* a été mis à l essai. (USA)

Booklets / Prospekte / Brochures

PHOTOGRAPHER / PHOTOGRAPH:

269–272 Joop der Weduwen
273, 274 Bill Farrell

DESIGNER / GESTALTER:

269–272 Paul Ibou
273, 274 Bob Pellegrini/
David Kaestle

ART DIRECTOR:

269–272 Paul Ibou
273, 274 Bob Pellegrini/
David Kaestle

AGENCY / AGENTUR:

273, 274 Pellegrini and
Kaestle, Inc.

274

275

279

275, 276 Cover and detail of an inside page of a folder about a CIBA antihypertensive drug. (USA)
277 Spread from a booklet for *Comifan,* makers of films for packaging applications. (ITA)
278 Cover of a book on the products of Elettromeccanica Razzoli. (ITA)
279 Detail of the cover of a folder about *Proost* papers. (NLD)
280 Cover of a *Geigy* folder for reprints of articles sent to doctors. Full colour. (USA)
281 Cover of a brochure about *Owens-Illinois* clear plastic bottles. Rich colours. (USA)
282 Cover of a booklet about suitcases made by Ronchi Valigeria, Padua. (ITA)
283, 284 Spreads with colour illustrations from a booklet on Carton y Papel de Mexico S.A. (MEX)

275, 276 Umschlag und Aufnahme aus einem Prospekt für ein Medikament von CIBA. (USA)
277 Doppelseite aus einem Prospekt für *Comifan,* Hersteller von Verpackungsfolien. (ITA)
278 Umschlag eines Katalogs über die Produkte von Elettromeccanica Razzoli. (ITA)
279 Detail der Vorderseite einer Faltmappe für Papier-Mustersendungen von *Proost.* (NLD)
280 Umschlag einer *Geigy*-Mappe für den Versand medizinischer Artikel an Ärzte. (USA)
281 Umschlagseite der Broschüre eines Herstellers von durchsichtigen Plastik-Behältern. (USA)
282 Aus einem Prospekt des Reisekoffer-Herstellers Ronchi Valigeria. (ITA)
283, 284 Farbige Doppelseiten aus einem Prospekt der Carton y Papel de Mexico S.A. (MEX)

275, 276 Couverture et détail d'une page d'un dépliant pour un médicament de CIBA. (USA)
277 Page double d'une brochure pour les feuilles d'emballage de *Comifan.* (ITA)
278 Couverture d'un catalogue présentant les produits d'Elettromeccanica Razzoli. (ITA)
279 Détail de la couverture d'un portfolio contenant des échantillons de papier. (NLD)
280 Couverture d'un portfolio de *Geigy* destiné au corps médical. (USA)
281 Couverture de la brochure d'un fabricant de récipients en matière plastique transparent. (USA)
282 Couverture d'une brochure présentant les valises de Ronchi Valigeria. (ITA)
283, 284 Pages doubles d'un prospectus de Carton y Papel de Mexico S.A. (MEX)

276

278

277

280

Owens-Illinois   Clear Barrier Plastic Packaging

281

PHOTOGRAPHER:

275, 276 Al Francekevich
277 R. Bazzani
279 Herman v. Haasteren
280 Ed Gallucci
281 Jim Rohman
282 G. Martin/G. Cecere
283, 284 Ruben Padova

DESIGNER / GESTALTER:

275, 276 Tom Hanifan
277 E. Lucini
278 L. Giovanetti/
T. Pantaleoni
279 Hans Versteeg
280 Larry Stires
281 Lesniewicz/Navarre
282 R. Rizzato
283, 284 Arie J. Geurts

ART DIRECTOR:

275, 276 Peter Belliveau
277 E. Lucini
279 Proost en Brandt Adv.
Department
280 Larry Stires
281 Lesniewicz/Navarre
282 G. DeBellis
283, 284 Arie J. Geurts

AGENCY / AGENTUR:

275, 276 William Douglas
McAdams, Inc.
277 Studio Elle
278 Graphic Design Studio
279 Proost en Brandt Adv.
Department
280 Ciba-Geigy
281 Lesnievicz/Navarre
282 Studio DeBellis
283, 284 Laboratorio de
Diseño y Analisis de
Mercado – Cartón y
Papel de Mexico S.A.

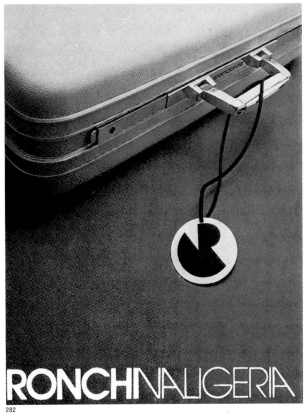

282

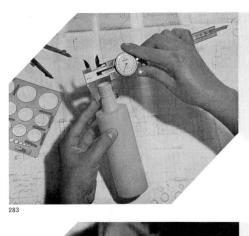

283

284

Booklets
Prospekte
Brochures

PHOTOGRAPHER:

285, 286 Richard Foster
287 Burk Uzzle
288 Hans Brorson
289, 290 Al Francekevich
291 Don Zimmerman
292 Robert Buyers

DESIGNER / GESTALTER:

285, 286 Dave Meade
287 Barry Ostrie
288 Holger Engholm
289 Vladimir Pechanec
290 Neil Ferrara
291 James C. Markle
292 Raymond Lee

ART DIRECTOR:

285, 286 Dave Meade
287 Barry Ostrie
288 Holger Engholm
289, 290 Peter Belliveau
291 James C. Markle
292 Raymond Lee

AGENCY / AGENTUR:

285, 286 Sieber & McIntyre,
Inc.
287 John Heiney
& Associates, Inc.
288 Holger Engholm
289, 290 William Douglas
McAdams, Inc.
291 Aves Advertising, Inc.
292 Raymond Lee
& Associates Ltd.

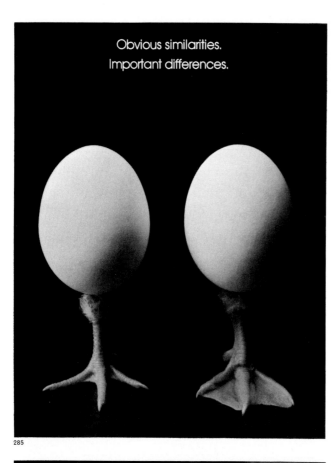

285

286

289

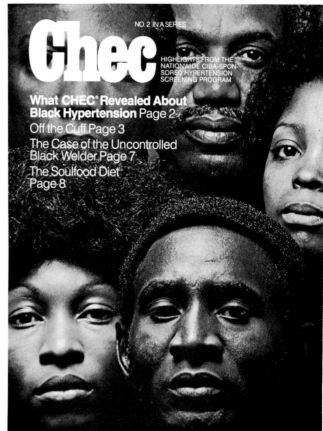

290

285, 286 Cover and inside page, both in full colour, from a folder comparing a *Bristol* broad-spectrum antibiotic with ampicillin. (USA)
287 Cover of a booklet about JLG Industries, makers of industrial lifts. The one shown on the cover is yellow against a deep blue sky. (USA)
288 Inside spread of a folder issued by the Holger Engholm design studio, which offers to crack the hard nuts of advertising. Nuts in colour. (SWE)
289 Cover of a folder about a CIBA drug for use in second-step antihypertensive therapy. Full colour. (USA)
290 Cover of a brochure reporting on the results of a CIBA-sponsored screening programme carried out by the Community Hypertension Evaluation Clinic (CHEC) among the black population of the United States. Full colour. (USA)
291 Cover of a folder about *Riviera* kitchens in oak. Brown shades. (USA)
292 Cover of a large brochure issued by National Film Finance Corporation about the investment of money in Canadian films. Full colour. (CAN)

285, 286 «Offensichtliche Ähnlichkeiten, bedeutende Unterschiede», eine Anspielung auf den Vergleich zwischen zwei Wirkstoffen. Vorderseite und Aufnahme aus einem Faltprospekt für das Medikament *Polymox* von *Bristol*. (USA)
287 Umschlagseite der Broschüre eines Kranherstellers. Gelb auf Blau. (USA)
288 Farbige Innenseiten des Eigenwerbungsprospekts einer Werbeagentur, die für ihre Kunden die Werbe-«Nüsse» knacken will. (SWE)
289 Vorderseite eines Faltprospekts von CIBA für ein Medikament, das für die Weiterbehandlung gegen zu hohen Blutdruck empfohlen wird. (USA)
290 Farbige Umschlagseite einer CIBA-Broschüre, die zu einer Serie gehört. Hier geht es um zu hohen Blutdruck innerhalb der schwarzen Bevölkerung. (USA)
291 Vorderseite eines Faltprospekts für Küchen-Kombinationsmöbel. Hier wird auf eine Variante in solider Eiche hingewiesen. (USA)
292 Umschlagseite der Broschüre einer Film-Finanzierungsgesellschaft. «Wie man in Filme investiert, ohne das Geld zum Fenster hinauszuwerfen.» (CAN)

JLG Industries

287

Nöten är en vanlig symbol för reklamproblem. Vem som helst kan få sina nötter knäckta, för det finns många världsmästare på det området! Men skalen är hårda och kostar pengar att knäcka.

Oavsett vilken nöt som knäcks, är det alltid kärnan man vill åt — den användbara goda biten. Skalet — överadministrationen — går inte att äta, men kostar ändå pengar. Varför skall man då betala för det?

Antingen det nu gäller en hel kampanj, en marknadskonsultation, några enstaka trycksaker, svensk eller engelsk reklamtext, displaymaterial, eller en fotografering, så erbjuder vi en skallös nöt! Stor eller liten. Ni betalar bara för det ni köper. Det är just det som är vår idé.

Vi ställer gärna upp och visar vad vi kan.

288

Cathedral Oak.
A kitchen that started
as a nut.

291

How to invest
in films and not
find your money gone
with the wind.

292

285, 286 Couverture et page intérieure (les deux en couleurs) tirées d'un dépliant qui compare un antibiotique à large spectre à l'ampicilline, deux médicaments évidemment semblables, mais d'une efficacité complètement différente. (USA)
287 Couverture de la brochure d'un fabricant de grues. Jaune sur fond bleu. (USA)
288 Panneau intérieur d'un dépliant autopromotionnel publié par un studio de design qui offre de «casser les noix dures» de la publicité. En polychromie. (SWE)
289 Recto d'un dépliant de CIBA en faveur d'un médicament pour le traitement consécutif de l'hypertension. En polychromie. (USA)
290 Couverture d'une brochure consacrée à un programme initié par CIBA. Elle présente les résultats d'examens que la Community Hypertension Evaluation Clinic a faits parmi la population noire des E.-U. qui souffre de l'hypertension. (USA)
291 Couverture d'un dépliant pour des meubles de cuisine en chêne. (USA)
292 Couverture d'une brochure grand format publiée par une société de financement de films: investissements dans l'industrie cinématographique canadienne. (CAN)

293

Kernig, saftig, fruchtig, frisch.

Da läuft einem das Wasser im Munde zusammen. Das sind Früchte, wie sie sein sollen. Wie in DEKA-Grundstoffen für Apfel-Limonaden mit natürlichen Fruchtauszügen und JAFFI-Grundstoffen für Orangen-Limonaden und hochsafthaltige Orangengetränke.

Ausgesuchte Früchte für erstklassige Grundstoffe. Apfel und Orange, zwei Beispiele – eine Sache: DEKA-Qualität.

Wenig ist oft mehr. Das ist auch die formale Auffassung des naiven jugoslawischen Malers Stefan Kečkeš. Seine suggestiven Bilder sind Ausdruck seiner täglichen Umgebung. Kečkeš sieht, was er malt. Kečkeš ist Bauer, daher sein besonderes Verhältnis zu den Früchten und der Landschaft. Erdnah, doch von surrealistischer Eindringlichkeit. Kennzeichen der Hinterglasbilder des Stefan Kečkeš.

Düning & Krausse GmbH
Hansestraße 33
3300 Braunschweig
Telefon: 0531-31581
Telex: 952486 deka d

295

Saftige Argumente
für fruchttrübe Zitrone

296

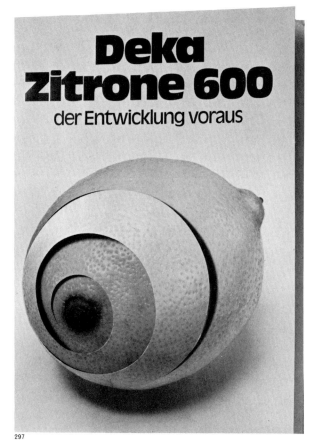

Deka
Zitrone 600
der Entwicklung voraus

297

294

299

293, 294 Detail of the colour shot and complete cover of a folder about H&R onion aromas and essences. (GER)
295 "Sound, juicy, fruity, fresh." Inside of a folder about *Deka* fruit essences. The real fruits merge with those in the picture. (GER)
296, 297 Folder about a *Deka* lemon essence. The yellow die-cut "peel" becomes three-dimensional when the folder is opened. (GER)
298 Catalogue cover for an exhibition of communication graphics organized by the American Institute of Graphic Arts. (USA)
299 Full-page illustration from a *Vogue* food diary. (GBR)
300 Call for photographic entries for an annual contest organized by the Seattle Art Directors Society. (USA)

293, 294 Farbige Aufnahme und komplette Vorderseite eines Prospektes für H&R-Rüstzwiebel-Produkte. (GER)
295–297 Farbige Innenseiten und Vorderseite eines Prospekts für *Deka*-Destillatessenzen. Hier echte und gemalte Früchte und eine Zitrone, deren eingeschnittene Schale beim Aufklappen zu einer geschälten Frucht auf der Innenseite des Prospektes führt. (GER)
298 Umschlag des Katalogs einer Ausstellung von Kommunikationsgraphik, organisiert vom American Institute of Graphic Arts. (USA)
299 Ganzseitige Illustration aus einer *Vogue*-Kochbuchagenda. (GBR)
300 Photographische Illustration einer Einladung zur Teilnahme an einem Photo-Wettbewerb der Art Directors Society, Seattle. (USA)

293, 294 Détail de la photo et couverture complète d'un dépliant présentant les arômes d'oignons de H&R. (GER)
295 «Sains, juteux, savoureux, frais.» Panneau d'un dépliant pour des essences de fruits. Les vrais fruits se mêlent à ceux du tableau. (GER)
296, 297 Dépliant pour des essences de citron. En ouvrant le dépliant, l'écorce jaune s'enlève en spirale. (GER)
298 Couverture du catalogue pour une exposition de travaux graphiques organisée par l'American Institute of Graphic Arts. (USA)
299 Illustration d'un agenda de cuisine publié par *Vogue*. (GBR)
300 Invitation de participer au concours annuel de photographie organisé par l'Art Directors Society de Seattle. (USA)

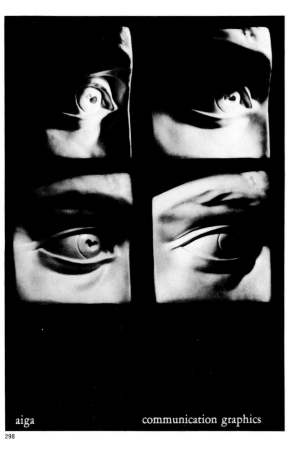

298

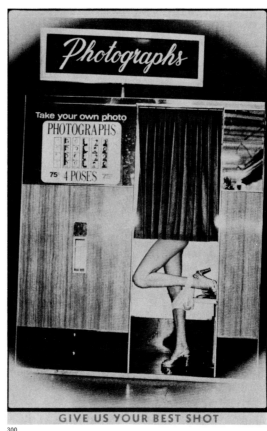

300

PHOTOGRAPHER / PHOTOGRAPH:

293, 294 Manfred G. Dietze
295–297 Peter Paxmann
298 James Cross
299 Tessa Traeger
300 Chuck Kuhn

DESIGNER / GESTALTER / MAQUETTISTE:

293, 294 Gert Jarke
295–297 Wenzel Schmidt
298 James Cross
299 Terry Stratton/Frances Ross Duncan

ART DIRECTOR / DIRECTEUR ARTISTIQUE:

293–295 Lothar F. Kümper
296, 297 Lothar F. Kümper/M. Blume
298 James Cross
299 Terry Stratton
300 Kelly Smith

AGENCY / AGENTUR / AGENCE – STUDIO:

298 Push Pin Studios

301

302

303

301, 302 Photographic illustration in actual size and complete cover of a folder about a *McGregor* summer collection of leisure apparel. (SWI)
303 Cover of a folder about *Mary Quant* cosmetics. (JPN)
304–307 Covers of fashion catalogues for the *Joseph Magnin* stores, with a spread from one of them. Fig. 304 shows a Christmas catalogue, Fig. 305 is for summer fashions, Fig. 306 for the fall. Fig. 307 shows the opening double spread of the fall catalogue. All covers and illustrations are in full colour. (USA)

301, 302 Aufnahme und komplette Vorderseite eines Faltprospekts für die «Sun'n Sand»-Kollektion von *McGregor*. (SWI)
303 Vorderseite eines Prospekts für *Mary-Quant*-Kosmetik, hier für Japan. (JPN)
304, 305 Farbige Umschlagseiten des Weihnachts- und des Sommerkatalogs des Kaufhauses *Joseph Magnin*, San Francisco. (USA)
306, 307 Umschlag- und Doppelseite in Farbe aus einem weiteren Modekatalog von *Joseph Magnin*, hier für die Herbstsaison. (USA)

301, 302 Illustration (en grandeur nature) et couverture complète d'un dépliant qui présente la nouvelle collection d'été de *McGregor*. (SWI)
303 Couverture d'un dépliant pour les produits cosmétiques de *Mary Quant*. (JPN)
304–307 Couvertures de divers catalogues de modes distribués par les grands magasins *Joseph Magnin* et page double tirée de l'un d'eux. Fig. 304: catalogue de Noël; fig. 305 présente la mode d'été et fig. 306 la mode d'automne; fig. 307: première page double du catalogue présentant la nouvelle collection d'automne. Toutes les couvertures et illustrations sont en couleurs. (USA)

304

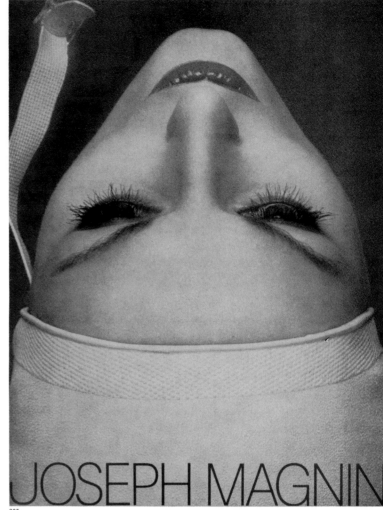

JOSEPH MAGNIN

305

JOSEPH MAGNIN

306

307

PHOTOGRAPHER / PHOTOGRAPH / PHOTOGRAPHE:

301, 302 Jost Wildbolz
303 Kou Chifusa
304—307 Robert Blakeman/Donald Miller

DESIGNER / GESTALTER / MAQUETTISTE:

301, 302 Paul A. Widrig
303 Hiroshi Serizawa
304—307 Donald Clark/David M. O'Grady

ART DIRECTOR / DIRECTEUR ARTISTIQUE:

301, 302 Werner Hofmann
303 Koosuke Tsukano
304—307 David M. O'Grady

AGENCY / AGENTUR / AGENCE – STUDIO:

301, 302 Paul A. Widrig
303 Cosmo Advertising
304—307 Joseph Magnin

**Booklets
Prospekte
Brochures**

308–312 Cover (red-brown wood), open folder with inserted sheets and three of these full-colour sheets. The cover is a rough textured board to heighten the impression of wood, the sheets are printed on coated stock. The whole folder promotes the vegetables and herbs of Armanino Farms in California, which are marketed in freeze-dried form. Information on each vegetable or herb is given on the verso of the colour sheets. (USA)
313, 314 Two double spreads in full colour showing bed-linen and tablecloths from the catalogue of the *habitat* stores. (GBR)
315 Shot to advertise the soft drink *7-Up* used as part of a self-promotion portfolio by the photographer. (USA)

308–312 Vorder- und Innenseite einer Faltmappe und drei Einzelblätter daraus. Die Mappe ist aus strukturiertem Karton, der den Holzcharakter des abgebildeten Kistenteils verstärkt. Armanino Farms sind Hersteller von gefriergetrockneten Gemüsen und Kräutern, von denen einige Beispiele auf den Einlageblättern farbig zu sehen sind. Auf der Rückseite dieser Blätter stehen detaillierte Angaben über das Angebot. (USA)
313, 314 Farbige Doppelseiten aus einem Katalog des Warenhauses *habitat*, hier mit einem Bett- und einem Tischwäsche-Angebot. (GBR)
315 Aus einer Eigenwerbungs-Broschüre des Photographen Robert Colton. Hier als Beispiel eine Werbeaufnahme für das Getränk *7-Up*. (USA)

PHOTOGRAPHER / PHOTOGRAPH:

308–312 Terry Heffernan/Jim Sadlon
315 Robert Colton

DESIGNER / GESTALTER / MAQUETTISTE:

308–312 Richard Garnas
313, 314 Fortescue/Lumsdale/Gavin/
Clive-Smith/Budwig
315 Robert Colton

ART DIRECTOR / DIRECTEUR ARTISTIQUE:

313, 314 Stafford Cliff
315 Robert Colton

AGENCY / AGENTUR / AGENCE – STUDIO:

308–312 Barile/Garnas and Light Language
313, 314 Conran Associates
315 Robert Colton

308

309

310

311

CHIVES

312

313

314

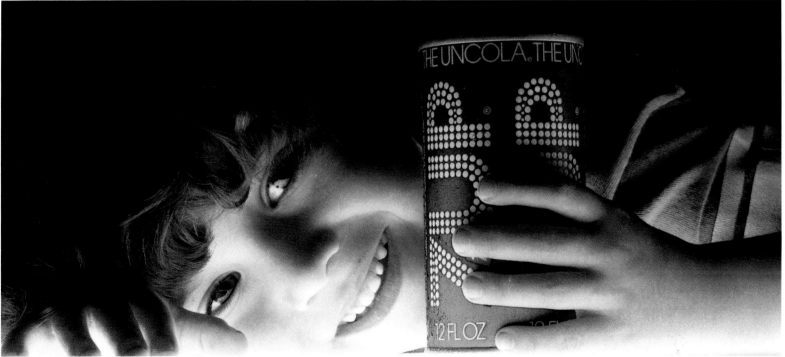

315

308–312 Couverture (bois rouge brun), dépliant ouvert avec feuilles insérées et trois feuilles volantes en couleurs. La couverture en carton structuré imite le bois; les feuilles sont imprimées sur papier couché. Elément de promotion en faveur des légumes et fines herbes des producteurs *Armanino* en Californie. Au verso de chaque feuille polychrome on trouve des informations concernant les légumes et fines herbes. (USA)
313, 314 Deux doubles pages couleur d'un catalogue des magasins *habitat,* présentant ici des draps de lits et des nappes. (GBR)
315 Elément de publicité en faveur de *7-Up*; il fait partie d'un portfolio autopromotionnel du photographe Robert Colton. (USA)

Booklets
Prospekte
Brochures

319

316, 317 Two double spreads from a catalogue of *Hermès* fashions for 1977/78. Both present handbags, one in tan, the other in grey, with full-colour insets. (FRA)
318 Front of a folder presenting a *Marc B.* fashion collection. (GER)
319–322 Cover illustration in actual size (Fig. 319), complete cover (Fig. 320), double spread referring to ranges of glasses and cosmetics (Fig. 321) and illustration from it in actual size (Fig. 322) from a catalogue of lingerie and accessories from *Bloomingdale's.* (USA)

316, 317 Zwei Doppelseiten aus dem *Hermès*-Katalog 1977/78. Hier wird ein Teil der Lederkollektion gezeigt; Abb. 316 in Brauntönen, Abb. 317 in Grautönen. (FRA)
318 Vorderseite eines Faltkataloges für Collection *Marc B.* Beige/Brauntöne. (GER)
319, 320 Illustration und komplette Umschlagseite eines Katalogs des New Yorker Kaufhauses *Bloomingdale's,* unter dem Titel «Intimacies» (Vertraulichkeiten). (USA)
321, 322 Aus demselben Katalog Doppelseite und Photo für *Helena-Rubinstein*-Produkte. (USA)

316, 317 Deux doubles pages figurant dans le catalogue pour les modes *Hermès* pour 1977/78. Les deux présentent des sacs à main en brun (fig. 316) et en gris (fig. 317). (FRA)
318 Couverture d'un dépliant présentant la nouvelle collection de *Marc B.* (GER)
319–322 Illustration de couverture en grandeur nature, couverture complète, page double se référant aux nouvelles gammes de lunettes et de cosmétiques et illustration en grandeur nature d'un catalogue de lingerie et d'accessoires de *Bloomingdale's.* (USA)

316

le cuir

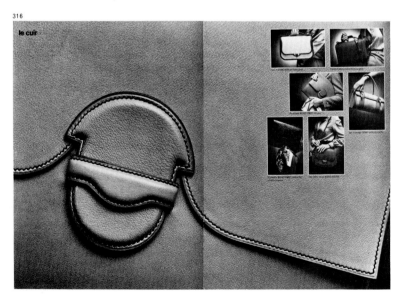

317

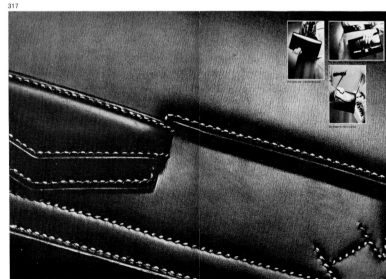

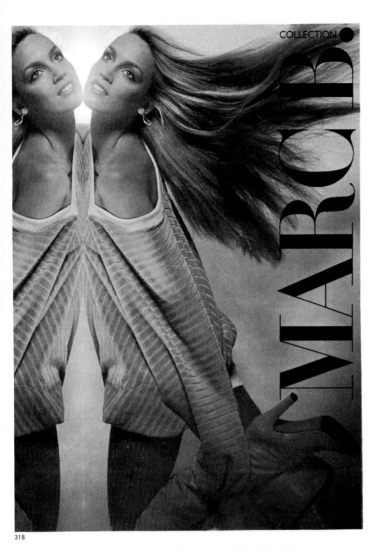

COLLECTION

MARCB.

PHOTOGRAPHER / PHOTOGRAPH / PHOTOGRAPHE:

316, 317 Patrice Tourenne
318 H. P. Mühlemann
319–322 David Hamilton

DESIGNER / GESTALTER / MAQUETTISTE:

318 Kreativ-Team Ulrich & Fehlmann
319–322 Richard Martino

ART DIRECTOR / DIRECTEUR ARTISTIQUE:

316, 317 Philippe Koechlin/Renate Malbec
319–322 Richard Martino

AGENCY / AGENTUR / AGENCE – STUDIO:

316, 317 Henri Addor & Associées
318 Kreativ-Team Ulrich & Fehlmann
319–322 Bloomingdale's

318

320

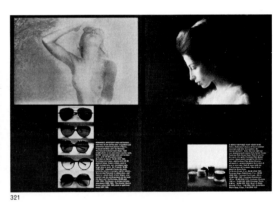

321

322

323

324

323, 324 Detail of the shot and complete inside spread of a folder issued to demonstrate the capabilities of Arthurs-Jones Lithographing Ltd. (USA)
325 Illustration from a brochure showing helicopter styling as part of a corporate indentity design programme for Hong Kong Air International. (HKG)
326, 327 Front and two panels of a concertina-type folder about *Microma* digital watches. Fig. 326 in blue shades, Fig. 327 on a sand background. (USA)
328 From a mailer used in a sales campaign of the *Isetan* department stores to popularize the Kyoto kimono. (JPN)

323, 324 Detail der Aufnahme und komplette Innenseite eines Faltprospektes für Arthurs-Jones Lithographing Ltd., als Beispiel für die von diesem Drucker geleistete Arbeit. (USA)
325 Aufnahme aus einer Broschüre der Hong Kong Air International. Der Helikopter ist in seiner Gestaltung Bestandteil eines einheitlichen Stils dieser Luftfahrtgesellschaft. (HKG)
326, 327 Vorderseite und Teil der Innenseite eines farbigen Faltprospekts for *Microma*-Uhren «die ersten automatischen Quarz-Uhren der Welt». (USA)
328 Teil eines Werbeprospekts, der im Rahmen einer Verkaufskampagne für Kyoto-Kimonos von dem japanischen Kaufhaus *Isetan* versandt wurde. (JPN)

323, 324 Détail de la photo et page entière d'un dépliant qui devrait mettre en évidence la capacité des photolithographes *Arthurs-Jones*. (USA)
325 Etude esthétique d'hélicoptère en tant qu'élément d'un programme global d'image de marque de la compagnie aérienne Hong Kong Air International. Page d'une brochure. (HKG)
326, 327 Couverture et deux panneaux d'un dépliant en accordéon pour les montres quartz *Microma.* Fig. 326 en tons bleus, fig. 327 sur fond de sable. (USA)
328 Volets d'un dépliant utilisé dans la publicité directe des grands magasins *Isetan* pour relancer les ventes de kimonos Kyoto. (JPN)

325

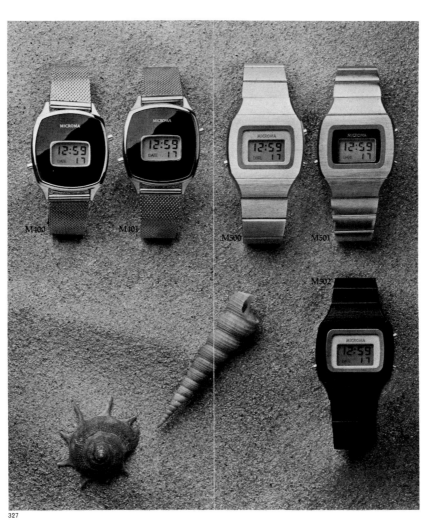

MICROMA®

The World's First
Continuous Time
Digital Watch

M400   M401   M500   M501

M502

326

327

PHOTOGRAPHER:

323, 324 Michel Tcherevkoff
326, 327 Ed Zak
328 Mamoru Sugiyama

DESIGNER / GESTALTER:

323, 324 Raymond Lee
325 Henry Steiner
326, 327 Barry Deutsch
328 Kenzo Nakagawa/
     Hiroyasu Nobuyama

ART DIRECTOR:

323, 324 Raymond Lee
325 Henry Steiner
326, 327 Barry Deutsch
328 Kenzo Nakagawa

AGENCY / AGENTUR:

323, 324 Raymond Lee
     & Associates
325 Graphic Communication
326, 327 Steinhilber & Deutsch
328 Nippon Design Center

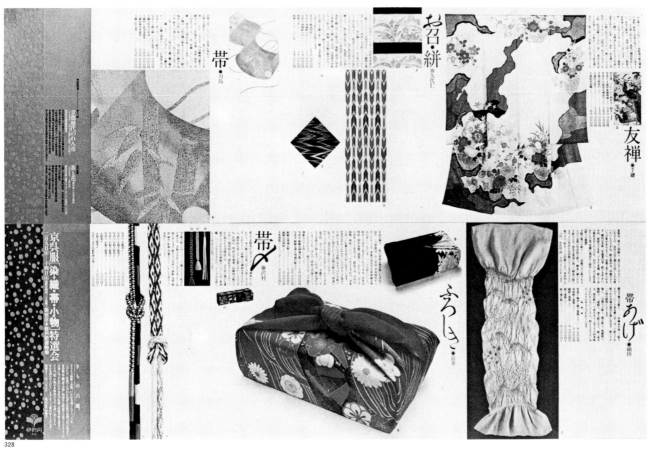

328

Booklets
Prospekte
Brochures

329

330

331

329 Black-and-white photograph used on a folder issued by a *Nikon* photo gallery and information centre in Zurich. (SWI)
330, 331 Double spreads, both in full colour, from spring and fall catalogues presenting *Polo* fashions for men. (USA)
332 Cover of a booklet presenting the National Ballet of Canada. Full colour. (CAN)
333, 334 Detail of the photography and complete double spread from a brochure in which compositions by several photographers are reproduced to demonstrate the printing quality that can be obtained on *Warren* papers. (USA)

329 Schwarzweiss-Aufnahme aus einem Prospekt der *Nikon* Foto-Galerie, Zürich, als Einladung zur Ausstellung «Fotografie und Werbung». (SWI)
330, 331 Zwei farbige Doppelseiten aus Katalogen für *Polo*-Kleidung von Ralph Lauren. «Wir glauben an Stil, nicht an Mode.» (USA)
332 Farbige Umschlagseite des vom National Ballet of Canada herausgegebenen Jahrbuches. Es stellt die Mitglieder des Balletts vor und bietet einen Rückblick auf das Vorjahr. (CAN)
333, 334 Detail der Aufnahme und komplette Doppelseite aus einer Broschüre der Papierfabrik E. T. Warren, in welchem verschiedene Photographen vorgestellt werden. (USA)

329 Photo en noir et blanc utilisée dans un dépliant de la galerie *Nikon*, Zurich, pour annoncer une exposition intitulée «La photographie et la publicité». (SWI)
330, 331 Pages doubles (les deux en couleurs) tirées de catalogues présentant les collections de printemps et d'automne lancées par *Polo*. (USA)
332 Couverture polychrome d'une brochure du Ballet National du Canada qui présente les membres de la troupe et donne une rétrospective sur les activités de l'année écoulée. (CAN)
333, 334 Détail de la photo et page double complète d'une brochure qui met en évidence la qualité des papiers *Warren* à l'aide de compositions de divers photographes. (USA)

PHOTOGRAPHER / PHOTOGRAPH / PHOTOGRAPHE:

329 Michael Müller
330, 331 Les Goldberg
332 David Street
333, 334 Rudy Muller

DESIGNER / GESTALTER / MAQUETTISTE:

330, 331 Les Goldberg
332 Raymond Lee
333, 334 Ralph Moxcey

Booklets / Prospekte / Brochures

120

The National Ballet of Canada Le Ballet National du Canada

332

333

ART DIRECTOR / DIRECTEUR ARTISTIQUE:

329 Peter Andermatt
330, 331 Les Goldberg
332 Raymond Lee

AGENCY / AGENTUR / AGENCE – STUDIO:

330, 331 Les Goldberg Studio
332 Raymond Lee & Associates
333, 334 Humphrey Browning McDougal

334

335

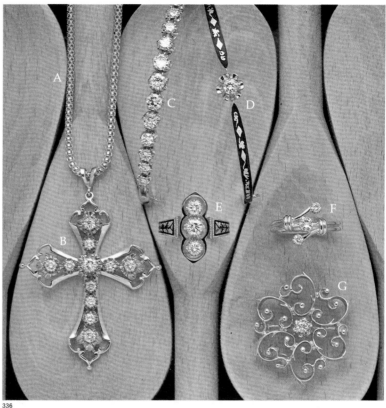

336

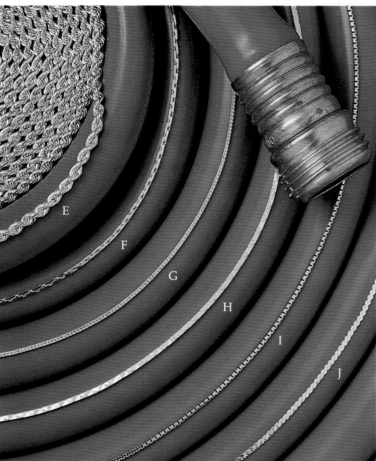

337

338

PHOTOGRAPHER / PHOTOGRAPH / PHOTOGRAPHE:

335–338 Eric Lindstrom
339 H. P. Mühlemann
340 Jyosui Tanaka/Hiro Kohayashi
341 Jerry Cosgrove

DESIGNER / GESTALTER / MAQUETTISTE:

335–338 Kitty Podgorski
339 Kreativ-Team Ulrich & Fehlmann
340 Jyosui Tanaka
341 Jerry Cosgrove

341

335–338 Four pages reproduced in roughly actual size from a small booklet prepared by The Fine Jewelers Guild of Dallas. (USA)
339 Cover of a brochure presenting the spring and summer collection of *Scherle* knitwear. Full colour. (GER)
340 Page (chiefly in white and blue shades) from a large booklet on Greek music, one of an "illustrated history of music" series issued by Toyo Electronics. (JPN)
341 Detail of the black-and-white cover of a folder on educational uses of *Sullivan* audio equipment. (USA)

335–338 Aufnahmen in Originalgrösse aus einer kleinformatigen Broschüre einer Juweliervereinigung. (USA)
339 Farbige Umschlagseite eines Prospektes für die Kollektion Frühjahr/Sommer '78 von *Scherle*-Tricots. (GER)
340 Ganzseitige Aufnahme (weisses Kleid, blauer Himmel) aus einer Broschüre der Toyo Electronics, die zu der Reihe «Illustrierte Geschichte der Musik» gehört. Hier ist das Thema Griechenland. (JPN)
341 Detail der Vorderseite eines Faltprospektes für ein Audio-Lernprogramm mit *Sullivan*-Geräten. (USA)

335–338 Pages (approx. en grandeur nature) d'une petite brochure publiée par une association de joailliers. (USA)
339 Couverture d'une brochure présentant la collection de printemps et d'été des tricots *Scherle*. Les illustrations sont en couleurs. (GER)
340 Page (prédominance de tons blancs et bleus) d'une brochure grand format consacrée à la musique grecque. Elle fait partie d'une série intitulée «histoire illustrée de la musique» de Toyo Electronics. (JPN)
341 Détail de la couverture d'un dépliant pour les équipements d'enregistrement pour l'enseignement. (USA)

340

ART DIRECTOR / DIRECTEUR ARTISTIQUE:

335–338 Kitty Podgorski
340 Jyosui Tanaka
341 Jerry Cosgrove

AGENCY / AGENTUR / AGENCE – STUDIO:

335–338 Glenn, Bozell & Jacobs
339 Kreativ-Team Ulrich & Fehlmann
340 Japan Ad Plan/Dentsu
341 Cosgrove Associates

342, 343 Cover and inside spread of a space promotion mailer in the shape of a folded newspaper sent out by the *Washington Post*. Black and white. (USA)
344 From a series of nostalgic covers for Beatles music for various instruments, published by Music Sales Ltd. (GBR)
345 Cover of a brochure about the sporting facilities offered by the town of Sindelfingen. Action shot reproduced in full colour. (GER)
346, 347 Page (full colour) and double spread from a brochure about forestry issued by the paper-makers *Westvaco*. (USA)
348–352 Four shots and a double spread from a large brochure by *Jovan*. The pictures lead up to the "man and woman" colognes, scents and perfumes marketed by this company. (USA)

342

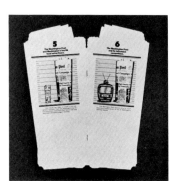

343

345

344

346

342, 343 Detail einer Aufnahme und ganze Doppelseite aus einem Werbeprospekt der Tageszeitung *Washington Post*, in einem Format, das einer zusammengefalteten Zeitung gleicht. (USA)
344 Aus einer Reihe nostalgischer Umschläge für Beatles-Musikpartituren für verschiedene Instrumente, hier Flötenmusik. (GBR)
345 Farbiger Umschlag einer Informationsbroschüre über die Sporthalle in Sindelfingen. (GER)
346, 347 Ganzseitige Aufnahme und komplette Doppelseite aus einer Broschüre des Papierherstellers *Westvaco*. Hier der Quelle ihres Rohstoffes, dem Wald, gewidmet. (USA)
348–352 «Denn was wäre die Welt ohne Mann und Frau?» Ganzseitige Aufnahmen und komplette Doppelseite aus einer Broschüre von *Jovan*. Das Produktionsprogramm und verwendete Flaschengestalttung dieses Parfumherstellers ist ganz auf das Thema Mann/Frau ausgerichtet. (USA)

342, 343 Couverture et page double d'un élément de publicité directe pour la promotion du journal *Washington Post*. Il a le format d'un journal plié. En noir et blanc. (USA)
344 Exemple d'une série de couvertures nostalgiques de partitions, pour divers instruments, de compositions des Beatles. (GBR)
345 Couverture d'une brochure consacrée au palais des sports de Sindelfingen. (GER)
346, 347 Page (en couleurs) et page double d'une brochure de *Westvaco*, fabricant de papiers. Celle-là est consacrée au bois, la matière première pour la fabrication du papier. (USA)
348–352 Quatre photographies pleine page et page double figurant dans une brochure publiée par *Jovan*. Le programme de production ainsi que la forme des flacons des parfums et eaux de Cologne s'orientent vers le sujet homme/femme. (USA)

348

349

350

351

347

352

353-358

PHOTOGRAPHER / PHOTOGRAPH / PHOTOGRAPHE:

353–358 Jay Maisel
359, 360 Jost Wildbolz
361 Larry Keenan

DESIGNER / GESTALTER / MAQUETTISTE:

359, 360 Domenig K. Geissbühler
361 Michael Manwaring

ART DIRECTOR / DIRECTEUR ARTISTIQUE:

359, 360 Domenig K. Geissbühler
361 Michael Manwaring

AGENCY / AGENTUR / AGENCE – STUDIO:

359, 360 Domenig K. Geissbühler
361 The Office of Michael Manwaring

359

126

353–358 Six shots on a self-promotion card for the photographer Jay Maisel, here shown in roughly actual size. (USA)
359, 360 Double spread and one page reproduced in actual size from a booklet about the Oversea Trading Co. Ltd., Zurich. (SWI)
361 Black-and-white shot of whales used on a self-promotion folder for the photographer. Silver lettering. (USA)

353–358 Aufnahmen eines Eigenwerbungsblattes des Photographen Jay Maisel, ungefähr in Originalgrösse. (USA)
359, 360 Aufnahme in Originalgrösse und komplette Doppelseite aus einem Katalog der Übersee-Handel AG, hier mit Bezug auf die von ihr exportierten europäischen Stoffe und Schuhe. (SWI)
361 Innenseite eines Eigenwerbungs-Faltprospektes in Schwarz-weiss für den Photographen. Schrift in Silber. (USA)

353–358 Six photos d'une carte autopromotionnelle du photographe Jay Maisel, reproduites ici approx. en grandeur nature. (USA)
359, 360 Photographie en grandeur nature et page double complète figurant dans le catalogue d'une entreprise de commerce d'outre-mer, se référant ici aux étoffes et chaussures exportées. (SWI)
361 Page intérieure d'un dépliant autopromotionnel (en noir et blanc) pour un photographe. Texte en argent. (USA)

361

360

362

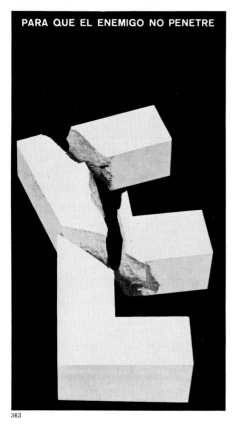

PARA QUE EL ENEMIGO NO PENETRE

363

BOKSTÄVER

364

Booklets / Prospekte / Brochures

DESIGNER / GESTALTER / MAQUETTISTE:

362 Thorgerson/Hardie/Christopherson
363 Felix Beltran
365 Bruce Blackburn
366, 367 Ford, Byrne & Associates
368 Eddie Byrd

PHOTOGRAPHER:

362 Thorgerson/Hardie/
    Christopherson
365 Ron Benvenisti
366, 367 Dan Moerder

365

366

367

ART DIRECTOR / DIRECTEUR ARTISTIQUE:

362 Storm Thorgerson
363 Felix Beltran
365 Danne & Blackburn
366, 367 Terry O'Brian
368 Eddie Byrd

AGENCY / AGENTUR / AGENCE – STUDIO:

362 Hipgnosis
363 Felix Beltran
364 Anders Beckmans Skola
365 Danne & Blackburn
366, 367 Ford, Byrne & Associates
368 Byrd Graphic Design, Inc.

368

3

369

370

PHOTOGRAPHER / PHOTOGRAPH:

369–371 John Olson
372–375 Otto C. Schürlein

DESIGNER / GESTALTER / MAQUETTISTE:

369–371 Jonson Pedersen Hinrichs
372–375 Otto C. Schürlein

ART DIRECTOR / DIRECTEUR ARTISTIQUE:

369–371 John Olson
372–375 Otto C. Schürlein

AGENCY / AGENTUR / AGENCE – STUDIO:

369–371 John Olson Productions, Inc.
372–375 R.O.S. Werbeagentur GmbH

371

369–371 Two of the large colour reproductions and complete sheet from a calendar for John Olson Productions, Inc. The twelve sheets humorously tell the story of an American family from 1909 to 1963. Here house renovation in 1912 and the call to arms in 1917. (USA)
372–375 Four motifs from a large calendar for the R.O.S. advertising agency, Stuttgart. All are in colour: Fig. 372, portrait in black caviar on a white plate; Fig. 373, grey, yellow-spotted fish, faded paper with recipes, orange pen, pink and green pot on grey tiles; Fig. 374, cigar with gold label; Fig. 375, red shoe and white mouse. (GER)

372

373

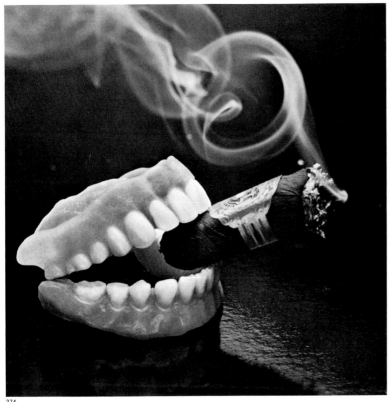

374

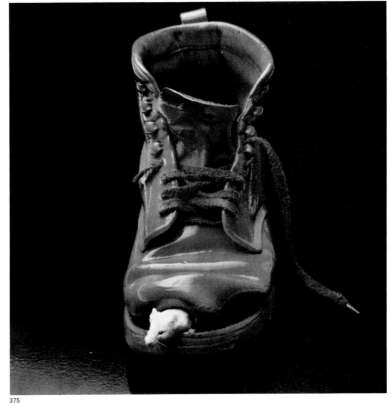

375

369–371 Farbige Aufnahmen und komplettes Blatt aus einem Kalender der John Olson Productions. Hier zwei Beispiele, Hausrenovierung 1912 und Einberufung 1917, aus der humoristisch dargestellten Geschichte einer amerikanischen Familie von 1909 bis 1963. (USA)
372–375 Vier Aufnahmen aus dem Kalender der R.O.S.-Werbeagentur. Abb. 372 schwarzer Kaviar auf weissem Teller, Abb. 373 roter Federhalter, Tintenfass mit violettem Inhalt und grünen Flecken, vergilbtes Papier und grau-brauner Fisch auf hellgrauen Kacheln, Abb. 374 naturgetreues Gebiss und Zigarre auf dunklem Hintergrund, Abb. 375 roter Schuh mit weisser Maus. (GER)

369–371 Deux illustrations polychromes et feuillet complet d'un calendrier des John Olson Productions. Elles présentent de façon humoristique quelques événements ayant bouleversés la vie d'une famille américaine, ici la rénovation de la maison en 1912 et l'appel en 1917. (USA)
372–375 Quatre photos du calendrier d'une agence de publicité. Fig. 372: caviar noir sur assiette blanche; fig. 373: porte-plume rouge, encrier violet avec des taches vertes, papier jauni et poisson gris brun sur des carreaux en bleu pâle; fig. 374: dentier avec cigare sur fond gris foncé; fig. 375: chaussure rouge avec souris blanche. (GER)

133

376

377

378

PHOTOGRAPHER / PHOTOGRAPH:

376, 377 Estudio Reprocolor Llovet, S.A.
378–381 Ulrich Pracht
382 Des Harding

DESIGNER / GESTALTER / MAQUETTISTE:

376, 377 Jose Luis Gimeno Londres
378–381 Kurt Kaizler
382 Des Harding

ART DIRECTOR / DIRECTEUR ARTISTIQUE:

376, 377 Premia De Mar
378–381 Ulrich Pracht
382 Bill Elders

AGENCY / AGENTUR / AGENCE – STUDIO:

376, 377 Reprocolor Llovet, S.A.
378–381 Studio Ulrich Pracht

376, 377 Two of the full-colour reproductions on the three-month sheets of a calendar for Reprocolor/Llovet SA, photolithographers, Barcelona. (SPA)
378–381 Complete sheet and three of the colour motifs from a six-month calendar for *Brian Scott* woollen fashions. Fig. 379: wools in grey shades; Fig. 380: blue, beige, white and black wools, carmine lips; Fig. 381: wools in blue shades, scarlet lips. (GER)
382 Shot from a calendar for SA Fine Worsteds in which the motifs all combine the patterns of men's suiting fabrics with female nudes. Here in shades of beige. (SAF)

376, 377 Zwei Beispiele der farbigen Reproduktionen auf Drei-Monats-Blättern eines Kalenders der Reprocolor/Llovet SA, Photolithographen, Barcelona. (SPA)
378–381 Komplettes Blatt und Aufnahmen aus einem Kalender des Garnherstellers *Brian Scott*. Mund in Abb. 380 in «shocking pink», in Abb. 381 in kräftigem Rot, jeweils als Gegensatz zu den Garnfarben. (GER)
382 Aufnahme aus dem Kalender eines Wollkammgarn-Herstellers. Auf allen Blättern sind Herrenanzugsstoffe mit Frauenakten kombiniert. Hier ein Anzugsstoff in Beigetönen, mit Webeffekt. (SAF)

376, 377 Deux photos couleur d'un calendrier mural de la Reprocolor/Llovet SA. Chaque feuillet est valable pour trois mois. (SPA)
378–381 Feuille complète et photos du calendrier d'un fabricant d'articles de tricot. Les bouches en «rose choc» (fig. 380) et en rouge foncé (fig. 381) devraient contraster avec les couleurs des tricots en laine. (GER)
382 Photo figurant dans un calendrier mural d'un fabricant de tissus en laine peignée. Etoffe en tons beiges. (SAF)

379

380

381

FRESCO STRIPE SUITING WITH WEAVE EFFECT   365 g PER METRE

Delta

382

135

383

384

385

386

387

383–387 Four of the shots for the months and one complete sheet from a *Stern* calendar for advertisers. Each colour photograph relates to a special feature and advertising area in the *Stern-Journal*: Fig. 383 to the cinema, Fig. 384 to investments and insurance. Fig. 385 to travel and Fig. 386 to the trades and crafts. (GER)
388 One of the twelve large studies contained in a calendar issued by *Asahi Pentax*. (JPN)

383–387 Aufnahmen und ein komplettes Blatt aus einem Kalender der Zeitschrift *Stern*. Die Abbildungen beziehen sich auf Themen, die im *Stern*-«Journal» behandelt werden. Hier «Kino» (Abb. 383) «Geld und Versicherung» (Abb. 384), «Reise» (Abb. 385) und «Handwerk» (Abb. 386). (GER)
388 Eine der zwölf grossen Aktstudien von Sam Haskins aus einem Kalender, der von dem Kamera-Hersteller *Asahi Pentax* herausgegeben wurde. (JPN)

383–387 Photos et feuille complète tirées du calendrier du *Stern-Journal*, où l'attention des annonceurs est attirée sur les sujets abordés dans les différents numéros, ici «cinéma» (383), «argent et assurances» (384), «voyages» (385) et «arts et métiers» (386). Sur les feuilles on indique la date limite pour la remise des annonces. Toutes les photos en polychromie. (GER)
388 L'une des douze études du calendrier d'*Asahi Pentax*. (JPN)

PHOTOGRAPHER / PHOTOGRAPH:

383–387 Holger Matthies
388 Sam Haskins

DESIGNER / GESTALTER / MAQUETTISTE:

383–387 Holger Matthies
388 Mitsuo Katsui

ART DIRECTOR / DIRECTEUR ARTISTIQUE:

383–387 Albers

AGENCY / AGENTUR / AGENCE – STUDIO:

383–387 Lintas

136

390

PHOTOGRAPHER / PHOTOGRAPH:

389, 390 Michael Friedel
391 Fritz Dressler

DESIGNER / GESTALTER / MAQUETTISTE:

389, 390 AEG-Telefunken, Zentralabt.
　　　　Firmenwerbung
391 Hartmut Brückner

ART DIRECTOR / DIRECTEUR ARTISTIQUE:

389, 390 Werner E. Müller

391

389, 390 Two of twelve landscape shots from all parts of the world contained in the AEG-*Telefunken* calendar for 1978. Here cliffs and tide in Hawaii and a white building set in grey and brown rock in the Cyclades, Greece, both photographed from the air. (GER)
391 From a large colour calendar showing buildings in Yemen, issued by a publishing company; here a house in the town of Sadah. (GER)

389, 390 Zwei von zwölf farbigen Landschaftsaufnahmen aus einem Wandkalender der AEG-*Telefunken*. Hier Luftaufnahmen von einer felsigen Küste Hawaiis (Abb. 389) und von Armorgos (Griechenland). (GER)
391 Farbige Aufnahme eines Hauses in der Stadt Sadah aus einem Architektur-Kalender des *Schmalfeldt*-Verlags unter dem Titel «Lehmbauten im nördlichen Jemen». Die aus sonnengetrockneten Lehmziegeln kunstvoll gemauerten obersten Stockwerke des Hauses sind ein Zeichen des Wohlstandes. (GER)

389, 390 Deux de douze paysages du monde entier contenu dans le calendrier de AEG-*Telefunken*. Ici on présente une vue aérienne de Hawaii et un bâtiment blanc à Armorgos en Grèce. (GER)
391 Photo couleur d'une maison à Sadah, d'un calendrier grand format d'une maison d'édition, consacré au bâtiments du Yemen. Le dernier étage, construit en briques en torchis séchées au soleil, indique qu'il s'agit de la maison d'une famille riche. (GER)

Calendars / Kalender / Calendriers

392

393

394

395

Calendars
Kalender
Calendriers

392, 393 Full-colour photographs from the calendar of Offset-Repro AG, lithographers. (SWI)
394, 395 Pages from a hard-cover book-cum-calendar issued by DSM and dealing with Roman remains found at Heerlen in the Netherlands—here samples of pottery (Fig. 394) and grindstones with a storage jar (Fig. 395). (NLD)
396, 397 Photographs on the extra-wide sheets of a *Swissair* calendar: an iceberg in McMurdo Sound, Antarctica, and the huge floating leaves of Victoria amazonica. (SWI)
398, 399 Cover (yellow sun, brown foreground) and sheet (tawny buildings, blue figure) of a *Bauer* calendar on the theme of man in the landscape. (GER)

392, 393 Farbige Aufnahmen aus einem Kalender der Offset-Repro AG, Zürich. (SWI)
394, 395 Farbige Beispiele aus einem Wandkalender mit Abbildungen und Informationen über Ausgrabungen in Heerlen (Holland) aus der römischen Zeit. Hier Krüge und Bruchstücke von Gefässen mit Inschriften (Abb. 394) und Mühlsteine mit Vorratsgefäss (Abb. 395). (NLD)
396, 397 Abbildungen aus einem *Swissair*-Kalender. Hier Eisberg im McMurdo Sound, Antarktis, und die riesigen schwimmenden Blätter der Victoria amazonica. (SWI)
398, 399 Deckblatt (gelbe Sonne, brauner Vordergrund) und Blatt (lehmbraune Gebäude, blaue Gestalt) aus einem *Bauer*-Kalender, dessen Thema Mensch und Umwelt ist. (GER)

392, 393 Photos couleur tirées du calendrier d'un photolithographe. (SWI)
394, 395 Exemples d'un calendrier avec des photographies et des informations sur les fouilles de Heerlen aux Pays-Bas. Les objects trouvés remontent à l'époque romaine: poteries et inscriptions sur céramique (fig. 394) et meules et pot à provision (fig. 395). (NLD)
396, 397 Deux feuilles d'un calendrier *Swissair*: Iceberg dans le détroit de McMurdo, Antarctique, et la Victoria amazonica dont les feuilles atteignent 2 m de diamètre. (SWI)
398, 399 Feuille de couverture et photo d'un calendrier consacré au sujet «L'homme et l'environnement». Les deux exemples sont en couleurs. (GER)

140

396

397

PHOTOGRAPHER / PHOTOGRAPH:

392, 393 Bertram Wolf
394, 395 Karel Van Straaten
396, 397 Emil Schulthess
398, 399 Hans Roth

DESIGNER / GESTALTER / MAQUETTISTE:

392, 393 Bertram Wolf/Franz Hörburger
394, 395 Martin Verjans
398, 399 Ursula Weckherlin

ART DIRECTOR / DIRECTEUR ARTISTIQUE:

392, 393 Horst Hagele/Dieter Segfried
394, 395 Martin Verjans
396, 397 Emil Schulthess

AGENCY / AGENTUR / AGENCE – STUDIO:

392, 393 HWS Werbestudio
394, 395 DSM Information Centre
396, 397 Swissair Advertising Division

398

399

401

SO	MO	DI	MI	DO	FR	SA	SO	MO	DI	MI	DO	FR	SA
					1	2	3	4	5	6	7	8	9
10	11	12	13	14	15	16	17	18	19	20	21	22	23
24	25	26	27	28	29	30	31						

Dezember   unbeschwert schlafen Mogadan Roche

402

PHOTOGRAPHER / PHOTOGRAPH / PHOTOGRAPHE:
400–402 Hans Schweiss

DESIGNER / GESTALTER / MAQUETTISTE:
400–402 Hans Schweiss

ART DIRECTOR / DIRECTEUR ARTISTIQUE:
400–402 Hans Schweiss

AGENCY / AGENTUR / AGENCE – STUDIO:
400–402 Schweiss-Gruppe

Calendars
Kalender
Calendriers

400–402 Calendars have been issued for some years as a means of promotion for the *Roche* soporific *Mogadon/Dalmadorm*. All of the sheets show people sleeping peacefully in more or less unusual surroundings. Here in the apple season in South Tyrol, 1979 calendar (Fig. 400); a shot in Sinai (tilted), 1978 calendar (Fig. 401); and a complete sheet with a picture from Lapland, 1977 calendar (Fig. 402). (GER)

400–402 Aufnahmen und komplettes Blatt aus Kalendern für die *Roche*-Schlafmittel *Mogadon/ Dalmadorm*, die in der Wirkung der Natur so nahe wie möglich kommen sollen. Abb. 400: Aufnahme zur Zeit der Apfel-Ernte in Süd-Tirol, aus dem Kalender 1979. Abb. 401: Photo (diagonal reproduziert), im Sinai aufgenommen, Juni-Blatt des Kalenders 1978. Abb. 402: Dezember-Blatt 1977 mit einer am Polarkreis in Lappland gemachten Aufnahme. (GER)

400–402 Photos et feuillet complet de calendriers *Roche* pour les somnifères *Mogadon/Dalma-dorm:* visualisation de l'effet de ces produits, qui est aussi près que possible au rythme de la nature. Fig. 400: cueillette des pommes au Tyrol du Sud; du calendrier pour 1979. Fig. 401: photo (repro-duite en biais) prise dans le Sinai; du calendrier pour 1978. Fig 402: feuillet de décembre (calendrier pour 1977) avec photo prise en Laponie, au cercle polaire. (GER)

PHOTOGRAPHER / PHOTOGRAPH:

403 Masanobu Fukuda
404 Pete Mecca
405 Melchior DiGiacomo
406 Gianni Grazia
407 Harry C. Suchland

DESIGNER / GESTALTER / MAQUETTISTE:

403 Kathuhiko Ishida
404, 405 David November/Ed Sobel
406 Gianni Grazia
407 Harry C. Suchland

403

ART DIRECTOR / DIRECTEUR ARTISTIQUE:

403 Kathuhiko Ishida
404, 405 David November
406 Gianni Grazia/Giorgio Vernizzi

AGENCY / AGENTUR / AGENCE – STUDIO:

403 Office 14
404, 405 CBS Advertising and
Promotion Department
406 Reno Grafica
407 Harry C. Suchland

404

405

406

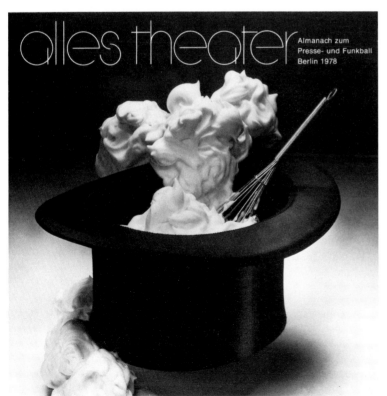

407

403 Photograph in actual size from a food calendar. (JPN)
404, 405 Black-and-white spreads from a large appointments calendar devoted to sports and issued by the CBS Television Network. Fig. 404 relates to American football (National Football League games), Fig. 405 to the tennis ace Chris Evert. (USA)
406 From a calendar on the subject of masks published by Industrie Chimiche OECE. Mask in flesh shades, blue eye on film strip. (ITA)
407 "All play-acting." Black-and-white cover of an almanac issued on the occasion of a press, radio and television ball in Berlin, 1978. (GER)

403 Aufnahme in Originalgrösse aus einem Kalender mit farbigen Abbildungen alltäglicher Nahrungsmittel mit besonderem ästhetischen Reiz. (JPN)
404, 405 Schwarzweiss-Aufnahmen aus einer vom amerikanischen Fernsehsender CBS herausgegebenen Agenda, hier dem Sport gewidmet. Abb. 404 bezieht sich auf die von CBS übertragenen «Football»-Spiele der Profiliga, Abb. 405 zeigt die Tennisspielerin Chris Evert. (USA)
406 Aufnahme aus einem Wandkalender zu dem Thema «Masken». Hier eine Maske in blassen, durchsichtigen Grautönen mit Filmabschnitt in Blautönen. (ITA)
407 Schwarzweisse Umschlagseite des Almanachs zum Presse- und Funkball, Berlin 1978. (GER)

403 Photo (en grandeur nature) tirée d'un calendrier qui est consacré à l'attrait ésthétique particulier des vivres. En polychromie. (JPN)
404, 405 Photos en noir et blanc tirées d'un agenda distribué par une station américaine de télévision. Il est entièrement consacré au sport. Fig. 404 se réfère aux jeux de football américain de la ligue des professionnels, émis par cette station; fig. 405 présente Chris Evert. (USA)
406 Photo d'un calendrier mural consacré aux masques. Masque en tons gris pâle, presque transparent, avec still en tons bleus. (ITA)
407 Couverture noir-blanc de l'almanach du bal de la presse et du radio de Berlin. (GER)

Calendars / Kalender / Calendriers

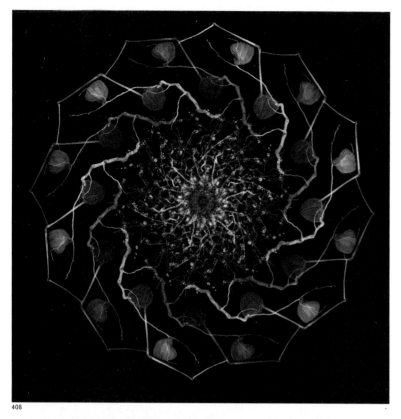

408

409

410

411

■ In organizing an annual contest for the best photographic calendars, staged as part of a large calendar exhibition in Stuttgart, *Kodak* is doing photography a real service; for the calendar, which this contest effectively promotes, offers the photographer the rare opportunity of presenting something like a small portfolio of his work, reproduced to the very highest standards, to a wide public that is going to contemplate it almost daily for the next twelve months. On the following pages (p. 151 excepted) we present a selection from the winning entries of the 1978 contest.

408–413 Photographic studies and one complete sheet from a calendar issued by *Kodak* in Vienna. The studies are taken from an extensive series of experiments in which the photographer attempts to bring out the intrinsic aesthetic qualities of plants and objects by using them to form new, symmetrical configurations. The materials used in these examples are flower bulbs, Japanese lantern seedpods, roots and peacock feathers. (AUT)

■ Mit der Organisation des jährlichen Farbphoto-Kalender-Wettbewerbs, der zusammen mit einer Kalenderschau des Graphischen Klubs Stuttgart und des Landesgewerbeamts Baden-Württemberg ausgetragen wird, erweist *Kodak* der Photographie einen grossen Dienst. Denn ein Kalender gibt dem Photographen die seltene Gelegenheit, eine Art Kleinportfolio mit erstklassigen Reproduktionen zu präsentieren, die von einem grossen Publikum während 12 Monaten fast täglich gesehen werden. Auf den folgenden Seiten (ausser S. 151) zeigen wir eine Auswahl des *Kodak*-Farbphoto-Kalender-Wettbewerbs 1978.

408–413 Photographische Studien und komplettes Blatt aus einem Kalender von *Kodak,* Wien. Die Studien sind Teil eines breit angelegten Experiments, bei dem der Photograph versucht, die verborgene Ästhetik von Gegenständen und Pflanzen sichtbar zu machen, indem er sie zu symmetrischen Konfigurationen umformt. Die in diesen Beispielen verwendeten Materialien sind Blumenzwiebeln, Lampionblumen und Pfauenfedern. (AUT)

412

En organisant chaque année un concours des meilleurs calendriers-photo débouchant sur une importante exposition de calendriers à Stuttgart, *Kodak* rend un service éminent à la photographie. En effet, le calendrier offre au photographe une rare occasion de présenter une espèce d'album miniature de spécimens de travail, reproduits à un niveau de technologie poussé, à un vaste public qui aura l'occasion de le feuilleter au sens propre du terme en s'en imprégnant tout au long des douze mois suivants. Nous présentons sur ces pages (sauf p. 151) une sélection du concours *Kodak* des calendriers couleurs, 1978.

408—413 Etudes photographiques et feuillet complet d'un calendrier publié par *Kodak*-Autriche à Vienne. Les études proviennent d'une série expérimentale importante aux cours de laquelle le photographe a essayé d'exprimer les qualités esthétiques intrinsèques de certaines plantes et objets en les assemblant en des configurations symétriques. Les matériaux employés ici sont des oignons, des lanternes vénitiennes et des plumes de paon. (AUT)

Calendars / Kalender / Calendriers

PHOTOGRAPHER / PHOTOGRAPH:
408—413 Karlheinz Koller

DESIGNER / GESTALTER / MAQUETTISTE:
408—413 Herbert Klaus

413

414, 415 Complete sheet and one of the photographs used in a *Mobil* calendar issued in Germany and entitled "Fly Me". Each sheet shows a vintage aircraft, such as the De Havilland Moth. (GER)
416 Cover picture of a calendar containing twelve BMW "impressions" printed on a silver ground. (GER)
417, 418 Photograph and complete corresponding sheet from a calendar devoted by the BMW car company to the fascination of the motorcycle. (GER)

414, 415 Komplettes Blatt und eine der Aufnahmen aus dem *Mobil*-Kalender «Fly me» (fliege mit mir). Jedes Kalenderblatt zeigt ein altes Flugzeugmodell, wie zum Beispiel die «De Havilland Moth». (GER)
416 Aufnahme und Vorderseite eines BMW-Kalenders 1978 mit zwölf «Impressionen», gedruckt auf silbrigem Grund. (GER)
417, 418 Aufnahme und komplettes Blatt aus dem BMW-Kalender «Faszination Motorrad». (GER)

414, 415 Feuille complète et l'une des photos illustrant un calendrier *Mobil* publié en Allemagne sous le titre de «Vole avec moi» et montrant divers avions de la première moitié du siècle, tels que le «De Havilland Moth». (GER)
416 Illustration de couverture du calendrier pour 1978 contenant douze «impressions» BMW imprimées sur fond argent. (GER)
417, 418 Feuillet et photo d'un calendrier BMW consacré à l'univers fascinant de la moto. (GER)

414

415

416

417

PHOTOGRAPHER / PHOTOGRAPH / PHOTOGRAPHE:

414, 415 Gert Wagner
416 Axel Krieger
417, 418 E.-H. Ruth

DESIGNER / GESTALTER / MAQUETTISTE:

414, 415 Eike Göpffahrt
416 Helmut Mätzler
417, 418 G. Gschwind

418

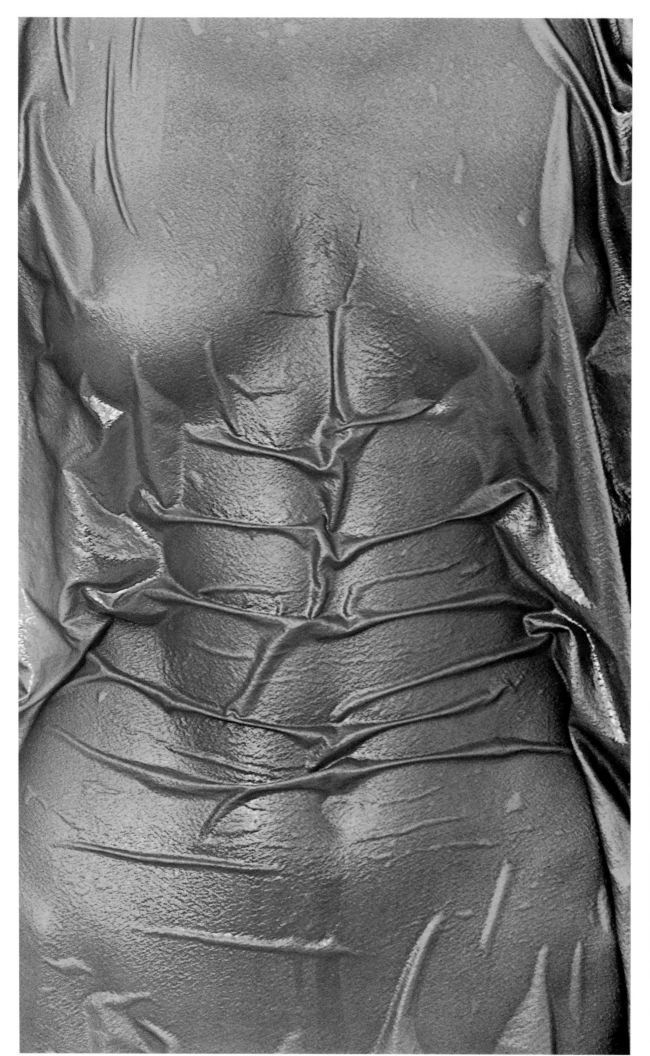

PHOTOGRAPHER / PHOTOGRAPH:

419–421 Hans Feurer
422 Phil Marco

DESIGNER / GESTALTER:

419–421 Mitsuo Katsui
422 Danne & Blackburn

ART DIRECTOR:

422 Phil Marco

AGENCY / AGENTUR / AGENCE:

422 Phil Marco, Inc.

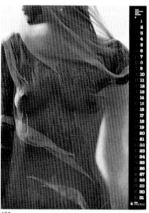

420

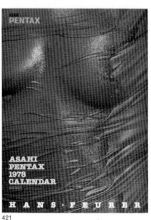

421

419

150

422

419–421 Two shots (Fig. 420 in lilac shades) and cover (blue shades) from a calendar for *Asahi Pentax* in which the photographer obtained sculpted effects with nudes and wet fabrics. (JPN)
422 Page from a desk calendar entitled "Images from the World of the Prosaic" and issued by the S. D. Scott Printing Company, Inc. (USA)

419–421 Blätter (Abb. 420 in Violett-Tönen) und Umschlag (Blautöne) aus einem *Asahi-Pentax*-Kalender. Das skulpturenartige Aussehen der Akte wird durch feuchte Tücher erzielt. (JPN)
422 Aufnahme in Originalgrösse aus einer Agenda der S. D. Scott Printing Company, Inc., «Bilder aus der Welt des Prosaischen». (USA)

419–421 Feuillets pour mars et pour janvier (tissu lilas) et couverture (tons bleus) d'un calendrier pour *Asahi Pentax* où le photographe revient inlassablement au sujet du nu voilé, en obtenant grâce à des tissus humidifiées des effets sculpturaux marqués. (JPN)
422 Photographie en grandeur nature figurant dans un agenda de la Scott Printing Co., intitulé «Images d'un monde prosaïque». (USA)

Calendars / Kalender / Calendriers

423

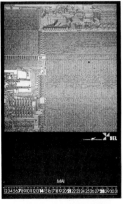

424

PHOTOGRAPHER / PHOTOGRAPH / PHOTOGRAPHE:
423–428 Manfred P. Kage

DESIGNER / GESTALTER / MAQUETTISTE:
423–428 Gebhardt & Lorenz

ART DIRECTOR / DIRECTEUR ARTISTIQUE:
423–428 Hans-Günter Grimm

AGENCY / AGENTUR / AGENCE – STUDIO:
423–428 Gebhardt & Lorenz

423–428 Complete sheet and five photographs taken from the research and development activities of Standard Elektrik Lorenz AG, a Stuttgart electronics company belonging to the ITT group. Figs. 423 and 424 show a detail of the crystal surface of a customer circuit magnified a hundred times; the colours are produced by elevations and depressions seen under an interference contrast microscope. Fig. 425 (blue and yellow) is a memory matrix of a semiconductor circuit under the electron microscope (magnified 6000 times). Fig. 426 shows an electrode structure (yellow) on a piezo-electric ceramic surface (brown); Fig. 427 (purple shades) a section through a ceramic condenser; and Fig. 428 (pink, green and white) a light-sensitive selenium surface, as used in photocopiers, under the electron microscope. (GER)

425

426

427

428

423–428 Kalenderblatt und fünf Aufnahmen aus dem Forschungs- und Entwicklungsbereich der Standard Elektrik Lorenz AG, einer Stuttgarter Elektronik-Firma der ITT-Gruppe. Abb. 423/424: Detail der Kristalloberfläche eines Kundenschaltkreises, 100× vergrössert; im Interferenzkontrast-Mikroskop werden die Höhen und Tiefen in Farben umgesetzt. Abb. 425 (blau und gelb) ist eine Speichermatrix eines Halbleiter-Schaltkreises im Rasterelektronen-Mikroskop, 6000× vergrössert. Abb. 426: Elektrodenstruktur (gelb) auf einer piezoelektrischen Keramikoberfläche (braun). Abb. 427 (Purpur-Töne) zeigt einen Querschnitt durch einen Keramik-Vielschichtkondensator. Abb. 428 (violett, meergrün und weiss): lichtempfindliche Selen-Oberfläche, wie in Photokopierern verwendet, unter dem Rasterelektronen-Mikroskop. (GER)

423–428 Feuillet et photos traitant des activités de recherche et de développement de la Standard Elektrik Lorenz SA, une société d'électronique de Stuttgart appartenant au groupe ITT. Les figs. 423 et 424 montrent un détail de la surface cristalline d'un microcircuit agrandie 100 fois; les couleurs résultent du relief de la surface vue au microscope interférentiel. La fig. 425 (bleu et jaune) est une matrice mémorielle d'un circuit à semiconducteurs telle qu'elle se présente sous le microscope électronique (grossissement 6000 fois). Fig. 426: structure d'électrode (jaune) sur une surface céramique piézo-électrique (brun). Fig. 427: coupe d'un condensateur en céramique (tons mauves). Fig. 428: surface de sélénium photosensible, pour photocopieur, vue au microscope électronique. (GER)

153

429

Brügmann 1978

Mit diesem Kalender
dankt Brügmann
für die gute Zusammenarbeit
und wünscht Ihnen
für 1978
Gesundheit, Freude und Erfolg

430

Calendars / Kalender / Calendriers

PHOTOGRAPHER / PHOTOGRAPH / PHOTOGRAPHE:
429–431 Siegfried Himmer

DESIGNER / GESTALTER / MAQUETTISTE:
429–431 Siegfried Himmer

429–431 Cover picture, complete sheet and detail of a motif from a calendar issued by the *Brüg-mann* group, suppliers of wood and plastic products. Double images of natural scenes combined with company products are used throughout, for instance cloud effects together with red cedar shingles in Fig. 431. (GER)

429–431 Aufnahme und komplette Umschlagseite sowie Detail des Maiblattes aus dem Kalender der *Brügmann*-Unternehmensgruppe, Hersteller von Holz- und Plastikprodukten. Es werden kombinierte Bilder mit Naturszenen und Firmenerzeugnissen verwendet, wie z. B. Holzschindeln mit Wolken in Abb. 431. (GER)

429–431 Illustration de couverture, couverture complète et détail du feuillet de mai d'un calen-drier publié par le groupe *Brügmann,* fabricant de produits en fibres de bois et plastiques. Emploi systématique de scènes de la nature en parallèle avec des produits du groupe. Fig. 431: bardeaux et nuages. (GER)

432

PHOTOGRAPHER / PHOTOGRAPH:
432–437 Manfred Vogelsänger

DESIGNER / GESTALTER / MAQUETTISTE:
432–437 F.G. Boes

432–437 A further example from the *Kodak* Colour Calendar Contest (see pages 146–155). F. G. Boes & Partner of Düsseldorf, who develop visual concepts for products and services, have come up with a highly original idea in a calendar which they call a permutable object and have entitled "The 365 faces of the year". The sheets for the months bear the grainy but skilfully photographed portraits of twelve "types". They are inserted in a folding box in such a way that they can only be torn out, and they are perforated for this purpose in squares corresponding to the days of the month, which are printed on the back of each square. The owner of the calendar tears off one of these squares each day and folds over the next, thus revealing the date, over which he slips a plastic envelope to hold it down. As he proceeds from day to day, he thus destroys the face of the month step by step and at the same time uncovers next month's face. Not only do the hybrid faces thus created produce some hilarious impressions; the process of change to which we and our world are subjected in time is also given visible expression in the calendar; and since the portraits for the months yet to come cannot be seen till we tear away the advancing present, we never know quite what the future—in this case the calendar—has in store for us. The game is thus one which has a deeper meaning as well as offering a daily ration of fun. We show here the calendar in use (Fig. 432) and five of the monthly portraits. (GER)

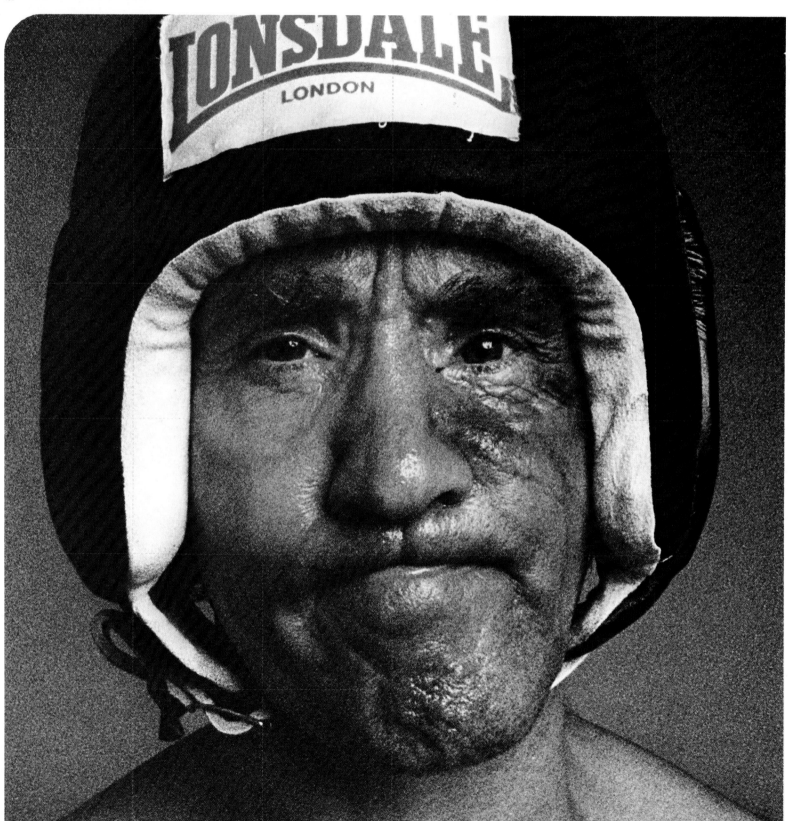

433

432–437 Ein weiteres Beispiel aus dem *Kodak*-Farbphoto-Kalender-Wettbewerb (siehe auch Seiten 146–155). F. G. Boes & Partner, die visuelle Konzepte und Dienstleistungen entwickeln, hatten eine sehr originelle Kalenderidee – ein «permutables Zeit-Objekt», dem sie den Titel «Die 365 Gesichter des Jahres 1978» gaben. Die Monatsblätter, mit grobkörnigen aber gekonnten Portrait-aufnahmen von 14 «Typen», sind so in einer Dosier-Faltschachtel untergebracht, dass man sie nur herausreissen kann. Zu diesem Zweck sind sie in Quadrate aufgeteilt und perforiert, entsprechend den Kalendertagen, die auf der Rückseite der einzelnen Quadrate aufgedruckt sind. Jeden Tag wird eines der Quadrate abgetrennt und das nächste umgeklappt, so dass das Datum erscheint. Mit einem Plexi-Schieber wird es festgehalten. Das jeweils umgeklappte Tagesquadrat eliminiert Stück für Stück das Gesicht des Monats und enthüllt gleichzeitig das Gesicht des folgenden Monats. Die so kombinierten Gesichter reizen nicht nur zum Lachen, sondern es wird dem kon-tinuierlichen Wandel, dem wir und unsere Welt unterworfen sind, im Kalender visuell Ausdruck verliehen. Und weil die Portraits für die kommenden Monate nicht sichtbar sind, bevor das gegen-wärtige abgerissen ist, wissen wir nie so genau, was die Zukunft – hier der Kalender – für uns bereithält. Das Spiel hat somit einen tieferen Sinn und vermittelt gleichzeitig eine tägliche Dosis Spass. Hier der Kalender im Gebrauch (Abb. 432) und fünf der monatlichen Portraits. (GER)

432–437 Voici un autre exemple du concours *Kodak* des calendries couleurs (voir pages 146–155). F. G. Boes & Partner à Düsseldorf, spécialisés dans la conception visuelle de produits et services, ont réalisé un calendrier très original sous forme d'un «objet permutable», sous le titre de «Les 365 visages de l'année». Les feuillets des différents mois sont ornés des portraits grenés, mais adroite-ment photographiés de 12 «types». Ils sont insérés dans une boite pliante de manière qu'on ne peut les en retirer qu'en les arrachant et sont perforés à cet effet en carrés correspondant aux jours du mois, qui sont imprimés au dos des carrés. La personne utilisant le calendrier arrache un rectangle par jour et replie le suivant, ce qui fait apparaître la date qu'il coiffe d'une cache plastique pour la maintenir visible. De jour en jour, le portrait du mois en cours se détruit, révélant celui du mois suivant. Il en résulte un mélange de traits parfois grotesque; mais ce que ce calendrier révèle surtout, c'est le changement incessant qui nous affecte, nous et notre environnement. Qui plus est, les portraits des mois à venir ne sont visibles qu'au fur et à mesure que nous arrachons une unité du temps présent – symbole vivant des tournures imprévues que nous réserve l'avenir. Ce calendrier satisfait ainsi notre instinct ludique de jour en jour tout en nous fournissant matière à réflexion. Nos lecteurs trouveront ici une représentation du calendrier à l'emploi (fig. 432), ainsi que cinq des portraits mensuels. (GER)

434

435

436

437

4

Editorial Photography
Magazine Covers
House Organs
Annual Reports

Redaktionelle Photographie
Zeitschriften-Umschläge
Hauszeitschriften
Jahresberichte

Photographie rédactionnelle
Couvertures de périodiques
Journaux d'entreprise
Rapports annuels

438

439

440

441

442

438, 440 Double spreads (both in full colour) from *Homemaker's Magazine,* opening features on pollution in the big cities and the plight of children whose parents divorce. (CAN)
439 Spread from a feature on Parisian fashion collections in *Harper's Bazaar.* (USA)
441 Spread from a feature in *Town & Country* about a golf course in the desert. (USA)
442 Spread from a feature in *The Sunday Times Magazine* on the perfect female image. (GBR)
443, 444 Double-spread feature on the photographer Deborah Turbeville from *Zoom,* and photographic illustration in just under actual size. (FRA)

438, 440 Einführende Doppelseiten in Farbe zu Artikeln über Umweltverschmutzung in Städten und Probleme der Kinder bei Ehescheidungen in *Homemaker's Magazine.* (CAN)
439 Doppelseite aus *Harper's Bazaar,* der neuen Pariser Mode gewidmet. (USA)
441 Doppelseite aus *Town & Country* mit Bericht über einen Golfplatz in der Wüste. (USA)
442 Doppelseite aus dem *Sunday Times Magazine* über das Image der perfekten Frau. (GBR)
443, 444 Komplette Doppelseite und ganzseitige Aufnahme aus der Zeitschrift *Zoom.* Der Text des Berichtes über die Photographin Deborah Turbeville besteht nur aus einzelnen Worten. (FRA)

438, 440 Deux pages doubles (en couleurs) introduisant deux articles, l'un sur la pollution de nos villes (fig. 438), l'autre sur les problèmes des enfants de parents divorcés (fig. 440). (CAN)
439 Page double d'un article de *Harper's Bazaar* présentant la nouvelle mode de Paris. (USA)
441 Page double figurant dans un rapport sur un terrain de golf dans le désert. (USA)
442 Page double du *Sunday Times Magazine* sur l'image parfaite de la femme. (GBR)
443, 444 Page double complète et photo pleine page du magazine *Zoom.* Le texte accompagnant ce portfolio sur la photographe Deborah Turbeville est composé de quelques mots seulement. (FRA)

DESIGNER / GESTALTER / MAQUETTISTE:

438, 440 Rod Della Vedova
441 Linda Stillman
443, 444 Christian Guillon

ART DIRECTOR / DIRECTEUR ARTISTIQUE:

438, 440 V. Georges Haroutiun
439 Jerold Smokler
441 Linda Stillman
442 Michael Rand
443, 444 Maurice Coriat

PUBLISHER / VERLEGER / EDITEUR:

438, 440 Homemaker's Mag.
439, 441 The Hearst Corporation
442 Sunday Times Magazine
443, 444 Publicness

PHOTOGRAPHER / PHOTOGRAPH / PHOTOGRAPHE:

438, 440 Michel Pilon
439 Peter Lindbergh
441 Robert Phillips
442 Allen Jones/Ronald Grant
443, 444 Deborah Turbeville

443

445

PHOTOGRAPHER / PHOTOGRAPH / PHOTOGRAPHE:

445, 446 Gianni Grazia
447 Jay Maisel
448, 449 Jean-Paul Goude/Pierre Houles

DESIGNER / GESTALTER / MAQUETTISTE:

445, 446 Alberto Piovani
448, 449 Don Menell

ART DIRECTOR / DIRECTEUR ARTISTIQUE:

445, 446 Alberto Piovani
447 Régis Pagniez
448, 449 Don Menell

PUBLISHER / VERLEGER / EDITEUR:

445, 446 Progresso Fotografico
447 Publications Filipacchi
448, 449 Playboy Publications, Inc.

445, 446 Shot and double spread from an article in *Progresso Fotografico* on the photographer Gianni Grazia of Bologna. Fig. 445 is an ironic commentary on the use of the female form in the modern media—it has lost all erotic meaning and become merely decorative. Fig. 446 illustrates Grazia's use of antithesis and parallel (two masks, old and young, ugly and beautiful) and of repetition (flight suggested by arms and wings): (ITA)
447 Sunset over New York, double spread from a series of photographs of New York by Jay Maisel, published in the magazine *Photo*. (GER)
448, 449 Two illustrations from an article in *Playboy* on fall fashions for men, which here have to stand the acid test of the rush hour in New York's subway. (USA)

gianni grazia

446

447

445, 446 Aufnahme und Doppelseite aus einem Bericht über den Photographen Gianni Grazia, aus *Progresso Fotografico*. Abb. 445 ist als ironischer Kommentar zur Photographie zu verstehen: der weibliche Körper verliert hier jegliche erotische Ausstrahlung, er wird zur blossen Dekoration. Die Aufnahmen in Abb. 446 sind Beispiele für die von Grazia verwendeten Ausdrucksmittel: Gegensätze und Ähnlichkeiten, Wiederholungen und Metaphern. (ITA)
447 «Sonnenuntergang über der Stadt.» Doppelseite aus einer Reihe von photographischen Impressionen Jay Maisels von der Stadt New York, erschienen in *Photo*. (GER)
448, 449 Zwei von vier Aufnahmen zu einem Artikel im *Playboy* über Herren-Herbstmode, die hier die härteste Bewährungsprobe, «Rush Hour» in der New Yorker U-Bahn, bestehen muss. (USA)

445, 446 Photo et page double d'un rapport consacré au photographe Gianni Grazia, publié dans le magazine *Progresso Fotografico*. Fig. 445: commentaire ironique sur la photographie: le corps féminin a perdu tout pouvoir d'attraction érotique, il n'est qu'un objet de décoration. Les photos sous fig. 446 présentent quelques exemples des moyens d'expression utilisés par Grazia: contrastes et ressemblances, répétitions et métaphores. (ITA)
447 «Coucher du soleil sur la ville.» Page double d'une série d'impressions photographiques de la ville de New York, publiée dans l'édition allemande de *Photo*. (GER)
448, 449 Deux photos de *Playboy* sur la mode masculine qui passe, vraisemblablement avec succès, l'une des plus dures épreuves – les heures de pointe dans le métro newyorkais. (USA)

448

449

163

450

451

450 Page in actual size from an article on Jost Wildbolz in *Progresso Fotografico*. (ITA)
451 Full page in colour from an article in *New York* on the New York dance season. (USA)
452 Full-page colour illustration from an article on torture published in *Gallery* magazine. (USA)
453 Opening spread of an article in *Gallery* on the sabotaging of White House plans. (USA)
454 Black-and-white scene from German football, from an issue of *Life* (1978 in pictures). (USA)

450 Aufnahme aus einem Artikel in *Progresso Fotografico* über Jost Wildbolz, Photograph. (ITA)
451 Ganzseitige Aufnahme zu einem Artikel in *New York* über New Yorks Ballett-Saison. (USA)
452, 453 Photographische Illustration und einleitende Doppelseite zu kritischen Berichten aus dem Magazin *Gallery*, hier über die amerikanische Beteiligung an Folterungen (Abb. 452) und Sabotage an Präsident Eisenhowers Friedensbemühungen (Abb. 453). (USA)
454 Schwarzweisse Doppelseite aus *Life*: Fussballspieler in Erwartung eines Freistosses. (USA)

450 Illustration d'un portfolio de *Progresso Fotografico* consacré à Jost Wildbolz. (ITA)
451 Photo pleine page d'un article sur les représentations de ballet à New York. (USA)
452, 453 Illustration pour un reportage sur la participation américaine dans divers cas de torture et page double introduisant un article critique sur les tentatives qui visaient à faire échouer les efforts du président Eisenhower en faveur de la paix. De *Gallery*. (USA)
454 Page double en noir et blanc du magazine *Life* avec photo dont le sense est évident. (USA)

PHOTOGRAPHER / PHOTOGRAPH:

450 Jost Wildbolz
451 Henry Wolf
452 Mark Ianacone
453 Kathy McGinnis

DESIGNER / GESTALTER / MAQUETTISTE:

450 Alberto Piovani
451 Walter Bernard/Milton Glaser
452, 453 Al Kahn

ART DIRECTOR / DIRECTEUR ARTISTIQUE:

450 Alberto Piovani
451 Walter Bernard/Milton Glaser
452, 453 Derek Burton
454 Charles Mikolaycak

AGENCY / AGENTUR / AGENCE – STUDIO:

452, 453 Al Kahn Design Associates

PUBLISHER / VERLEGER / EDITEUR:

450 Progresso Fotografico
451 New York Magazine
452, 453 Gallery Magazine
454 Time, Inc.

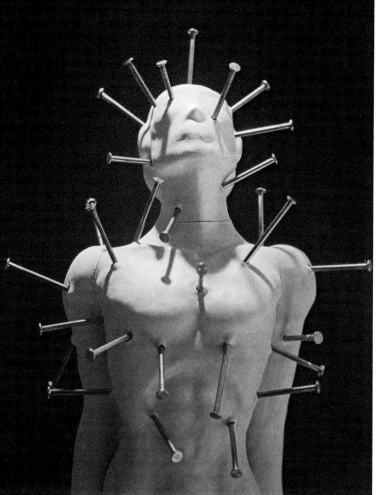

452

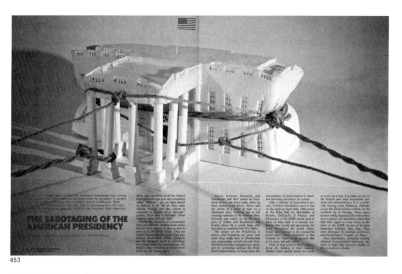

453

454

455, 456 Two double spreads from an article in *Photo* magazine about a love affair between the artist and his model. (FRA)
457 Double spread in full colour opening a feature in *Skeptic* magazine about illegal immigration into the United States. (USA)
458 Spread from the annual magazine of the National Hot Rod Association. Full colour. (USA)
459 Opening spread of a feature in *Town & Country* about cold soups, here showing (in full colour) a strawberry cream soup. (USA)
460 Detail of a full-page illustration from *Visual Message*, a new magazine. (JPN)

455, 456 Zwei Doppelseiten und Detail einer dritten, alle farbig, aus *Photo:* Eine Liebeserklärung des Photographen Art Kane an sein Modell, Marcella Klep. (FRA)
457 Einleitende Doppelseite in Farbe zu einem Artikel über das Problem illegaler Einwanderung in die Vereinigten Staaten, aus *Skeptik*. (USA)
458 Farbige Doppelseite aus dem Jahresmagazin der National Hot Rod Association. (USA)
459 Einleitende Doppelseite in Farbe aus *Town & Country* zu einem Artikel über kalte Suppen, die für den Sommer empfohlen werden. (USA)
460 Photographische Illustration aus *Visual Message*, einer neuen Zeitschrift. (JPN)

455

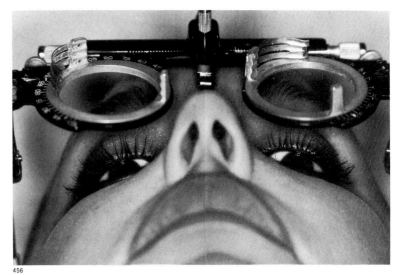

456

457

458

459

PHOTOGRAPHER / PHOTOGRAPH:

455, 456 Art Kane
457 Barrie M. Schwortz
458 James Joern
459 Michel Tcherevkoff
460 Ken Mori

DESIGNER / GESTALTER / MAQUETTISTE:

457 Gordon Mortensen
458 Steve Phillips
459 Linda Stillman

ART DIRECTOR / DIRECTEUR ARTISTIQUE:

455, 456 Eric Colmet Daâge
457 Gordon Mortensen
458 Steve Phillips
459 Linda Stillman

AGENCY / AGENTUR / AGENCE – STUDIO:

458 Steve Phillips Design, Inc.

455, 456 Pages doubles (en couleurs) tirées d'un portfolio du magazine *Photo*, publié en tant que faire-part de mariage d'Art Kane avec son modèle, Marcella Klep. (FRA)
457 Page double (en polychromie) introduisant un article sur le problème de l'immigration illégale aux Etats-Unis. Elément de *Skeptic*. (USA)
458 Page double du magazine annuel de la National Hot Rod Association. En couleurs. (USA)
459 Page double en couleurs introduisant un article du magazine *Town & Country* sur les soupes froides, recommandées pour l'été. (USA)
460 Illustration tirée du *Visual Message*, un nouveau magazine japonais. (JPN)

PUBLISHER / VERLEGER / EDITEUR:

455, 456 Publications Filipacchi
457 Skeptic Magazine, Inc.
458 Bold Horizons Publishing, Inc.
459 The Hearst Corporation
460 Visual Message

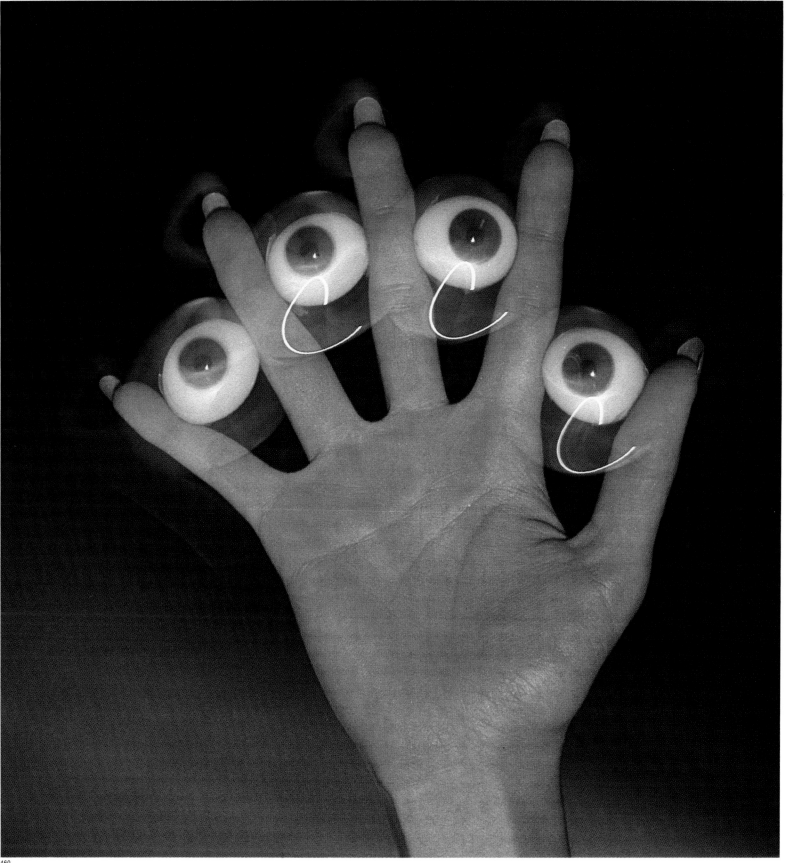

460

461

Editorial Photography

PHOTOGRAPHER / PHOTOGRAPH / PHOTOGRAPHE:

461, 461a, 461b Maureen Bisilliat

ART DIRECTOR / DIRECTEUR ARTISTIQUE:

461, 461a, 461b Regastein Rocha

PUBLISHER / VERLEGER / EDITEUR:

461, 461a, 461b Praxis Artes Gráficas Ltda.

461a

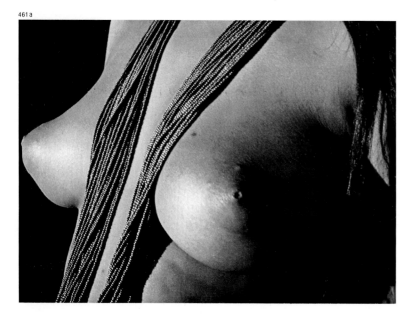

461—461 b Three of the photographs contained in the large portfolio *Xingu* issued by the agency and publishing company Praxis. These shots were taken in 1974—77 in the Xingu National Park, an Indian reservation in the Amazon region, and they show the ornaments and body painting of the Indians. The accompanying text was written by Orlando and Claudio Villas-Bôas, two leading authorities on the Indian tribes of Brazil. The portfolio was the subject of an exhibition in the Art Museum of São Paulo. Fig. 461 shows urucú, the red dye much used by the Indians; Fig. 461a blue beads of a type often obtained by barter from white traders; and Fig. 461b a blue parrot feather worn as an ornament by an Indian warrior. (BRA)

461—461 b Drei Aufnahmen aus einem Album mit dem Titel *Xingu,* das von «Praxis», Agentur und Verlag, herausgegeben wurde. Diese Aufnahmen wurden zwischen 1974 und 1977 im Xingu Nationalpark, einem Indianer-Reservat im Amazonasgebiet, gemacht. Gezeigt werden die Ornamente und Körperbemalungen der Indianer. Den Begleittext schrieben Orlando und Claudio Villas-Bôas, die sich jahrzehntelang mit den brasilianischen Indianerstämmen befasst haben. Abb. 461 zeigt den von den Indianern häufig verwendeten roten Farbstoff Urucú, Abb. 461a blaue Glasperlen, die für die Tauschgeschäfte mit weissen Händlern typisch sind, Abb. 461b eine blaue Papageienfeder als Ornament auf der dunkel gefärbten Haut eines indianischen Kriegers. (BRA)

461—461 b Trois photos reproduites dans un portfolio grand format intitulé *Xingu* (publication de Praxis, agence et maison d'édition). Les photos ont été prises entre 1974 et 1977 dans le Parc National Xingu, un territoire réservé aux Indiens dans la région de l'Amazone. On y montre les ornements et tatouages des Indiens. Le texte a été ecrit par Orlando et Claudio Villas-Bôas, qui ont étudié pendant des dizaines d'années les tribus d'Indiens brésiliens. Le portfolio a paru à l'occasion d'une exposition au Musée des Beaux-Arts de São Paulo. Fig. 461 montre l'urucú, un colorant fréquemment utilisé par les Indiens; fig. 461a: perles bleues que les marchands blancs ont échangées; fig. 461b: guerrier indien portant une plume de perroquet. (BRA)

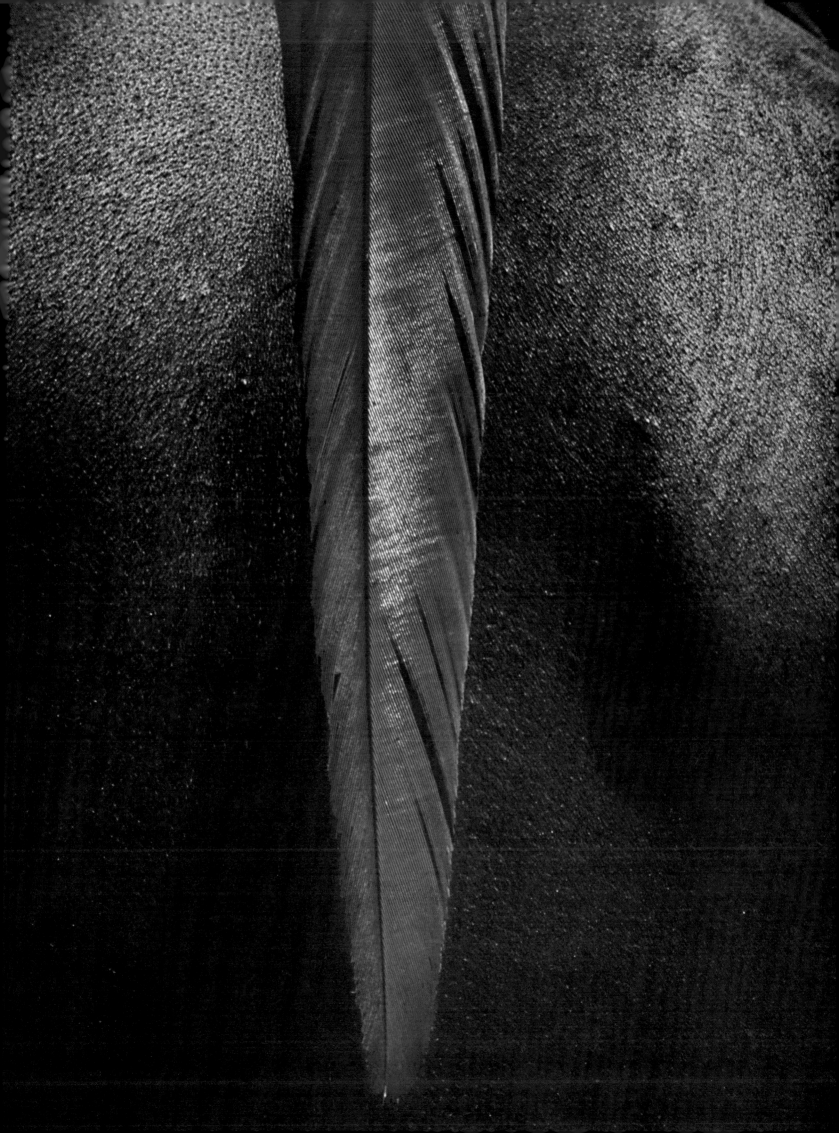

462

463

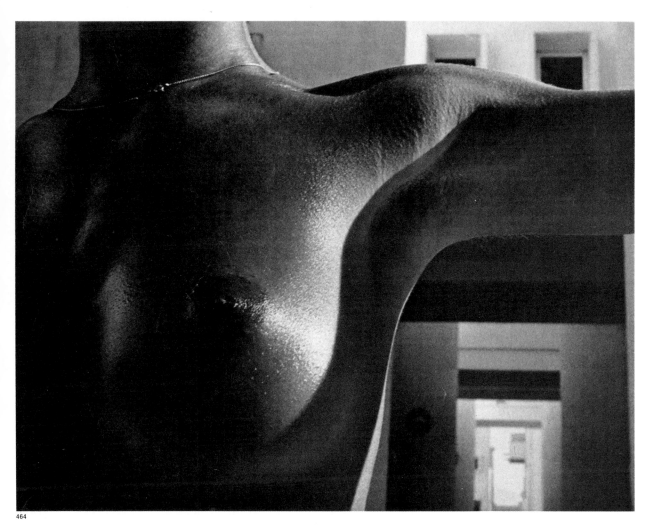

465

464

PHOTOGRAPHER / PHOTOGRAPH:

462, 463, 466, 467 Thomas Höpker/
Heinz Mack
464, 465 Frank Rheinboldt

DESIGNER / GESTALTER:

462, 463, 466, 467 Detlef Conrath
464, 465 Irmgard Voigt

ART DIRECTOR:

462, 463, 466, 467 Rolf Gillhausen
464, 465 Rainer Wörtmann

PUBLISHER / VERLEGER / EDITEUR:

462, 463, 466, 467 Gruner & Jahr
464, 465 Heinrich Bauer Verlag

Editorial Photography

462, 463, 466, 467 Double-spread illustrations from an article in the magazine *Stern* entitled ''Expedition into artificial gardens''. The luminodynamic sculptures of Heinz Mack are often so large that they are only really effective in the landscape. A photographer accompanied him to take these shots of his artefacts in the Algerian desert and the Greenland ice. (GER)
464, 465 Illustration and complete spread, in full colour, from a feature in the German *Playboy*, here on the theme of the curve. (GER)

462, 463, 466, 467 Doppelseitige Illustrationen aus einem Artikel in der Zeitschrift *Stern* über das im gleichen Verlag erschienene Buch *Expedition in künstliche Gärten* von Heinz Mack. Die Plastiken des Bildhauers Mack sind so gewaltig, dass sie nur in der freien Natur zur Wirkung kommen. Seine Expeditionen in die Arktis und die Sahara unternahm er zusammen mit dem Photographen Thomas Höpker, der Macks Artefakte im Bild festhielt. (GER)
464, 465 Farbige Aufnahme und ganze Seite aus *Playboy*, zum Thema «Kurve». (GER)

462, 463, 466, 467 Pages doubles d'un article du magazine *Stern* intitulé «Expédition au pays des jardins artificiels». Heinz Mack est un sculpteur allemand dont les œuvres lumino-dynamiques sont souvent de si grandes dimensions qu'elles ont besoin d'être implantées dans un paysage pour s'affirmer. Le photographe Thomas Höpker a accompagné Mack au Groenland et en Algérie pour y enregistrer l'impression qu'y font ces artefacts. (GER)
464, 465 Photo couleur et page entière de *Playboy*. Thème: «courbes». (GER)

466

467

468

469

Editorial Photography

470

471

472

468, 469, 471 Double spreads, partly in colour, and black-and-white illustration from an article in *Pardon* on James Wedge, who gave up textile design to become a photographer. (GER)
470 Detail of a full-page black-and-white illustration from a feature in the magazine *New York* about a CBS series starring a baseball pitcher who wrote the script and will also play the leading role in the series. (USA)
472 Double spread in full colour opening a feature on steaks in *Playboy*. The pun in the title is visualized in the shot of a steak in the form of the United States. (USA)
473 Spread opening an article in *Penthouse* on modern stereo equipment. Full colour. (GBR)
474 Spread opening an article in *Penthouse* on teenage relationships in the fifties. Bright colours, pink ground. (GBR)
475 Black-and-white spread from the German edition of *Playboy*. (GER)

468, 469, 471 Zwei Doppelseiten und Detail einer Aufnahme aus einem Artikel über den Photographen James Wedge in *Pardon*. «Das Wunder der Kings Road» war ursprünglich Textil-Designer. Als Photograph hat er sich aufs Handkolorieren spezialisiert. (GER)
470 Detail einer Schwarzweiss-Illustration zu einem Artikel über einen Baseball-Star, der in einer amerikanischen Fernsehserie zu sehen sein wird. Aus der Zeitschrift *New York*. (USA)
472 «Die vereinigten Steaks von Amerika.» Einleitende Doppelseite zu einem Artikel über Steaks (Steak in der Form der Vereinigten Staaten), aus *Playboy*. (USA)
473, 474 Einleitende Doppelseiten in Farbe zu einem Artikel über supermoderne Musikanlagen der siebziger Jahre (Abb. 473) und über Teenager in den fünfziger Jahren (Abb. 474): «Vergangen sind die Tage...», aus dem Magazin *Penthouse*. (GBR)
475 Doppelseite in Schwarzweiss, aus *Playboy*, mit Anspielung auf «Sex-Astrologie». (GER)

473

474

468, 469, 471 Doubles pages complètes et photo d'un article que le magazine *Pardon* a consacré au photographe James Wedge. Dessinateur de tissus, le «miracle de la Kings Road» s'est spécialisé maintenant à colorier des photos. (GER)
470 Détail d'une illustration noir-blanc accompagnant un article sur un champion de base-ball qui prendra part à une série présenté à la TV américaine. Du magazine *New York*. (USA)
472 «Les steaks unis de l'Amérique.» Page double introduisant un article sur les steaks (steak en forme des Etats-Unis). Elément du magazine *Playboy*. (USA)
473, 474 Pages doubles (en polychromie), l'une introduisant un article sur les appareils de musique hypermodernes des années 70 (fig. 473) et l'autre sur les teenagers des années 50 (fig. 474): «Les jours sont passés...». Eléments du magazine *Penthouse*. (GBR)
475 Page double en noir-blanc de *Playboy*, avec allusion à «l'astrologie du sexe». (GER)

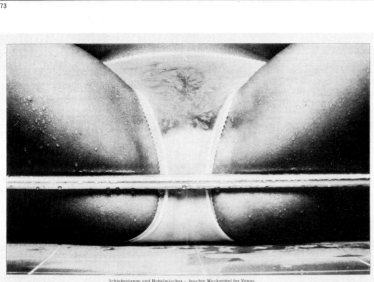

475

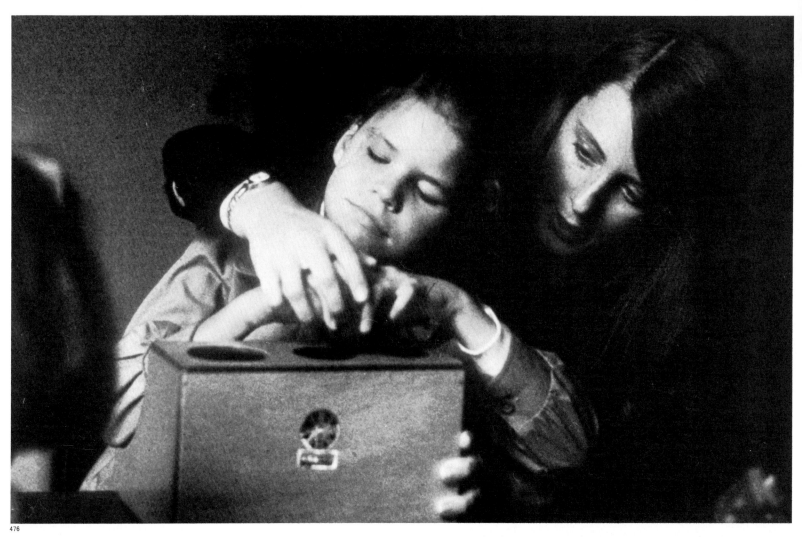

476

477

174

478

479

PHOTOGRAPHER / PHOTOGRAPH / PHOTOGRAPHE:

476–478, 481 Lord Snowdon
479, 480 Shig Ikeda

DESIGNER / GESTALTER / MAQUETTISTE:

476–478, 481 Gilvrie Misstear
479, 480 John C. Jay

ART DIRECTOR / DIRECTEUR ARTISTIQUE:

476–478, 481 Michael Rand
479, 480 John C. Jay

AGENCY / AGENTUR / AGENCE – STUDIO:

479, 480 John Jay Designs

PUBLISHER / VERLEGER / EDITEUR:

476–478, 481 Sunday Times Magazine
479, 480 Argosy, Popular Publications

480

Editorial Photography

476–478, 481 Three double spreads in black and white and cover photograph from an issue of *The Sunday Times Magazine* chiefly devoted to the problem of caring for the mentally handicapped, with shots taken in institutions by the Earl of Snowdon. The title of the feature is "Love and Affection". (GBR)
479, 480 Full-page illustration, and opening page with the following double spread, from an article in the magazine *Argosy* on the psychic effects of the full moon. Illustrations in pale grey shades, blue window and title. (USA)

476–478 Doppelseiten und photographische Illustration des Umschlags einer Ausgabe des *Sunday Times Magazine*, die hauptsächlich den Problemen geistig Behinderter gewidmet ist. Die Aufnahmen machte Lord Snowdon in verschiedenen Heimen. (GBR)
479, 480 Ganzseitige, farbige Aufnahme und einleitende Seite mit kompletter nachfolgender Doppelseite (Abb. 480) aus der Zeitschrift *Argosy*, mit einem Artikel über häufig festgestelltes, aussergewöhnliches Verhalten von Menschen bei Vollmond. (USA)
481 Aus dem Bericht im *Sunday Times Magazine* über Behinderte. Siehe auch Abb. 646–478. (GBR)

476–478 Deux pages doubles et photo de couverture d'un numéro du *Sunday Times Magazine*, consacré pour l'essentiel aux problèmes des retardés mentaux et illustré d'un reportage d'asiles par l'Earl of Snowdon. (GBR)
479, 480 Photo pleine page (en polychromie) et triple page introduisant un article du magazine *Argosy*: l'influence de la pleine lune sur le comportement d'un grand nombre de personnes. (USA)
481 Page double du reportage du *Sunday Times Magazine* sur les retardés mentaux. Voir aussi les figs. 476–478. (GBR)

481

PHOTOGRAPHER / PHOTOGRAPH / PHOTOGRAPHE:

482, 483 Michael Furman
484 Ron Seymour
485, 486 Peter Knapp
487 Lucky Curtis

DESIGNER / GESTALTER / MAQUETTISTE:

482, 483 Jim Minnich
484 Michael Brock
485, 486 John Tennant
487 Bill Lowry

482

483

484

Editorial Photography

485

486

482 Double spread from a feature in *Philadelphia* magazine on the large range of running shoes. (USA)
483, 484 Complete double spread and detail of the photography from a feature in *Oui* magazine on fashionable briefs for men. Full colour. (USA)
485, 486 Cover and illustration (in colour) from an issue of *The Sunday Times Magazine* featuring sun-bathing holidays and beach fashions. (GBR)
487 Opening page of a feature in *Chicago* magazine with an inside story about baseball. (USA)

482 Aufnahme zu einem Artikel über die neuen Schuhe, die speziell für das populär gewordene Laufen entwickelt wurden. Aus der Zeitschrift *Philadelphia*. (USA)
483, 484 Komplette Doppelseite und Detail der Aufnahme (farbig) zu einem Artikel über modische Herrenunterwäsche, aus dem Magazin *Oui*. (USA)
485, 486 Umschlag und Illustration einer Ausgabe des *Sunday Times Magazine* zum Thema Strand. (GBR)
487 Einführende Seite in Farbe zu einem Insider-Bericht über Baseball (der amerikanische Sport) aus *Chicago*. (USA)

482 Photo accompagnant un article du magazine *Philadelphia* sur les nouvelles chaussures développées spécialement pour les courses, un sport très populaire aux Etats-Unis. (USA)
483, 484 Page double complète avec détail de la photo (en couleurs) d'un article sur les sous-vêtements masculins à la mode. Eléments tirés du magazine *Oui*. (USA)
485, 486 Couverture et illustration d'un numéro du *Sunday Times Magazine* présentant des programmes de vacances au soleil et les nouvelles modes de plage. (GBR)
487 Page introduisant un reportage pour insiders sur le baseball, le sport le plus populaire aux Etats-Unis. Photo couleur du magazine *Chicago*. (USA)

ART DIRECTOR / DIRECTEUR ARTISTIQUE:

482, 483 Jim Minnich
484 Michael Brock
485, 486 Michael Rand
487 Jack Lund

AGENCY / AGENTUR / AGENCE – STUDIO:

482, 483 Philadelphia Magazine

PUBLISHER / VERLEGER / EDITEUR:

482, 483 Philadelphia Magazine
484 Playboy Publications, Inc.
485, 486 Sunday Times Magazine
487 Chicago Magazine

487

488

PHOTOGRAPHER / PHOTOGRAPH / PHOTOGRAPHE:

488–490 Sacha
491 Gianni Fabrizio
492 André Carrara

DESIGNER / GESTALTER / MAQUETTISTE:

488–490 Gilvrie Misstear
491 Roberto Orlandi

ART DIRECTOR / DIRECTEUR ARTISTIQUE:

488–490 Michael Rand
491 Claudio Zamperini
492 Peter Knapp/Antoine Kieffer

PUBLISHER / VERLEGER / EDITEUR:

488–490 Sunday Times Magazine
491 Harper's Bazar-Italia
492 Elle France Editions et Publications

489

490

per l'immaginario viaggio intorno al mondo come il 'navigatore solitario'

PRONTI...VIA!

con la blusa antivento e gli shorts di Deni-Cler disegnati da Giuliana Alberti. Per proteggersi dagli spruzzi e dal sole, il berretto con visiera di Brigatti, gli stivaloni di Superga... e il make-up coloratissimo di Ellen Betrix. Su tutto il corpo e sul viso Ultra Brown Sun Jelly per epidermidi già abbronzate che sopportano bene il sole. Per questo Ellen Betrix ha creato una gamma completa di prodotti solari suddivisi a seconda del tipo di fragilità (o resistenza) della pelle. Ci sono preparati per epidermidi delicate facilmente irritabili, per pelli resistenti ai raggi ultravioletti e agli agenti atmosferici. Inoltre, ogni linea Ultra Brown è completata, a sua volta, da una linea dopo-sole con leggero effetto autoabbronzante, estremamente idratante. Sulle guance, per ravvivare l'incarnato, Creamy Rouge tonalità Soft Copper. La bocca, molto importante d'estate, dovrà sempre essere ultraprotetta. Qui Lip Pencil una matita cremosa che ha il pregio di poter essere usata in due modi: come contorno e come rossetto. Nello stesso tempo lucida ed idrata le labbra. Nella foto, la tonalità è Red Fire. Lo smalto è Young Colors N. 77.

491

Editorial Photography

492

488–490 Complete cover, cover photograph and double spread from an issue of *The Sunday Times Magazine* containing a feature on warm socks for the winter. (GBR)
491 Double spread from an issue of the Italian edition of *Harper's Bazaar:* fashions and make-up for sun and sports. (ITA)
492 Full-page illustration from a fashion feature ("Rhapsody in blue") from the women's magazine *Elle.* Clothes in shades of blue, blue and white ground. (FRA)

488–490 Kompletter Umschlag, Detail der Farbaufnahme und Doppelseite einer Ausgabe des *Sunday Times Magazine,* worin die Nützlichkeit warmer Socken im Winter behandelt wird. (GBR)
491 Doppelseite aus der italienischen Ausgabe von *Harper's Bazaar* mit Ratschlägen zu Make-up und Mode für Sport und Sonne. (ITA)
492 Ganzseitige Aufnahme aus der Zeitschrift *Elle* unter dem Titel «Rhapsodie in Blau». Kleidung in verschiedenen Blautönen auf blau-weissem Hintergrund. (FRA)

488–490 Couverture complète, détail de la photo et double page d'un numéro du *Sunday Times Magazine,* où il est question de l'utilité de chaussettes chaudes en hiver. (GBR)
491 Page double de l'édition italienne du magazine de mode *Harper's Bazaar* avec des conseils et propositions de maquillage et de mode. (ITA)
492 Photo pleine page (en couleurs) d'un article de modes intitulé «Rapsodie en bleu» qui a paru dans le magazine féminin *Elle.* Divers tons bleus sur fond en bleu et blanc. (FRA)

493, 494 "A good start" for the one-piece swimsuit: complete double spread and illustration in roughly actual size from a feature on bathing fashions in *Vogue*. (FRA)

493, 494 «Ein guter Start für den einteiligen Schwimmanzug». Komplette Doppelseite und Illustration (ungefähr Original-grösse) zu einem Bericht über Bademode in *Vogue*. (FRA)

493, 494 «Bon départ pour le maillot style nageuse»: double page complète et illustration approx. grandeur originale d'un article sur les modes en matière de costumes de bain. Eléments du magazine féminin *Vogue*. (FRA)

PHOTOGRAPHER / PHOTOGRAPH / PHOTOGRAPHE:

493, 494 Helmut Newton

ART DIRECTOR / DIRECTEUR ARTISTIQUE:

493, 494 Jocelyn Kargère

AGENCY / AGENTUR / AGENCE – STUDIO:

493, 494 Vogue Studios

PUBLISHER / VERLEGER / EDITEUR:

493, 494 Condé Nast SA

Editorial Photography

493

494

495

Editorial Photography

PHOTOGRAPHER / PHOTOGRAPH / PHOTOGRAPHE:

495 Barbara Bordnick
496, 497 Art Kane
498, 499 Guy Bourdin

DESIGNER / GESTALTER / MAQUETTISTE:

495 Will Hopkins

ART DIRECTOR / DIRECTEUR ARTISTIQUE:

495 Will Hopkins
496–499 Jocelyn Kargère

AGENCY / AGENTUR / AGENCE – STUDIO:

496–499 Vogue Studios

PUBLISHER / VERLEGER / EDITEUR

495 New York Times Magazine
496–499 Condé Nast SA

496

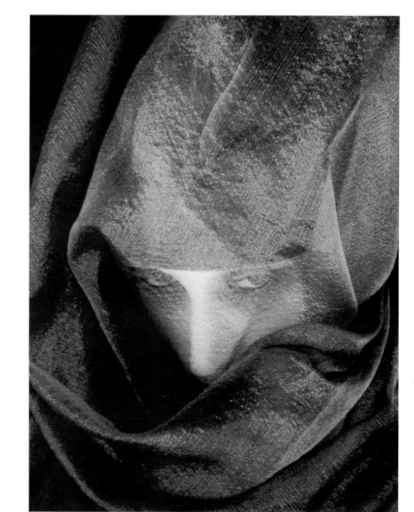

497

495 Double spread from a feature on faces as seen by fashion designers, published in *The New York Times Magazine*. (USA)
496, 497 Two full-page illustrations from a review of beauty products published each month in the women's magazine *Vogue*. (FRA)
498 Colour spread on winter fashions from *Vogue*: Karl Lagerfeld has combined "the most feminine with the most masculine". (FRA)
499 Colour spread from *Vogue*: fashion design to which Claude Montana was inspired by Elgar's *Pomp and Circumstance*. (FRA)

495 Einleitende Doppelseite zu einem Artikel im *New York Times Magazine*, unter dem Titel: «Was berühmte Designer über Gesichter zu sagen haben». (USA)
496, 497 Ganzseitige Aufnahmen zu einem Artikel in der Modezeitschrift *Vogue* über dekorative Kosmetik: «Das Fest der Farbe». (FRA)
498 Farbige Doppelseite über Wintermode aus *Vogue*: Karl Lagerfeld kombinierte «die weiblichste mit der männlichsten Mode». (FRA)
499 Eine weitere Doppelseite aus *Vogue*, farbig. Zu der gezeigten Mode wurde Claude Montana durch Elgars *Pomp and Circumstance* inspiriert. (FRA)

495 Double page initiale d'un article du *New York Times Magazine* sur le visage féminin. (USA)
496, 497 «La fête de la couleur.» Photos pleines pages parues dans le magazine de mode *Vogue* dans un article sur les nouveaux maquillages et des soins raffinés. (FRA)
498 Double page couleur du magazine de mode *Vogue* sur la mode d'hiver, où Karl Lagerfeld combine «le plus féminin et le plus masculin». (FRA)
499 Page double en couleurs du magazine *Vogue* avec la mode que *Pomp and Circumstance*, d'Elgar, a inspiré à Claude Montana. (FRA)

LA MODE ENCHANTÉE DE L'HIVER

KARL LAGERFELD OU LES JEUX DE L'HUMOUR ET DE LA MODE. "C'est la nouvelle féminité aux frontières indécises," dit Karl Lagerfeld qui compose, pour Chloé, le plus féminin avec le plus masculin, la dentelle avec le cuir, la botte avec la lingerie. Des tulles brodés et des barbes festonnées animent des chemises et des corsages aussi légers que des souffles. Les jambes sont allongées et enveloppées dans des écrins de satin noir. On trouve des blouses à la Fragonard, des décolletés à la Watteau, des culottes de satin du chevalier d'Éon. La démarche est plus vive, les gestes plus aériens.

De gauche à droite, robe en crêpe romain de Biní, rebrodé par Chaste, au décolleté plongeant garni de martre et de Chantilly. Blouse en dentelle noire de Hurel et pantalon à la française en satin noir. Blouse en tulle rebrodé ivoire de Forster Willi - St. Gall et pantalon en satin noir à la française. Karl Lagerfeld pour Chloé. Cuissardes. Guido Pasquali pour Chloé. Fleurs et nœud de dentelle de Jeannine Montel pour Chloé. Coiffures Valentin pour Jean-Louis David. Maquillages "Soft Tender" de Heidi Moravetz pour Lancaster : teint "Sahara"; aux yeux, eye shadow "Boréal".

498

499

500

501

kim ono

502

503

PHOTOGRAPHER / PHOTOGRAPH / PHOTOGRAPHE:

500–503, 505 Guy Bourdin
504 Darrell E. Arnold

ART DIRECTOR / DIRECTEUR ARTISTIQUE:

500–503, 505 Jocelyn Kargère
504 Ernest Scarfone

AGENCY / AGENTUR / AGENCE – STUDIO:

500–503, 505 Vogue Studios

PUBLISHER / VERLEGER / EDITEUR:

500–503, 505 Condé Nast SA
504 Nikon, Inc.

Editorial Photography

500–503, 505 Four double spreads, all in full colour, and one page in roughly actual size from a feature in the French fashion magazine *Vogue* presenting ten ceremonial kimonos for unmarried girls created by the Japanese fashion designer Kenichi Takizawa, whose family has been designing kimonos for two centuries. The pages are a good example of the presentation of fashion in this magazine in a form which does not merely display the clothing but gives the photographer full scope for the deployment of his art. (FRA)
504 Double spread from a feature in *Nikon World*, an American magazine published by the Japanese camera manufacturers. (USA)

500–503, 505 Vier farbige Doppelseiten und ganzseitige Aufnahme (ungefähr Originalgrösse) aus einem Artikel in der französischen Modezeitschrift *Vogue*, worin zehn zeremonielle Kimonos für unverheiratete Mädchen präsentiert werden. Sie wurden von Kenichi Takizawa kreiert, dessen Familie seit zwei Jahrhunderten Kimonos entwirft. Hier wird deutlich, dass für *Vogue* Modephotographie nicht nur blosse Aufzeichnung ist, sondern dass sie eine eigene kreative und darstellerische Dimension haben muss. (FRA)
504 Doppelseite aus einem Artikel in *Nikon World*, Hauszeitschrift des japanischen Kameraherstellers *Nikon*, die in Amerika herausgegeben wird. (USA)

500–503, 505 Quatre doubles pages (en polychromie) et page au format approx. original d'un article du magazine de mode *Vogue*. On y présente dix kimonos de cérémonie pour filles nubiles créés par Kenichi Takizawa, dont la famille s'est spécialisée dans la conception de kimonos depuis deux siècles. Cet article montre qu'un magazine de mode n'est pas un simple instrument d'enregistrement, mais doit faire état d'une dimension créatrice et interprétative et garantir à cet effet le maximum de liberté à ses collaborateurs. (FRA)
504 Page double d'un article publié dans *Nikon World*, le journal d'entreprise du fabricant japonais d'appareils photographiques. (USA)

504

 506

MAILLOTS D'AVRIL

507

PUBLISHER / VERLEGER / EDITEUR:

506 Penthouse International Ltd.
507, 508, 511 Condé Nast SA
509 Haymarket Publishing
510 Playboy Publications, Inc.
512 Nikon, Inc.

506 Double spread opening an article on cognac in *Penthouse* magazine. (USA)
507 Double spread in full colour in the fashion magazine *Vogue*, opening a feature on new popular one-piece swimsuits. (FRA)
508 Illustration from a fashion feature in *Vogue*, with a pink featherweight on the barbell. (FRA)
509 Double spread opening an article in *Management Today* on a young entrepreneur who has risen to success fast in the electronics field. (GBR)
510 Double spread opening a feature on candy bars in *Oui* magazine. (USA)
511 Illustration ("a new romantic face") from a *Vogue* beauty feature. (FRA)
512 Shot of a balloon watering, from *Nikon World*. (USA)

506 Erste Doppelseite eines Artikels über Cognac in der Zeitschrift *Penthouse*. (USA)
507 Farbige Doppelseite aus *Vogue*. Hier werden die neuen, raffinierten einteiligen Badeanzüge vorgestellt, die stark im Kommen sein sollen. (FRA)
508 Farbige Aufnahme zu einem Schönheitsartikel in *Vogue*. Hier ein «Federgewicht». (FRA)
509 Doppelseite aus dem Wirtschaftsmagazin *Management Today* zu einem Artikel über den umstrittenen jungen Unternehmer Sinclair, Hersteller von microelektronischen Geräten. (GBR)
510 Doppelseite aus der Zeitschrift *Oui* zu einem Artikel über Süsswaren. (USA)
511 Illustration («ein neues romantisches Gesicht») aus einem Kosmetikartikel in *Vogue*. (FRA)
512 Aufnahme einer Ballon-Wasserung aus *Nikon-World*. (USA)

506 Double page initiale d'un article sur le cognac publié dans le magazine *Penthouse*. (USA)
507 Page double en couleurs du magazine de mode *Vogue*. On y présente la nouvelle collection des une-pièce très fantaisistes, très fantasques. (FRA)
508 Illustration en tons atténués figurant dans un article du magazine *Vogue* sur les produits de beauté. Ici on voit une femme poids-plume en robe de tulle. (FRA)
509 Page double du magazine économique *Management Today* accompagnant un article sur un jeune entrepreneur assez discuté (fabricant d'équipements micro-électroniques). (GBR)
510 Page double du magazine *Oui* introduisant un article sur l'industrie de sucreries. (USA)
511 Illustration («un nouveau visage romantique») tirée d'un article de *Vogue*. (FRA)
512 Photo d'un amerrissage de ballon, publiée dans *Nikon World*. (USA)

508

509

510

511

512

Editorial Photography

STILL LIFE WITH HORSES

Seventy years ago there were more than a million working horses in the country; 10 years ago only 2000 were left. But now they are coming back, like this Clydesdale on Hugh Ramsay's farm at Garliestown, Wigtownshire. Photographs by Kenneth Griffiths

513

514

515

PHOTOGRAPHER / PHOTOGRAPH / PHOTOGRAPHE:

513 Kenneth Griffiths
514 David Hamilton
515, 516 Guy Bourdin

DESIGNER / GESTALTER / MAQUETTISTE:

513 Gilvrie Misstear

ART DIRECTOR / DIRECTEUR ARTISTIQUE:

513 Michael Rand
514–516 Jocelyn Kargère

AGENCY / AGENTUR / AGENCE – STUDIO:

514–516 Vogue Studios

PUBLISHER / VERLEGER / EDITEUR:

513 Sunday Times Magazine
514–516 Condé Nast SA

513 Double spread opening a feature on working horses in *The Sunday Times Magazine.* Full colour. (GBR)
514 Illustration from an article on a "return to nature in long skirts", from *Vogue* magazine. (FRA)
515, 516 Colour illustration of dramatic "more feminine" fashions by Karl Lagerfeld and full page in black and white on the "crinoline line", with a dress designed by Constantin Guys, from a fashion feature in *Vogue.* (FRA)

513 Erste Doppelseite eines Artikels über Arbeitspferde, deren Bestand in England nach einem Rückgang auf 2000 wieder beträchtlich zunimmt. Aus *Sunday Times Magazine.* (GBR)
514 Illustration zu einem Artikel über einen «Zurück-zur-Natur»-Modesommer in langen Röcken. Aus *Vogue.* (FRA)
515, 516 Farbillustration mit dramatischer «weiblicherer» Mode von Karl Lagerfeld und ganze Seite in Schwarzweiss mit einem Modell von Constantin Guys («Krinoline-Linie»), beide aus dem gleichen Modebericht in *Vogue.* (FRA)

513 Page double initiale d'un article sur les chevaux de labour paru dans le *Sunday Times Magazine.* (GBR)
514 Illustration d'un article du magazine *Vogue* sur le «retour à la nature en jupes longues». (FRA)
515, 516 Illustration couleur de modes dramatiques «plus féminines» par Karl Lagerfeld et pleine page noir-blanc consacré à la «ligne crinoline», avec une robe dessinée par Constantin Guys, figurant toutes deux dans le même article de mode publié dans le magazine *Vogue.* (FRA)

516

517

518

519

517 Full-page colour illustration for an article on wine in the magazine *House Beautiful.* (USA)

518, 519 Two colour pages from a feature on high fashion and the new designers in *Chicago* magazine. (USA)

520 Full-page illustration in black and white for a feature in the magazine *Avenue.* (NLD)

521, 523 Full-page illustration in full colour and complete opening spread of a critical article on Jimmy Carter's presidency in *Skeptic* magazine. (USA)

522, 524 Two illustrations from an article in the German *Playboy* entitled "The Sexth Dimension". The photographs are taken with various tricks and technical aids. (GER)

520

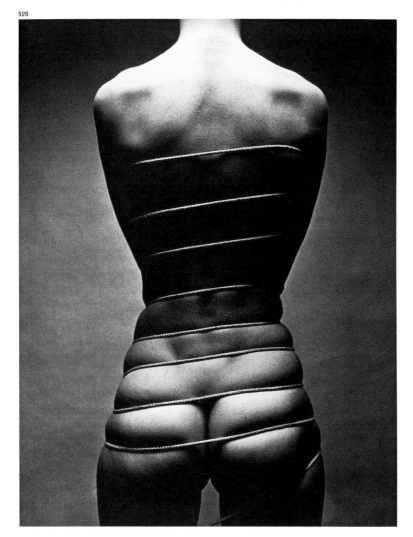

521

PHOTOGRAPHER / PHOTOGRAPH / PHOTOGRAPHE:

517 Henry Wolf
518, 519 Victor Skrebneski
520 Jan Henderik
521, 523 Barrie M. Schwortz
522, 524 Gerhard Vormwald

DESIGNER / GESTALTER / MAQUETTISTE:

517 Henry Wolf
518, 519 Jack Lund
521, 523 Gordon Mortensen

ART DIRECTOR / DIRECTEUR ARTISTIQUE:

517 Henry Wolf
518, 519 Jack Lund
520 Dick de Moei
521, 523 Gordon Mortensen
522, 524 Rainer Wörtmann

AGENCY / AGENTUR / AGENCE – STUDIO:

517 Henry Wolf Productions

PUBLISHER / VERLEGER / EDITEUR:

517 House Beautiful
518, 519 Chicago Magazine
520 De Geillustreerde Pers N.V.
521, 523 Skeptic Magazine, Inc.
522, 524 Heinrich Bauer Verlag

Editorial Photography

517 Ganzseitige, farbige Aufnahme aus der Zeitschrift *House Beautiful* zu einem Artikel über Weine. (USA)
518, 519 Farbige Seiten zu einem Artikel über neue Mode-schöpfer in Chicago, aus der Zeitschrift *Chicago.* (USA)
520 Ganzseitige Schwarzweiss-Aufnahme aus der Zeitschrift *Avenue* unter dem Titel «Spannkraft». (NLD)
521, 523 Farbige Aufnahme und komplette Doppelseite zu einem kritischen Artikel über Präsident Carters erstes Jahr im Amt aus dem Magazin *Skeptic.* (USA)
522, 524 Aufnahme, ungefähr Originalgrösse, und Detail einer weiteren Aufnahme aus *Playboy* unter dem Titel «Die sexte Dimension». (GER)

517 Pleine page en couleurs d'un article sur les vins. (USA)
518, 519 Deux pages (en polychromie) d'un article du magazine *Chicago* présentant les nouveaux créateurs de modes de Chicago. (USA)
520 Photo pleine page en noir et blanc intitulée «élasticité». Elément du magazine *Avenue.* (NLD)
521, 523 Photo couleur et page double complète d'un article critique sur la première année de présidence de Jimmy Carter. Du magazine *Skeptic.* (USA)
522, 524 Deux illustrations d'un article de l'édition alle-mande de *Playboy,* intitulé «La sexième dimension». Les photos ont été prises avec divers trucs techniques. (GER)

522

523

524

525, 526 Two full-page illustrations from a series entitled *Fiches-consommation* in the women's magazine *Elle*. The series was a survey of the raw materials used in cooking, a single page of information being backed by a more or less imaginative illustration; here on peas from a series of garden vegetables and on eggs from a series of farm products. (FRA)
527 "Gloves... for the feet." Opening spread of a feature in the Russian edition of *America Illustrated* on the fashion of socks with individual toes. (USA)
528, 529 Complete cover of a *Fortune* listing of the 500 largest industrial corporations. (USA)
530 Full-page illustration of the various agrarian products from the magazine *Economic Impact*. Full colour. (USA)

525, 526 Zwei Beispiele aus einer speziellen Beitragsfolge in der Zeitschrift *Elle*, unter dem Titel *Fiches-consommation*, eine Art kleiner Warenkunde, die gründlich über die in der Küche verwendeten Rohstoffe informiert. Hier eine Illustration für «Zuckererbsen» aus der Folge «Gartengemüse» und für «Das Ei» aus der Folge «Vom Bauernhof». (FRA)
527 «Handschuhe... für die Füsse.» Erste Doppelseite eines Artikels, der in der russischen Ausgabe von *America Illustrated* veröffentlicht wurde. (USA)
528, 529 «Die 500 grössten Industrie-Unternehmen in den USA.» Kompletter Umschlag und Vorderseite des Wirtschaftsmagazins *Fortune*. (USA)
530 Farbige Aufnahme zu einem Artikel in *Economic Impact* (Wirtschaftsmagazin). (USA)

528

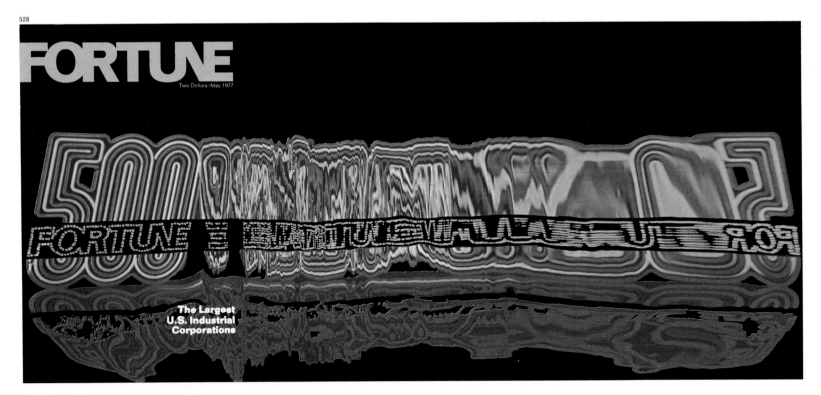

ФОТО МАЙКА МИТЧЕЛЛА

ПЕРЧАТКИ ...ДЛЯ НОГ

В мире молодежной моды набирает популярность новый вид носков. На манер перчаток, носки имеют пальцы. Носить их одно удовольствие, хотя бы потому, что в них каждый палец сам себе хозяин и может шевелиться как ему угодно. Некоторые поклонники новой моды даже уверяют, что такой покрой носков способствует кровообращению и придает устойчивость. Так это или не так, очевидно одно: носки необыкновенно практичны. Изготовляют их из чистой шерсти или из смеси ее с искусственными волокнами, и зимой ногам в них тепло даже в сандалиях.

527

525, 526 Le magazine féminin français *Elle* a entrepris la publication d'une série de *Fiches-consommation* présentant les matières premières utilisées dans la cuisine: «Petits pois» de la série «Légumes du potager» – vision kafkaïenne d'un flot de petits pois montant à l'assaut d'une maison – et «L'Œuf» de la série des «Produits de la ferme». (FRA)
527 «Des gants... pour les pieds.» Double page initiale d'un article de l'édition russe d'*America Illustrated* sur la nouvelle mode des chaussettes à orteils séparés. (USA)
528, 529 «Les 500 entreprises les plus importantes des Etats-Unis.» Recto et verso de la couverture du magazine économique *Fortune*. (USA)
530 Photo couleur accompagnant un article du magazine économique *Economic Impact*. (USA)

AGENCY / AGENTUR / AGENCE – STUDIO:

527, 530 U.S. Information Agency

PUBLISHER / VERLEGER / EDITEUR:

525, 526 Elle France Editions et Publications
527 U.S. Information Agency
528, 529 Fortune Magazine
530 Economic Impact Magazine

529

PHOTOGRAPHER / PHOTOGRAPH:

525 Bouillaud
526 Sarah Moon
527 Mike Mitchell
528, 529 Michel Tcherevkoff
530 Robert Banks

DESIGNER / GESTALTER / MAQUETTISTE:

527 Dorothy Fall
528, 529 Ron Campbell
530 Robert Banks

ART DIRECTOR / DIRECTEUR ARTISTIQUE:

525, 526 Peter Knapp/Antoine Kieffer
527 David Moore
528, 529 Ron Campbell
530 Robert Banks

Editorial Photography

530

531

АМЕрика

533

532

534

535

PHOTOGRAPHER / PHOTOGRAPH:

531, 532 Peter Lindbergh
538 Tony Duffy

DESIGNER / GESTALTER / MAQUETTISTE:

531, 532 Wolfgang Behnken
536, 537 Gilvrie Misstear
538 John Tennant

Magazine Covers

194

THE SUNDAY TIMES *magazine*

THE FOURTH OF JULY

JULY 4, 1976

Today is the 200th anniversary.
Will Jimmy Carter
be the 39th President of
the United States?

J. CARTER

536

531, 532 Photograph and complete cover of the illustrated magazine *Stern*. It was a casual shot but a very successful cover, and one that caused quite a stir. (GER)
533 Cover of the Russian edition of *America Illustrated*. It shows the Lone Star flag executed in neon in the Institute of Texan Cultures, San Antonio, Texas. (USA)
534, 535 Complete cover of an issue of *New York* carrying a feature on gambling houses, and detail of the colour photograph. (USA)
536–538 Covers of *The Sunday Times Magazine*. The references are to features on the "peanut farmer" Jimmy Carter (Fig. 536); on the jubilee of Queen Elizabeth II (Fig. 537); and on special rinks for skateboard enthusiasts (Fig. 538). (GBR)

531, 532 Aufnahme und kompletter Umschlag einer Ausgabe der Zeitschrift *Stern*. Diese Aufnahme steigerte den Absatz dieser *Stern*-Nummer erheblich. (GER)
533 Umschlag der russischen Ausgabe von *America Illustrated* Dargestellt ist die aus Neonröhren konzipierte Fahne von Texas, wie sie im Institut für Texanische Kultur zu sehen ist. (USA)
534, 535 Kompletter Umschlag und farbige Aufnahme der Zeitschrift *New York*, mit Bezug auf einen Artikel über die neuen Spielhöhlen in New York. (USA)
536–538 Drei Umschlagseiten des *Sunday Times Magazine*. Abb. 536 zeigt den Erdnussfarmer Jimmy Carter, dargestellt mit einem dreidimensionalen Modell, vor seiner Wahl zum US-Präsidenten. Abb. 537 bezieht sich auf das 25. Regierungsjubiläum von Königin Elisabeth II – mit wenig schmeichelhaften Figuren, Abb. 538 auf einen Artikel über Rollbrett-Bahnen. (GBR)

531, 532 Photo et couverture complète d'un numéro du magazine *Stern*. La publication de cette couverture a eu pour conséquence que le tirage du magazine a considérablement augmenté. (GER)
533 Couverture de l'édition russe d'*America Illustrated*. On y voit le drapeau du Texas composé de tubes néon, tel qu'on peut l'admirer à l'Institut des Cultures Texanes, San Antonio. (TEX)
534, 535 Couverture complète et photo couleur d'un numéro du magazine *New York*, se référant à un article sur les nouvelles maisons de jeu à New York. (USA)
536–538 Trois couvertures du *Sunday Times Magazine*. Fig. 536 présente le producteur de cacahouètes Jimmy Carter dans un modèle tridimensionnel avant son accession à la présidence; fig. 537: représentation sans aucun fard à l'occasion des 25 ans de règne d'Elisabeth II; fig. 538 se réfère à un numéro où figure un article sur les pistes pour planches à roulettes. (GBR)

ART DIRECTOR / DIRECTEUR ARTISTIQUE:

531, 532 Wolfgang Behnken
536–538 Michael Rand

PUBLISHER / VERLEGER / EDITEUR:

531, 532 Gruner & Jahr AG & Co
534, 535 New York Magazine
536–538 Sunday Times Magazine

THE SUNDAY TIMES *magazine*

JUNE 5, 1977

Meanwhile,
what is
Prince Andrew
up to?

537

THE SUNDAY TIMES *magazine*

MARCH 19, 1978

Skatopia!

538

539 Cover of the design magazine *form* with a three-dimensional graph of its growing popularity over a period of twenty years. In colour. (GER)
540 Cover of an issue of the magazine *Horizon* containing a feature on the film in which the dancer Nureyev acted the part of Rudolph Valentino. (USA)
541 Cover of *Home*, weekly magazine of the *Los Angeles Times*. The issue carried a feature on fashions for "action-oriented" children. Full colour. (USA)
542, 546 Shot and complete cover of the magazine *Elle*, with an article on beach fashions. (FRA)
543, 545 Shot and complete cover of an issue of *Pardon* featuring an article on rising bank charges: "Rescue your money!" (GER)
544 Cover of the magazine *Photo*, with a view of Los Angeles in the background. Full colour. (FRA)

539 Umschlag für *form*, Zeitschrift für Gestaltung, mit einem photographischen Diagramm zum Thema «20 Jahre *form*». (GER)
540 Umschlag einer Ausgabe der Zeitschrift *Horizon* mit einem Artikel über den Film, in dem der Tänzer Nurejew die Rolle von Rudolph Valentino spielt. (USA)
541 Farbiger Umschlag einer Ausgabe von *Home* (Beilage der *Los Angeles Times*) mit einem Bericht über die neue Herbstmode für aktive Kinder. (USA)
542, 546 Aufnahme und kompletter Umschlag der Zeitschrift *Elle*, hier zum Thema Bademode. (FRA)
543, 545 Aufnahme und kompletter Umschlag der Zeitschrift *Pardon*, hier zu einem Artikel über höhere Bankgebühren: «Rettet Euer Geld!». (GER)
544 Umschlag des Magazins *Photo*. In Farbe. Im Hintergrund Los Angeles. (FRA)

539 Couverture de *form*, un magazine d'art graphique avec un diagramme photographique se référant au sujet des «20 ans de *form*». (GER)
540 Couverture d'un numéro du magazine *Horizon* se référant ici à un article sur un film dans lequel Nurejev joue le rôle de Rudolph Valentino. (USA)
541 Couverture polychrome d'un numéro de *Home*, supplément hebdomadaire du *Los Angeles Times* qui présente un article sur la nouvelle collection d'automne pour les enfants actifs. (USA)
542, 546 Photo et couverture complète du magazine *Elle*: la nouvelle mode de plage. (FRA)
543, 545 Photo et couverture complète d'un numéro du magazine *Pardon*, ici se raportant un article sur les frais bancaires élevés, intitulé «Sauvez votre argent!» (GER)
544 Couverture (en polychromie) du magazine *Photo*. Au fond on voit Los Angeles. (FRA)

PHOTOGRAPHER / PHOTOGRAPH / PHOTOGRAPHE:

539 Hanswerner Klein
540 Steve Shapiro/Sygma
542, 546 Oliviero Toscani
543, 545 Gerhard Vormwald
544 Jeff Dunas

539

540

Nureyev Takes On Valentino

HORIZON

SEPTEMBER 1977 $2.50

F 2887 F

form

ZEITSCHRIFT FÜR GESTALTUNG 79-III-1977

1957   1964   1971   1977

541

LOS ANGELES TIMES, AUGUST 8, 1976

HOME   TASTE SURPRISES   HOME IMPROVEMENT:
         IN ICES & ICE CREAMS   HOW TO FIND AN ATRIUM

FASHION TUNE-UP FOR FALL'S ACTION-ORIENTED KIDS

542

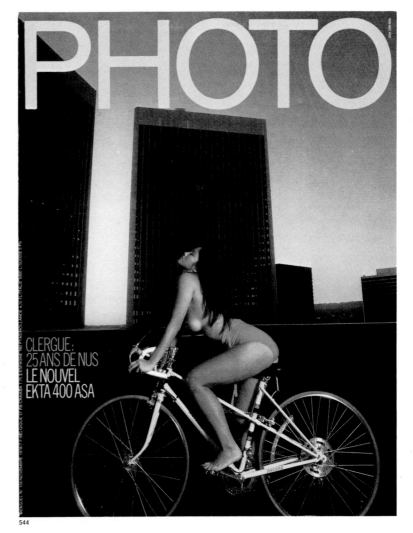

544

DESIGNER / GESTALTER / MAQUETTISTE:

539 Hanswerner Klein
540 Ken Munowitz
541 Hans Albers
543, 545 Gerhard Kromschröder

ART DIRECTOR / DIRECTEUR ARTISTIQUE:

539 Hanswerner Klein
540 Ken Munowitz
541 Hans Albers
542, 546 Antoine Kieffer
543, 545 Gerhard Kromschröder
544 Eric Colmet Daâge

AGENCY / AGENTUR / AGENCE – STUDIO:

539 Klein & Partner
540 American Heritage Publishing

PUBLISHER / VERLEGER / EDITEUR:

539 Verlag form GmbH
540 USIA
541 Los Angeles Times
542, 546 Elle France Editions et Publications
543, 545 Pardon Verlagsgesellschaft mbH
544 Publications Filipacchi

543

545

546

Magazine Covers

197

547

547, 549 Complete cover of an issue of *New York* containing articles on the power of the homosexual movement, and detail of the shot in roughly actual size. (USA)
548 Cover of *New York* illustrating Venturi and Monroe effects of the winds in New York's skyscraper canyons. Full colour. (USA)
550 Cover of *Playboy*. Blue balloon and bikini. (USA)
551 Cover of an issue of *Esquire* carrying an article on "sex among the species". (USA)
552 Cover of the humorous magazine *National Lampoon*. Moustache drawn in. (USA)
553 Introductory page of a "Wild West" issue of *National Lampoon,* with a reference to the branding of cattle on the ranches. (USA)

548

549

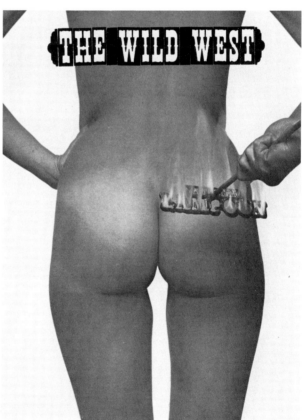

PHOTOGRAPHER / PHOTOGRAPH:

547, 549 John Olson
548 Henry Wolf
550 Claude Maugin
551 Robert Grossman
552, 553 Chris Callis

DESIGNER / GESTALTER:

548 Tom Tarnowsky
550 Kerig Pope
551 Bob Ciano
552, 553 Peter Kleinman

ART DIRECTOR:

548 Tom Tarnowsky
550 Arthur Paul
551 Bob Ciano
552, 553 Peter Kleinman

PUBLISHER / VERLEGER / EDITEUR:

547–549 New York Magazine
550 Playboy Enterprises, Inc.
551 Esquire, Inc.
552, 553 National Lampoon/
21st Century
Communications, Inc.

550

551

552

553

547, 549 Kompletter Umschlag und Detail der Aufnahme der Zeitschrift *New York*, mit Bezug auf die Homosexuellen-Bewegung. (USA)
548 «Die bösen Winde in New York.» Umschlag von *New York*. (USA)
550 *Playboy*-Umschlag. Hase und Kleidung blau, Schrift rot und blau. (USA)
551 Umschlag der Zeitschrift *Esquire*. Thema ist hier das Paarungsverhalten von Vögeln (USA)
552 Umschlag (Hitler-Ausstattung schwarz auf rotem Hintergrund) des Magazins *National Lampoon*: «Ausblick auf den Frühjahrs-Faschismus». (USA)
553 Einleitende Seite zu einer Ausgabe des *National Lampoon* über den Wilden Westen. (USA)

547, 549 Couverture complète et détail de la photo d'un numéro de *New York* avec une allusion aux homosexuels. (USA)
548 «Les vents méchants à New York.» Couvert du magazine *New York*. (USA)
550 Couverture de *Playboy*. Lapin et vêtement bleus, typo rouge/bleue. (USA)
551 Couverture du magazine *Esquire*. Elle se réfère à un article sur la parade des oiseaux (USA)
552 Couverture du magazine *National Lampoon*: «Les perspectives d'un fascisme de printemps». Uniforme hitlérienne noire sur fond rouge. (USA)
553 Page introduisant un article du magazine *National Lampoon* sur le Wild West. En polychromie. (USA)

554

555

554 Illustration from the ICI magazine *Plastics Today* showing two injection-moulded acrylic lenses. Red flower on orange background. (GBR)
555 Full-page illustration from *Pentax Photography*. Full colour. (FRA)
556 Cover of *Aluminium by Alcoa*, a magazine for shareholders of the company. Metallic shades. (USA)
557 Cover of Contact, the magazine of Haarmann & Reimer GmbH, makers of essences and flavouring substances. "Flower" made of biscuits on a brown ground. (GER)
558 Cover of *Stethoscope*, house organ of Sankyo Co. Ltd. Blue-grey hinge, yellowish ground. (JPN)
559 Double-spread illustration, originally an advertising shot for a perfume, reproduced in the photographic magazine *Pentax Photography*. (FRA)

554 Aufnahme aus *Plastics Today*, Hauszeitschrift von ICI. Hier geht es um Linsen aus Kunststoff (Acryl). Rote Blume vor orangefarbenem Hintergrund. (GBR)
555 Detail einer farbigen Aufnahme aus *Pentax Photography*, Hauszeitschrift von Asahi Pentax. (FRA)
556 Umschlag der Aktionärs-Zeitschrift der Aluminium Company of America. (USA)
557 Farbiger Umschlag der internationalen Hauszeitschrift *Contact* (in englischer Sprache) des Essenzen- und Aromastoff-Herstellers Haarmann & Reimer GmbH. (GER)
558 Umschlag der Hauszeitschrift *Stethoscope* von Sankyo Co. Ltd. In Farbe. (JPN)
559 Doppelseite aus einem Artikel über die Photographin Sarah Moon in *Pentax Photography*. Die Aufnahme wurde ursprünglich in der Werbung für das Parfum «Bal à Versailles» eingesetzt. (FRA)

554 Photo de *Plastics Today*, journal d'entreprise d'ICI. Ici il est question de lentilles en matière plastique. Fleur rouge sur fond orange. (GBR)
555 Détail d'une photo couleurs figurant dans le journal d'entreprise d'*Asahi Pentax*. (JPN)
556 Couverture d'un magazine destiné aux actionnaires de l'Aluminium Company of America. (USA)
557 Couverture (en polychromie) de l'édition internationale en langue anglaise du journal d'entreprise d'un fabricant d'essences et d'aromates. (GER)
558 Couverture du journal d'entreprise d'une compagnie de produits pharmaceutiques. (JPN)
559 Page double de *Pentax Photography*, journal d'entreprise d'*Asahi Pentax*. On y présente une photo publicitaire pour le parfum *Bal à Versailles* de Jean Desprez. (JPN)

PHOTOGRAPHER / PHOTOGRAPH:

554 Sandy Hedderwick
555 Karin Szekessy
550 Nick Fasciano
557 von Mannstein Fotoatelier
558 Akio Suyama
559 Sarah Moon

House Organs
Hauszeitschriften
Journaux d'entreprise

Aluminum by Alcoa

556

DESIGNER / GESTALTER / MAQUETTISTE:

554 Len Harvey
555, 559 Bill Chevallier
556 Thomas D. Morin
557 Coordt von Mannstein
558 Kenji Itoh

ART DIRECTOR / DIRECTEUR ARTISTIQUE:

554 Len Harvey
555, 559 Bill Chevallier
556 Jack Hough
557 Coordt von Mannstein
558 Kenji Itoh

AGENCY / AGENTUR / AGENCE – STUDIO:

554 Kynoch Graphic Design
555, 559 Advertising Publicité Sàrl
556 Jack Hough Assoc., Inc.
557 von Mannstein Werbeagentur

PUBLISHER / VERLEGER / EDITEUR:

554 ICI Plastics Division
555, 559 Asahi Optical Europe N.V.
556 Aluminium Company of America
557 Haarmann & Reimer GmbH
558 Sankyo Co., Ltd.

557

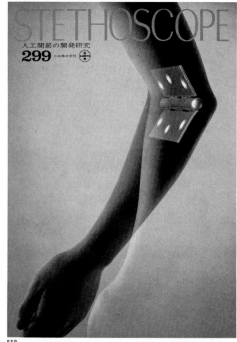

558

559

560

Trade Magazines
Fachzeitschriften
Revues professionnelles

560 Detail of the photograph used on the cover of an issue of the *Kodak* magazine *Bulletin für angewandte Fotografie*. (GER)
561 Photographic composition (full colour) used as a cover for *Revue Fotografie*. (CSR)
562 Illustration from an article on the work of the photographer in the magazine *Nueva Lente*. Black and white. (SPA)
563 From a portfolio of work by the same photographer as in Fig. 562, this time in the magazine *Fotografia*. Black and white. (GRE)
564, 565 Covers of the trade magazine *Real Estate Today*. (USA)

560 Detail der Aufnahme auf einem Umschlag des *Bulletins für angewandte Fotografie*, herausgegeben von *Kodak*. (GER)
561 Farbiger Umschlag der *Revue Fotografie*, eine vierteljährlich erscheinende tschechische Fachzeitschrift. (CSR)
562 Schwarzweiss-Aufnahme aus dem Magazin *Nueva Lente*. (SPA)
563 Schwarzweiss-Aufnahme vom gleichen Photographen wie in Abb. 562 aus einer Fachzeitschrift für Photographie. (GRE)
564, 565 Farbige Umschläge von *Real Estate Today*, Fachzeitschrift auf dem Immobilien-Sektor. (USA)

560 Détail de la photo de couverture d'un bulletin de la photographie appliquée, publié par *Kodak*. (GER)
561 Couverture (en polychromie) de la *Revue Fotografie*, revue spécialisée tchèque qui paraît tous les trois mois. (CSR)
562 Photo noir-blanc figurant dans la revue *Nueva Lente*. (SPA)
563 Photo noir-blanc parue dans une revue photographique. (GRE)
564, 565 Couvertures (en polychromie) de deux numéros de *Real Estate Today*, une revue destinée au marché immobilier. (USA)

562

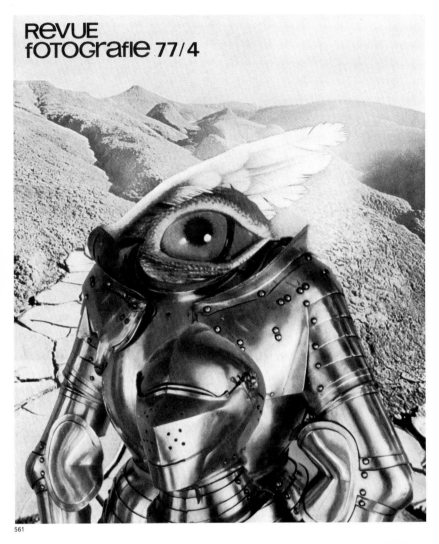

REVUE
fotografie 77/4

561

AUGUST 1977   real estate today

564

MARCH 1977   real estate today

565

563

PHOTOGRAPHER / PHOTOGRAPH / PHOTOGRAPHE:

560 Eugen Leu
561 Dagmar Bromové
562, 563 Jay Seeley
564, 565 Tom Zamiar

DESIGNER / GESTALTER / MAQUETTISTE:

560 Beni Schalcher
561 Jiří Šalamoun/Karel Divina

ART DIRECTOR / DIRECTEUR ARTISTIQUE:

560 Eugen Leu
562 Jorge Rueda
563 Stavros Moresopoulos
564, 565 Carl Hofmann

AGENCY / AGENTUR / AGENCE – STUDIO:

560 Humbert & Vogt

PUBLISHER / VERLEGER / EDITEUR:

560 Kodak SA
561 Revue Fotografie
562 Nueva Lenta
563 S. Moresopoulos Publishing Co.
564, 565 Realtors National Marketing Institute

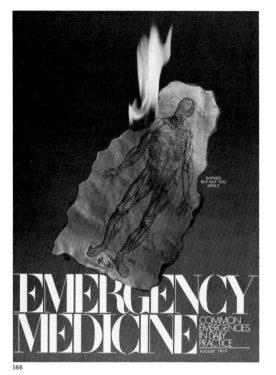

566

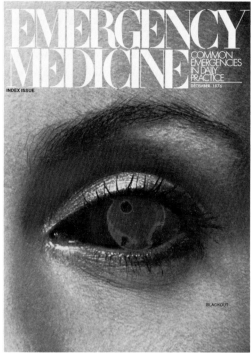

567

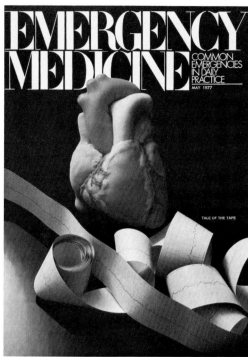

568

569

570

571

Trade Magazines

Fachzeitschriften

Revues professionnelles

566–568 Three covers of the magazine *Emergency Medicine*, all in full colour. They refer to features on burns, loss of sight and cardiac therapies. (USA)
569 Cover of an issue of *Psychologie* containing an article entitled "Sexual liberty or sexual prison?" Full colour. (FRA)
570, 571 Spring and autumn covers of *Top,* a fashion magazine for men. Full colour. (ITA)
572, 573 Double spreads from the issues of *Emergency Medicine* whose covers are shown in Figs. 567 and 568. They open articles on loss of sight and the interpretation of electrocardiograms. Full colour. (USA)
574 Composition of 24 shots taken from the same position over a period of 45 minutes. From *Minolta Mirror.* (JPN)

566–568 Drei farbige Umschlagseiten der medizinischen Fachzeitschrift *Emergency Medicine.* Hier zu den Themen Verbrennung, Erblindung und EKG. (USA)
569 Farbiger Umschlag der Fachzeitschrift *Psychologie,* hier zum Thema «Sexuelle Freiheit oder Gefangenschaft?». (FRA)
570, 571 Farbige Umschlagseiten von *Top,* Zeitschrift für Herrenmode, hier die Frühjahrs- und Herbstausgabe. (ITA)
572, 573 Erste Doppelseiten von Artikeln über Erblinden und Elektrokardiographie, aus *Emergency Medicine.* (Siehe auch Abb. 567 und Abb. 568.) (USA)
574 Komposition einer Serie von Aufnahmen, die an einem Ort innerhalb von 45 Minuten gemacht wurden. Aus der Photo-Hauszeitschrift *Minolta Mirror.* (JPN)

566–568 Trois couvertures (en couleurs) d'un périodique médical, se référant ici aux brûlures, à la cécité et à l'électrocardiogramme. (USA)
569 Couverture du magazine *Psychologie* se référant à un article intitulé «Liberté sexuelle ou prison sexuelle?». (FRA)
570, 571 Couvertures (en couleurs) de *Top,* magazine de mode masculin, ici des éditions de printemps et d'automne. (ITA)
572, 573 Pages doubles initiales, l'une pour un article sur la cécité, l'autre pour un article sur l'électrocardiogramme. D'un périodique médical (v. fig. 567 et 568). (USA)
574 Composition d'une série de photos prises au cours de 45 minutes du même endroit. Elément tiré d'un numéro du journal d'entreprise *Minolta Mirror.* (JPN)

572

573

574

PHOTOGRAPHER:

566, 567, 572 Shig Ikeda
568, 573 Phil Gottheil
569 Edouard Rousseau
570, 571 Giorgio
    & Valerio Lari
574 Harald Mante

DESIGNER / GESTALTER:

566 David Komitav
567, 572 Tom Lennon/
    Irv Cohen
568, 573 Judith Jampel/
    Tom Lennon
570, 571 Rinaldo DelSordo/
    Giuseppe Berlinghieri
574 Fred O. Bechlen

ART DIRECTOR:

566 Tom Lennon
567, 568, 572, 573
    Tom Lennon/
    Ira Silberlicht
569 Daniel Sinay
570, 571 Rinaldo DelSordo/
    Giuseppe Berlinghieri
574 Fred O. Bechlen

AGENCY / AGENTUR / AGENCE:

569 Hollenstein Création
570, 571 Studio Giob
574 Bechlen & Fong, Ltd.

PUBLISHER / VERLEGER / EDITEUR:

566–568, 572, 573 Fischer
    Medical Publications
569 Psychologie
570, 571 Lanificio
    Ermenegildo Zegna
    & Figli
574 Katsusaburo Nakamura

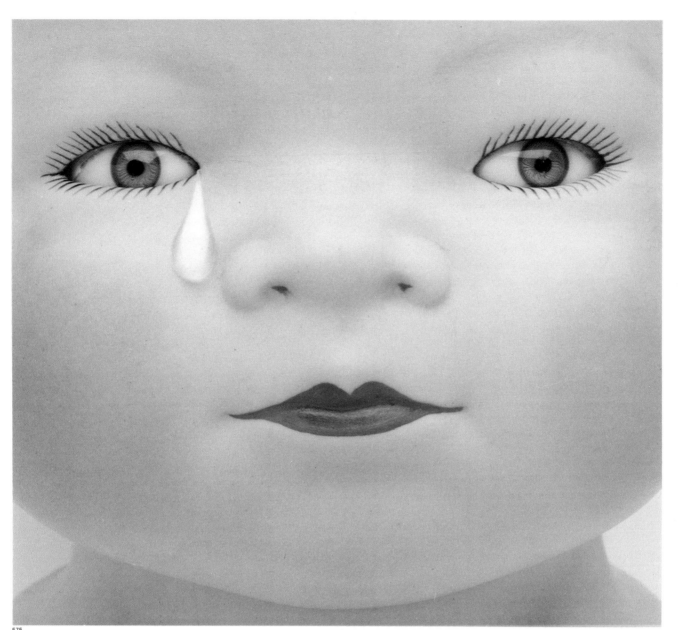

575

PHOTOGRAPHER:

575, 576 David Hedrich
577, 578 John Moss
579 Wolfgang Klein

DESIGNER / GESTALTER:

575, 576 John C. Jay
577, 578 Elton S. Robinson
579 Dietmar Meyer
580, 581 Jim Lienhart
582 Christian Piper

ART DIRECTOR:

575, 576 John C. Jay
577, 578 Elton S. Robinson
579 Dietmar Meyer
580, 581 Jim Lienhart
582 Eiko Ishioka

PUBLISHER / VERLEGER:

575, 576 MBA
Communications, Inc.
577, 578 Exxon Corporation
579 Theobald
& Sondermann
580, 581 Savings
& Loan News
582 Kadokawa

576   577

579

575, 576 Shot and cover of an issue of *Medical Dimensions* with a feature on death in infancy. (USA)
577, 578 Double spread and illustration in actual size from an article on Belgium in the *Exxon* house organ *The Lamp.* Fig. 578 is a scene at the carnival in Veurne. (USA)
579 Cover of the psychological magazine *Warum!* (meaning "Why"). Green leaf. (GER)
580, 581 Colour covers of the magazine *Savings & Loan News.* Themes: women at the top, energy. (USA)
582 Cover of a magazine published by *Kadokawa.* Pharmaceuticals in bright colours on green. (JPN)

575, 576 Aufnahme und Umschlag einer medizinischen Zeitschrift. Thema: Babysterblichkeit. (USA)
577, 578 Doppelseite und Aufnahme aus *The Lamp,* Hauszeitschrift von *Exxon.* Thema: Belgien. (USA)
579 Farbiger Umschlag von *Warum!,* Fachzeitschrift für Psychologie und Lebenstechnik. (GER)
580, 581 Farbige Umschläge der Bank-Publikation *Savings & Loan News.* Die Themen: Frauen als Führungskräfte und Energie-Darlehensprogramme. (USA)
582 Umschlag der Publikation eines Pharmazeutika-Herstellers. Farbige Pillen auf Grün. (JPN)

575, 576 Détail de la photo et couverture complète d'un numéro du périodique médical *Medical Dimensions.* Dans ce numéro il est question de la mortalité infantile. (USA)
577, 578 Page double et photo du journal d'entreprise *The Lamp* se référant à la Belgique. (USA)
579 Couverture (en polychromie) de *Warum!,* périodique de psychologie. (GER)
580, 581 Couvertures d'une publication financière: les cadres féminins et un programme de prêts. (USA)
582 Couverture (capsules polychromes) du journal d'une fabrique de produits pharmaceutiques. (JPN)

578

Trade Magazines
Fachzeitschriften
Revues professionnelles

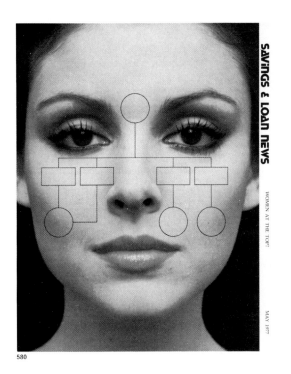

580

SAVINGS & LOAN NEWS

WOMEN AT THE TOP?

MAY 1977

581

SAVINGS & LOAN NEWS

ENERGY LOAN PROGRAMS
FIGHT THE ELEMENTS

OCTOBER 1977

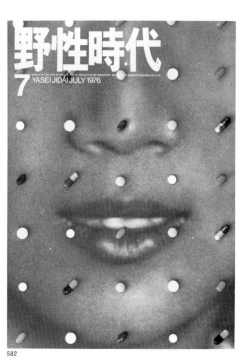

野性時代

7 YASEI JIDAI JULY 1976

582

584

Annual Reports

DESIGNER / GESTALTER:

583, 584 Walter Ender
585, 586 Bob Ciano
587 Bob Nemser
588 Thomas D. Morin

ART DIRECTOR:

583, 584 Walter Ender
585, 586 Bob Ciano
587 Bob Nemser
588 Jack Hough

PHOTOGRAPHER:

583, 584 Gary Bishop
585, 586 Jerry Sarapochiello
587 Simpson Kalisher
588 George Haling

AGENCY / AGENTUR:

583, 584 Ender & Associates
587 Robert S. Nemser Assoc.
588 Jack Hough Assoc., Inc.

583, 584 Full page in actual size and complete double spread from an annual report of Alcon Laboratories, Inc. The reference is to ophthalmic pharmaceuticals. (USA)
585, 586 Double spreads from an annual report of The Risdon Manufacturing Company. The colour shots show containers and sewing products, from the company's production range. (USA)
587 Shot from an annual report of Arkwright-Boston Insurance. Full page, full colour. (USA)
588 Children work with *Xerox* materials. Page from an annual report of the Xerox Corp. (USA)

583, 584 Ganzseitige Aufnahme und komplette Doppelseite aus einem Jahresbericht der Alcon Laboratories, Inc., hier im Zusammenhang mit Medikamenten gegen Augenkrankheiten. (USA)
585, 586 Doppelseiten mit farbigen Aufnahmen aus einem *Risdon*-Jahresbericht. Hier werden Alternativen zu Sprays und ein Teil des Nähzubehör-Sortiments gezeigt. (USA)
587 Farbige Aufnahme aus einem Jahresbericht der *Arkwright-Boston* Versicherung. (USA)
588 Farbige Aufnahme aus einem Jahresbericht der Xerox Corporation. (USA)

583, 584 Photo pleine page et page double complète d'un rapport annuel des Laboratoires *Alcon*. Elles figurent dans un article sur les médicaments pour les maladies des yeux. (USA)
585, 586 Pages doubles avec photos couleur d'un rapport annuel. On y discute les flacons atomiseurs et leurs alternatives et présente une gamme d'outils à coudre. (USA)
587 Photo couleur figurant dans le rapport annuel d'une compagnie d'assurances. (USA)
588 Photo couleur d'un rapport annuel de la Xerox Corporation. (USA)

585

586

587

588

589

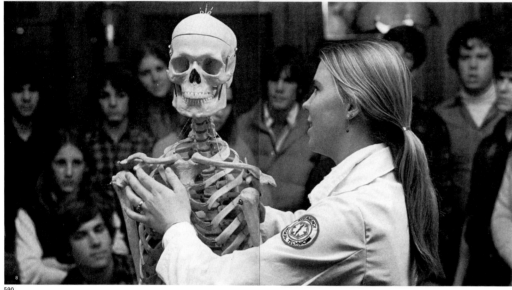

Seconds To Save A Life. What do you do when someone chokes at the dinner table? How do you try to restore heartbeat in an emergency? What do you put on a burn? People who know the right answers are the 60 teenagers and adult advisors who comprise Boy Scout Explorer Post 63, Emergency Medical Service, Darien, Connecticut. They learn in classes like those shown below.

Their example, captured in a 28-minute film produced by Johnson & Johnson's Health Care Division, is designed to make viewers want to learn first-aid techniques themselves.

Nearly 500 prints of the film, "Prepared To Care," are currently in circulation among first-aid squads, hospitals, parent-teacher organizations, police departments, schools and service organizations. Viewers see members of the squad meet emergencies—in car accidents, on ski slopes, in schools and even at the scenes of crimes. The film shows how those skilled young people are keeping alive a great tradition of volunteerism in health care delivery in the United States. In the process, it is inspiring millions of others to do the same.

590

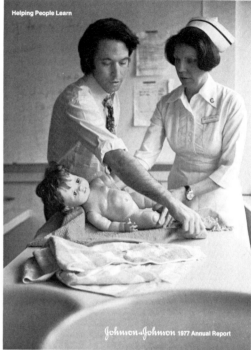

Helping People Learn

Johnson&Johnson 1977 Annual Report

591

PHOTOGRAPHER / PHOTOGRAPH / PHOTOGRAPHE:

589–592 Gary Gladstone
593 Burk Uzzle
594 Burt Glinn
595–597 David Deahl

DESIGNER / GESTALTER / MAQUETTISTE:

589–592 George Tscherny
593 Arnold Saks/Taris Charysyn
594 Ingo Scharrenbroich/Arnold Saks
595–597 Joseph Essex

ART DIRECTOR / DIRECTEUR ARTISTIQUE:

589–592 George Tscherny
593, 594 Arnold Saks

AGENCY / AGENTUR / AGENCE – STUDIO:

589–592 George Tscherny, Inc.
593, 594 Arnold Saks, Inc.
595–597 Burson/Marsteller

594

Union Special Corporation
1977 Annual Report

595

210

592

593

589, 592 Komplette Doppelseite und ganzseitige Aufnahme aus dem Jahresbericht von *Johnson & Johnson.* Hier geht es um die von J&J unterstützte Kinder-Nahrungsmittel-Forschung. (USA)
590, 591 Farbige Doppelseite und Umschlag des *Johnson-&-Johnson*-Jahresberichtes. Die Themen sind hier das Erste-Hilfe- und Baby-Pflegeprogramm. (USA)
593 Farbige Aufnahme aus einem Jahresbericht der Öl-Gesellschaft Amerada Hess Corp. (USA)
594 Doppelseitige Farbaufnahme aus dem Bericht des Spirituosen-Herstellers *Seagram.* (CAN)
595–597 Umschlag und farbige Doppelseiten aus einem Jahresbericht der Union Special Corporation, Hersteller von Nähmaschinen für die Bekleidungsindustrie. (USA)

589–592 Spreads, cover and page from an annual report of *Johnson & Johnson.* Figs. 589 and 592 refer to company research into child nutrition, Fig. 590 to first-aid instruction for young people, and Fig. 591, the cover, shows a father learning to handle a baby. All shots are in full colour. (USA)
593 Page with a shot of a plant from an annual report of Amerada Hess Corporation. (USA)
594 Double spread from the 1977 annual report of the Seagram Company Ltd. Full colour. (CAN)
595–597 Cover, showing ski jackets, and two colour spreads, showing special stitching, from an annual report of Union Special Corporation, makers of industrial sewing equipment. (USA)

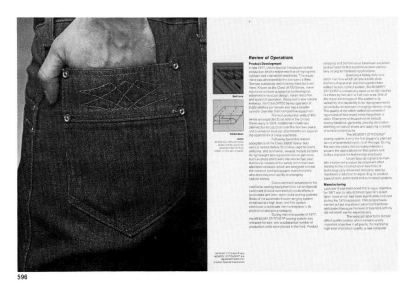

596

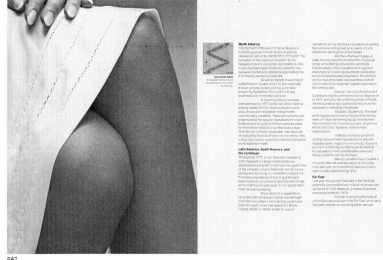

597

589–592 Pages doubles, couverture photo pleine page d'un rapport annuel de *Johnson & Johnson.* Elles se réfèrent à la recherche dans le domaine de la nourriture pour enfants, favorisée par J&J, et à un programme de secours et de puériculture. (USA)
593 Photo couleur figurant dans le rapport annuel d'une compagnie pétrolière. (USA)
594 Illustration sur page double du rapport annuel d'une distillerie. (USA)
595–597 Du rapport d'un fabricant de machines à coudre utilisées dans l'industrie de l'habillement.

598

Annual Reports

598, 602 *Maremont* have made shock absorbers for 100 years. Detail and cover of report. (USA)
599 Page from an annual report of Brenton Banks, which cater for business and farming. (USA)
600 Page from the 1976 annual report of The Seagram Company Ltd. Full colour. (CAN)
601 Cover of an annual report of *Inland Steel*. Work on the steel shell of a blast furnace. (USA)
603, 604 Cover and detail of an annual report of the U.S. Leasing Company. (USA)

601

602

603

PHOTOGRAPHER:

598, 602 Richard Foster
599 Kent Severson
600 Farrell Grehan
601 Burt Glinn
603, 604 Keehn Gray

DESIGNER / GESTALTER:

598, 602 Gene Rosner
599 Sue Crolick
600 Ingo Scharrenbroich/
      Arnold Saks
601 Norman Perman
603, 604 Rex Simmons

ART DIRECTOR:

598, 602 Gene Rosner
599 Sue Crolick
600 Arnold Saks
601 Sam Saran
603, 604 Rex Simmons

AGENCY / AGENTUR / AGENCE – STUDIO:

598, 602 Wallace & Brown
599 Martin Williams Advertising
600 Arnold Saks, Inc.
601 Norman Perman, Inc.
603, 604 Corporate Graphics

Our executive committee:
Bankers who know both sides of Iowa.

599

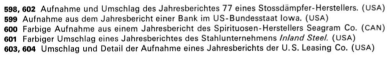

600

598, 602 Aufnahme und Umschlag des Jahresberichtes 77 eines Stossdämpfer-Herstellers. (USA)
599 Aufnahme aus dem Jahresbericht einer Bank im US-Bundesstaat Iowa. (USA)
600 Farbige Aufnahme aus einem Jahresbericht des Spirituosen-Herstellers Seagram Co. (CAN)
601 Farbiger Umschlag eines Jahresberichtes des Stahlunternehmens *Inland Steel*. (USA)
603, 604 Umschlag und Detail der Aufnahme eines Jahresberichts der U.S. Leasing Co. (USA)

598, 602 Photo et couverture du rapport annuel 77 d'un fabricant d'amortisseurs. (USA)
599 Photo publiée dans le rapport annuel d'une banque de l'Iowa. (USA)
600 Photo couleur figurant dans le rapport annuel d'une distillerie. (CAN)
601 Couverture (en polychromie) du rapport annuel publié par l'aciérie *Inland Steel*. (USA)
603, 604 Recto et détail de la photo du rapport annuel de l'U.S. Leasing Co. (USA)

604

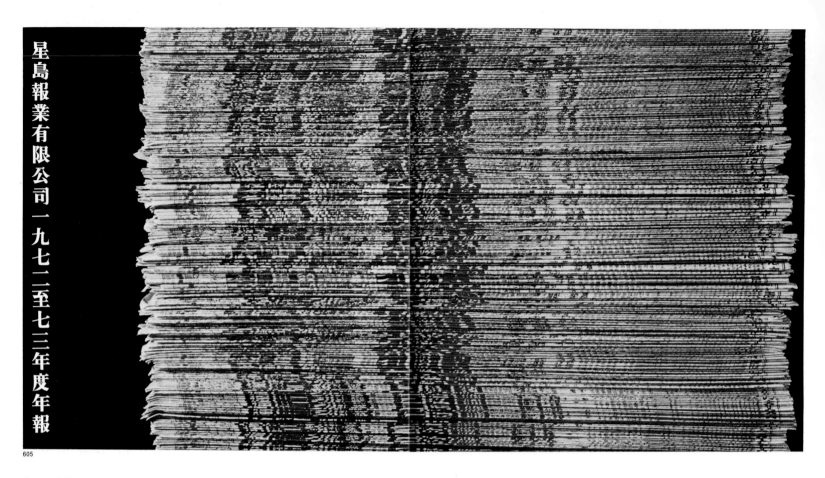

星島報業有限公司一九七二至七三年度年報

605

Annual Reports
Jahresberichte
Rapports annuels

605 Complete cover (back and front) of an annual report of Sing Tao Newspapers Ltd. (HKG)
606 Cover of an annual report of the Brown Group, Inc., cloth manufacturers and retailers. Yellow scissors, black-and-white striped cloth. (USA)
607–609 Double spread and cover, with detail of the photograph in actual size, of an annual report of the First Boston Corporation, investment bankers. Fig. 607 (full colour) shows rice fields in the Philippines (a World Bank development programme), Figs. 608 and 609 show a refinery near New Orleans financed by First Boston. (USA)

605 Vollständiger Umschlag eines Jahresberichtes des Zeitungs-verlegers Sing Tao Newspapers Ltd. (HKG)
606 Umschlag eines Jahresberichtes der Brown Group, Inc., deren Fabrikationsprogramm auch Stoffe umfasst. (USA)
607 Farbige Doppelseite aus einem Jahresbericht der Bankge-sellschaft First Boston, Inc. Hier philippinische Reisfelder als Hinweis auf die Anlage-Tätigkeit der Bank. (USA)
608, 609 Detail der Aufnahme und kompletter Umschlag eines Jahresberichtes der First Boston, Inc. (Siehe auch Abb. 607.) Die Aufnahme bezieht sich auf die von dieser Bank abgewickelte Finanzierung einer Ölraffinerie. (USA)

605 Couverture complète d'un rapport annuel de Sing Tao Newspapers Ltd. (HKG)
606 Couverture du rapport annuel du Brown Group, Inc., com-pagnie diversifiée qui fabrique aussi des tissus. (USA)
607 Page double en polychromie figurant dans le rapport annuel d'une banque. La rizière philippine devrait représenter l'un des domaines de placement de cette banque. (USA)
608, 609 Détail de la photo et couverture complète du rapport annuel d'une banque (voir aussi fig. 607). La prise de vue se réfère au financement d'une raffinerie de pétrole garantie par cette banque. (USA)

606

Brown Group, Inc. Annual Report for 1976

Rice fields in the Philippines are part of the World Bank's many development programs which are helping to improve the economic conditions of poor people in developing countries. First Boston is investment banker to the International Bank for Reconstruction and Development. We are also investment banker to regional development banks, such as the Asian Development Bank and the European Investment Bank, as well as to numerous national development banks around the world. In 1976, we managed development bank issues totaling $2 billion.

607

608

609

PHOTOGRAPHER / PHOTOGRAPH / PHOTOGRAPHE:

605 Henry Steiner
608, 609 Elliot Erwitt/Magnum

DESIGNER / GESTALTER / MAQUETTISTE:

605 Henry Steiner
606 Morton Goldsholl
607–609 Richard Danne

ART DIRECTOR / DIRECTEUR ARTISTIQUE:

605 Henry Steiner
606 Morton Goldsholl
607–609 Richard Danne

AGENCY / AGENTUR / AGENCE – STUDIO:

605 Graphic Communication Ltd.
606 Goldsholl Associates
607–609 Danne & Blackburn, Inc.

610

611

PHOTOGRAPHER / PHOTOGRAPH / PHOTOGRAPHE:

610 Greg Booth
611 Jerry Sarapochiello
612, 613 Clint Clemens
614 William Kuykendall
615, 616 Jason Haley

DESIGNER / GESTALTER / MAQUETTISTE:

610 Ron Sullivan
611 Richard Perleman
612, 613 Sid Herman
614 Marcel Itin

ART DIRECTOR / DIRECTEUR ARTISTIQUE:

610 Ron Sullivan
611 Richard Perleman
612, 613 Mason Morfit/Sid Herman
614 Marcel Itin

AGENCY / AGENTUR / AGENCE – STUDIO:

610 The Richards Group
612, 613 Herman & Lees Associates
614 Visualconcepts, Inc.
615, 616 James Cross Design Office, Inc.

The Stride Rite Corporation   Annual Report 1976

612

Annual Reports
Jahresberichte
Rapports annuels

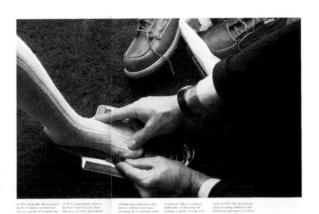

613

615

616

614

618

PHOTOGRAPHER / PHOTOGRAPH:

618 Cheryl Rossum/Burt Glinn
619 Silano
620 Photostudio Giob
621, 622 Studio SDE

DESIGNER / GESTALTER:

618 Victor Gialleonardo
619 Susan Heydt
620 Rinaldo DelSordo/
    Giuseppe Berlinghieri
621, 622 Studio SDE

ART DIRECTOR:

618 Brian O'Neill
619 Susan Heydt
620 Rinaldo DelSordo/
    Giuseppe Berlinghieri
621, 622 Studio SDE

AGENCY / AGENTUR:

618 Doremus & Company
619 Ong & Associates, Inc.
620 Studio Giob

618 Shot used for the cover of an annual report of The Bank of Tokyo Trust Company. (JPN)
619 Cover of an annual report of the J.C. Penney Company, Inc., operators of clothing and department stores and a mail order business. (USA)
620 Page from an annual report of Comital s.p.a., an aluminium company. Black and white. (ITA)
621, 622 Cover (in full colour) and double spread (illustration in subdued whites and light browns) from an annual report of *Sommer Allibert,* an international manufacturer of household furnishings, surfacing materials and industrial equipment. (FRA)

618 Aufnahme für den Umschlag eines Jahresberichtes der Bank of Tokyo Trust Co. (JPN)
619 Farbige Aufnahme des Umschlags eines Jahresberichtes der J.C. Penney Company, ein grosses Versandhaus für Textilien, das auch Kaufhäuser besitzt. (USA)
620 Aufnahme aus einem Jahresbericht von *Comital,* Hersteller von Aluminium. (ITA)
621, 622 Umschlag und Doppelseite, beide mit farbigen Aufnahmen, aus einem Jahresbericht der *Sommer-Allibert*-Unternehmensgruppe, Hersteller von Einrichtungsgegenständen für privaten und industriellen Bedarf. Hier Beispiele aus dem Produktionsprogramm. (FRA)

J.C. Penney Company, Inc.
1977 Annual Report

619

SOMMER ALLIBERT . 1976

621

Relazione del
consiglio d'amministrazione

620

RAPPORT
DU CONSEIL
D'ADMINISTRATION

622

618 Photo figurant dans le rapport annuel d'une grande banque. (JPN)
619 Photo de couverture (en polychromie) du rapport annuel de la J.C. Penney Company, une importante chaîne de grands magasins. (USA)
620 Photo tirée du rapport annuel de *Comital,* producteur d'aluminium. (ITA)
621, 622 Couverture et page double (les deux avec des illustrations en couleurs) du rapport annuel du groupe *Sommer-Allibert,* une société largement diversifiée. On montre ici quelques exemples du programme de production. (FRA)

623

624

Annual Reports
Jahresberichte
Rapports annuels

625

626

627

628

623, 624 Double spreads in black and white from an annual report of the Northrop Corporation, showing two product lines – aircraft and a building complex. (USA)
625–628 Detail of the cover (orange on black) and three double spreads from an annual report of the Itel Corporation. Figs. 626 and 628 relate to the leasing of equipment for transport and industry, Fig. 627 to computer services. Full-colour illustrations. (USA)
629, 630 Detail and complete cover of an annual report of Litton Industries, Inc. (USA)
631 Monochrome cover of an annual report of Group Property Services Ltd. (AUS)

623, 624 Doppelseitige Schwarzweiss-Aufnahmen aus dem Jahresbericht der Northrop Corporation, mit Beispielen aus dem Tätigkeitsbereich dieses Unternehmens. (USA)
625-628 Umschlag eines Jahresberichtes der Itel Corporation, mit gelbem Namenszug auf schwarzem Hintergrund, und drei komplette Doppelseiten daraus, alle mit Farbaufnahmen. (USA)
629, 630 Detail der Aufnahme und kompletter Umschlag eines Jahresberichtes der Litton Industries, Hersteller von elektrischen und elektronischen Geräten. (USA)
631 Umschlag des Jahresberichtes 76/77 einer Anlageberatungsfirma. (AUS)

629

Group Property Services Limited   Annual Report 1976|77

631

PHOTOGRAPHER / PHOTOGRAPH / PHOTOGRAPHE:

623, 624 Burk Uzzle
625, 626, 628 Tom Tracy
627 Ted Kurihara
629, 630 Ken Whitmore
631 Ken Cato

DESIGNER / GESTALTER / MAQUETTISTE:

623, 624 Carl Seltzer
625–628 Thom LaPerle
629, 630 Ronald Jefferies
631 Ken Cato

ART DIRECTOR / DIRECTEUR ARTISTIQUE:

623, 624 James Cross
625–628 Thom LaPerle
629, 630 Robert Miles Runyan/Richard Rice
631 Ken Cato

AGENCY / AGENTUR / AGENCE – STUDIO:

623, 624 James Cross Design Office, Inc.
625–628 LaPerle/Assoc., Inc.
629, 630 Runyan & Rice
631 Cato Hibberd Design Pty Ltd

630

623, 624 Photo noir-blanc sur page double figurant dans le rapport annuel de la Northrop Corp. Les illustrations se réfèrent à divers domaines d'activité. (USA)
625–628 Couverture complète d'un rapport annuel de l'Itel Corporation – logo jaune sur fond noir – et trois doubles pages qui y figurent avec des illustrations en couleurs. (USA)
629, 630 Détail de la photo et couverture complète d'un rapport annuel de Litton Industries, fabricant d'équipements électriques et électroniques. (USA)
631 Couverture du rapport 76/77 d'une société de gérance et de placement. (AUS)

632 Annual report cover: *Cluett* clothing. (USA)
633 Report cover of the Barber Oil Corporation, showing a coking test. (USA)
634 Cover of an annual report of the Charter New York Corporation, showing a vault door in gold and bronze shades. (USA)
635, 636 Shot in roughly actual size and complete cover of an annual report of Deere & Company, showing a new model of a farm tractor. (USA)
637, 638 Cover and page (yellow ground) from an annual report of the Wallace Murray Corporation, building products and industrial equipment. (USA)
639 Cover (red shades) of a report of Nolex Corporation, papermakers. (USA)
640 Cover of an annual report of Cadillac Fairview Corp. Ltd. (housing). (CAN)

636

632
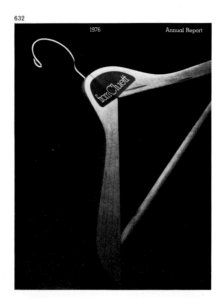

633
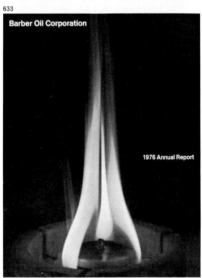

634

635

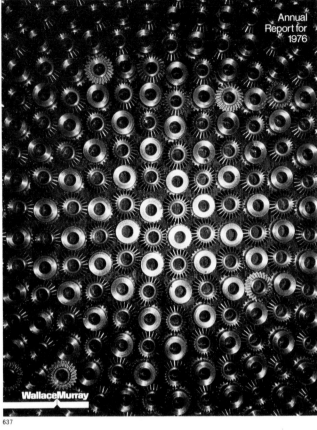

637

638

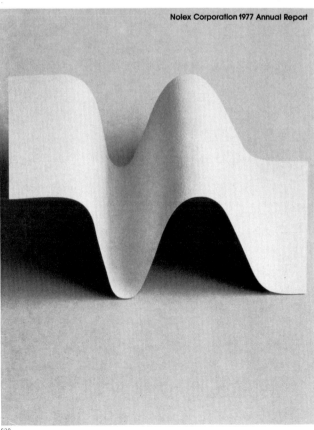

639

640

641

642

643

644

Editorial Photography

645

641 Double spread (full colour) from an annual report of the Pneumo Corp., active in the aerospace industry. (USA)
642 Double spread with narrower interleaved pages from an annual report of Warner Communications, Inc.: music copyrights and sheet music. (USA)
643 Colour spread from a report of Denney's, Inc., food services. (USA)
644 Covers of a two-part annual report of the Hongkong and Shanghai Banking Corporation. (HKG)
645 Complete cover of an annual report of Hongkong Land Co. Ltd. (HKG)
646 Detail of a page from a report of the textile company Burlington Industries: fabrics for industry. (USA)

641 Farbige Doppelseite aus dem Jahresbericht 1976 der Pneumo Corp. (Flugzeugbau-Industrie). (USA)
642 Doppelseite mit schmaleren Innenseiten aus einem Jahresbericht der Warner Communications, Inc. (USA)
643 Farbige Doppelseite aus einem Jahresbericht von Denney's, Restaurant- und Lebensmittelkette. (USA)
644 Umschläge eines zweiteiligen Jahresberichtes für die Hongkong und Shanghai Banking Corp. (HKG)
645 Vollständiger Umschlag des Jahresberichtes einer Baufirma. (HKG)
646 Aufnahme aus einem Jahresbericht der Burlington Industries, Hersteller von Textilien und Garnen. (USA)

641 Page double (en couleurs) du rapport annuel d'une société qui construit des trains d'atterrissage. (USA)
642 Page double avec des pages intercalées du rapport annuel de Warner Communications, Inc. (USA)
643 Page double en couleurs du rapport annuel d'une chaîne de restaurants et de magasins d'alimentation. (USA)
644 Couvertures de deux tomes d'un rapport annuel de la Hongkong & Shanghai Banking Corp. (HKG)
645 Couverture du rapport annuel d'une société immobilière. (HKG)
646 Détail d'une photo tirée du rapport annuel d'un fabricant de tissus. (USA)

PHOTOGRAPHER / PHOTOGRAPH:

641 Bruce Davidson
642 John Olson
644 Frank Fischbeck
645 Nicholas Tsui
646 Peggy & Ronald Barnett

DESIGNER / GESTALTER:

641 Barry Ostrie
642 Kit Hinrichs
643 Alfred Briggs
644, 645 Henry Steiner
646 Arnold Saks/Ingo Scharrenbroich

ART DIRECTOR:

641 Barry Ostrie
642 Kit Hinrichs
643 Robert Miles Runyan/Richard Rice
644, 645 Henry Steiner
646 Arnold Saks

AGENCY / AGENTUR:

641 John Heiney & Associates, Inc.
642 Jonson Pedersen Hinrichs
643 Runyan & Rice
644, 645 Graphic Communication Ltd.
646 Arnold Saks, Inc.

646

PHOTOGRAPHER / PHOTOGRAPH / PHOTOGRAPHE:

647, 648 Paul Fusco
649 Farrell Grehan
650 Jean-Pierre Ronzel
652 Stephen L. Feldman
653 Burk Uzzle

ART DIRECTOR / DIRECTEUR ARTISTIQUE:

647, 648 Reginald Jones
649 Arnold Saks
650 Michel Anne
652 Michael Reid
653 Barry Ostrie

647

DESIGNER / GESTALTER / MAQUETTISTE:

647, 648 Dawson Zaug/Ellen Smith
650 Michel Anne
652 Michael Reid
653 Barry Ostrie

647, 648 Complete cover and illustration in actual size from an annual report of Victoria Station, Inc., a chain of restaurants with headquarters in San Francisco. (USA)
649 Cover of an annual report of Pfizer, Inc., pharmaceuticals. (USA)
650 Page from the annual report of a sleeping-car company. Full colour. (FRA)
651 Page from an annual report of the *Hoechst* chemical company: plant protection. (GER)
652 Page from a *Morton-Norwich* annual report, here referring to special chemicals. (USA)
653 Illustration from a report of Automatic Data Processing, Inc.: retirement accounts. (USA)

647, 648 Kompletter Umschlag eines Jahresberichtes der Restaurantkette *Victoria Station* und Aufnahme daraus, die eine Strassenbahn in San Francisco zeigt. (USA)
649 Farbiger Umschlag eines Jahresberichtes von *Pfizer,* Hersteller von Pharmazeutika. (USA)
650 Farbige Aufnahme aus einem Jahresbericht der französischen Schlafwagengesellschaft. (FRA)
651 Aufnahme in Grüntönen aus einem Jahresbericht von *Hoechst.* (GER)
652 Farbige Aufnahme, mit Produktbeispiel, aus einem Jahresbericht von *Morton-Norwich.* (USA)
653 Aufnahme aus einem Jahresbericht der Computer-Firma Automatic Data Processing, Inc. (USA)

647, 648 Couverture complète d'un rapport annuel de la chaîne de restaurants *Victoria Station* et photo qui y figure: tram de San Francisco. (USA)
649 Couverture du rapport annuel d'une compagnie de produits pharmaceutiques. (USA)
650 Photo du rapport annuel de la Comp. Internationale des Wagons-Lits et du Tourisme. (FRA)
651 Photo (prédominance de tons verts) du rapport annuel de *Hoechst.* (GER)
652 Photo couleur avec représentation d'un produit, du rapport annuel de *Morton-Norwich.* (USA)
653 Photo du rapport annuel d'une société d'équipements électroniques. (USA)

648

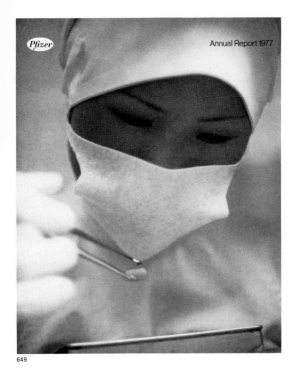

649

650

651

AGENCY / AGENTUR / AGENCE – STUDIO:

647, 648 Unigraphics
649 Arnold Saks, Inc.
652 Michael Reid Design, Inc.
653 John Heiney & Associates, Inc.

**Annual Reports
Jahresberichte
Rapports annuels**

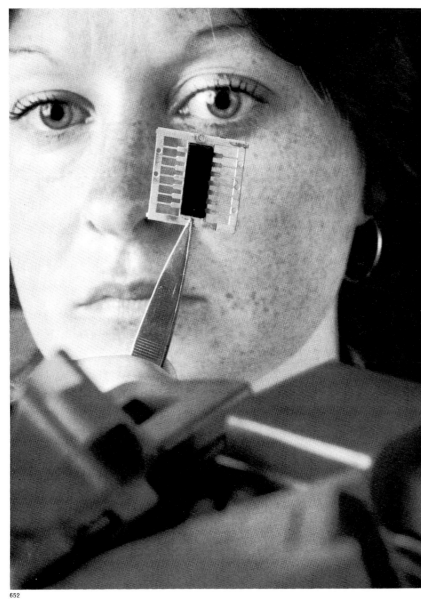

652

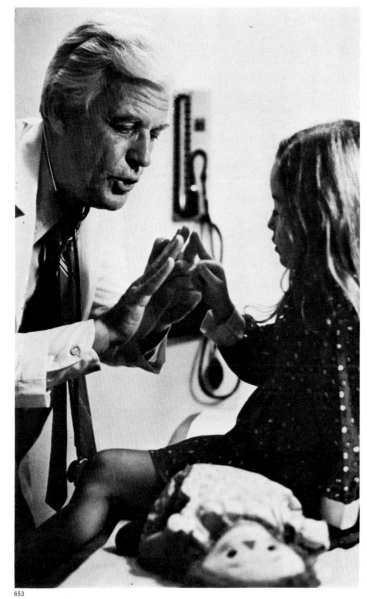

653

Paper/Papier: Papierfabrik Biberist – Biber GS SK3, blade coated, pure white 120 gm2 and Biber Offset SK3, pure white, machine-finished, 140 gm2 / Biber GS SK3, hochweiss, satiniert, 120 gm2 und Biber-Offset SK3, hochweiss, maschinenglatt, 140 gm2

Printed by / gedruckt von: J. E. Wolfensberger AG, Zürich (Colour pages / Farbseiten), Merkur AG, Langenthal (black and white / schwarzweiss)

Cover / Einband: Buchbinderei Schumacher AG, Bern / Schmitten
Glossy lamination / Glanzfoliierung: Durolit AG, Pfäffikon SZ